The Structure of Thinking

The Structure of Thinking

A Process-Oriented Account of Mind

Laura E. Weed

ia

IMPRINT ACADEMIC

Published in the UK by Imprint Academic
PO Box 200, Exeter EX5 5YX, UK

Published in the USA by Imprint Academic
Philosophy Documentation Center
PO Box 7147, Charlottesville, VA 22906-7147, USA

ISBN 0 907845 27 4

A CIP catalogue record for this book is available from the
British Library and US Library of Congress

other titles of interest:
www.imprint-academic.com

Contents

Introduction 1

1. Mental Activity and Computation 5

2. Causation 29

3. Objections and Replies 43

4. Cognitive Science on Kausation Rather Than Causation . . . 73

5. Semantical Causation 87

6. What Objects Are 109

7. The Concept of an Object 137

8. Stalnaker vs. Husserl 155

9. Relation Between X-type & Y-type Thinking Processes . . . 165

10. The Third Man 181

11. Is Platonic Heaven All That Pure? 201

12. Overview and Conclusion 217

Bibliography 221

Index 231

Introduction

In the introduction to *Reclaiming Cognition*, Raphael Núñez and Walter J. Freeman claim that a revolution is taking place in the understanding of what a human mind is and how it works. Núñez and Freeman observe:

> We believe that the cognitive sciences have reached a situation in which they have been frozen into one narrow form by the machine metaphor. There is a need to thaw that form and move from a reductionist, atemporal, disembodied, static, rationalist, emotion- and culture-free view, to fundamentally richer understandings that include the primacy of action, intention, emotion, culture, real-time constraints, real-world opportunities, and the peculiarities of living bodies.[1]

The *Structure of Thinking* is a book dedicated to developing some aspects of the fundamentally richer philosophy of thinking that Núñez and Freeman are seeking.

This book has had a very long genesis. The oldest section is chapter ten, 'The Third Man', which originated as my master's thesis, supervised by Dr. José Benardete at Syracuse University in 1979. That chapter was re-written and folded into my doctoral dissertation, which also included the rest of the chapters, except for the current chapter four, 'Cognitive Science on Kausation Rather Than Causation' which is completely new. I received the doctorate from Syracuse University in 1992, under the direction of Dr. Stuart Thau, to whom I owe many thanks for his guidance and assistance. But chapters nine, 'The Relation between X-type and Y-type Thinking Processes', and eleven, 'Is Platonic Heaven all that Pure?' have been substantially re-written, as well, and are more new than recycled.

Despite the age of some of the arguments in *The Structure of Thinking*, I suspect that most of the Imprint Academic audience will still not have seen either them or anything like them. This is so because the form of philosophical inquiry, driven by the machine metaphor, to which Núñez and Freeman referred in my opening

[1]   Raphael Núñez and Walter J. Freeman, eds., *Reclaiming Cognition, the primacy of action, intention and emotion*. Imprint Academic, Exeter, UK, 1999, p. ix.

quotation, has completely dominated philosophical inquiry, at least in the prestigious universities and journals in the United States, for all of the time period over which these arguments have been in existence. I believe it is important to publish these arguments at this time, and I am most grateful to Keith Sutherland at Imprint Academic for giving me the opportunity to do so, for at least three reasons.

First, I believe the arguments in this book indicate that the twentieth century underpinnings of the logical and mechanical reductivist program in philosophy are basically unsound. The arguments from philosophers such as Bertrand Russell, G.E. Moore, Carl Hempel, J.L. Mackie, Rudolph Carnap, Alan Turing and Gottlob Frege, and from behaviorists such as B.F. Skinner, on which dominant philosophers at the end of the century, such as W.V.O. Quine, Daniel Dennett and Fred Dretske have been relying and expanding are basically flawed in their underpinning premises. And even in cases in which the early twentieth century philosophers had it right, their late century followers took some of their arguments in directions that were unsupported by the earlier claims on which they were based. Across the analytical tradition there is a general assumption that a small number of principles, limited to the tools of symbolic logic, computational mathematics, and experimental science, (construed on an early-twentieth century paradigm), are adequate to explain all that exists, and that any purported existents that are not analyzable in terms compatible with those few methods of analysis are fictitious and dispensable entities. Blindness to the need for first-person experience to understand reality, even in science, math and logic, let alone in respects such as language use and understanding of brains and minds has resulted from this devout reverence for too few principles of understanding. The arguments in this book point out some of the flaws and multiple areas of blindness of the dominant but narrow philosophical methodology in the United States, today.

Second, and more specifically, the mechanistic notion of causation with which the dominant tradition has intellectually shackled itself is preventing productive advances in a number of areas of inquiry which I find particularly important — such as philosophy of mind, philosophy of language, philosophy of religion and philosophical inquiry into understanding the social behavior of human beings in politics and economics.

Third, I believe now is a good time to bring the philosophical arguments in *The Structure of Thinking* to the foreground in public intellectual life, because the extensive research on the brain and in the neurosciences that is taking place at present is indicating that the flaws in the logical and mechanical reductivist methodology that I pointed out, starting more than twenty years ago, are seriously hampering the development of new understandings about humans and our world. The genesis of the *Journal of Consciousness Studies*, the importance of David Chalmers' arguments in favour of panpsychism, and the recent development of research methodologies for studying first and second person experience, all indicate that the time is ripe for an intellectual re-examination of the experiential roots of human intellectual life. This book undertakes that task.

I would like to thank my many mentors without whose guidance, assistance and advice this book would not have come to fruition. First of all, I would like to thank my parents, Peter and Loretta Van Buren, for their patience, support and encouragement with my philosophical obsession, which they never quite understood. In addition, I would like to thank my many mentors at Syracuse University, but especially, Stuart Thau, and José Benardete, who mentored me through my dissertation and master's thesis, respectively, and Clyde Hardin, and Ted Denise, of the Philosophy Department who also served on my dissertation committee. I would also like to thank my colleagues and mentors at SUNY Empire State College, especially John Spissinger, Dora Ingolfsdottir, Mike Andolina, and Mike Fortunato, and my colleagues at the College of St. Rose, especially, Bruce Johnston, Jeannie Wiley, Jeffrey Marlett, Steve Strazza, Kate Cavanaugh, Ben Clansy Melissa Clarke and David McCarthy.

The administration of the College of St. Rose, especially President Mark Sullivan and Vice President Bill Lowe deserve special thanks for supporting my sabbatical leave for the 2002–2003 academic year. And, of course, I owe an enormous debt of gratitude to Keith Sutherland at Imprint Academic, for his suggestions, edits and patience in the preparation of this text for publication.

Laura Weed
The College of St. Rose
September, 2002

Chapter 1

Mental Activity and Computation

Marking off the areas of mental activity for which a computational analysis is not appropriate

Argument for the Need for a Non-Computational Analysis of Sensory, Experiental and Existential Phenomena

Among cognitive scientists and researchers in artificial intelligence are some who still argue for what John Searle calls 'strong AI'.[1] This is a strong thesis that claims that the workings of a computer constitute a model of the workings of a mind, and that a mind is just a biochemical computer. According to this thesis, brain 'wet ware' and computer hardware are the same type of thing, which can be instantiated in either a biochemical or silicon chip medium .

For these claims to be true, the brain's operations must parallel the structure of the symbolic logic system with which computers are programmed, and must have many of the same functional and operational properties as a logical system. For example, the brain must be primarily a computational device that calculates mathematical and symbolic functions, if strong AI is to maintain its claims. While I think that artificial intelligence research has brought impressive insights and progress to recent study about the mind, there are certain features of mental operation that I think can be better explained. Certainly, much of the operation of a mind is computational and does operate as a symbol manipulator, in the way that advocates of

[1]   John R. Searle, *The Rediscovery of the Mind*, MIT Press, Cambridge MA, 1994, p. 44.

strong AI claim. But I shall argue in this book that there are many key features of thinking that can be better understood in another way.

At the outset, I might indicate the direction that my analysis will take by pointing out that I think that the proponents of strong AI are concentrating on the products of thinking; the propositionally structured mental representations that might be said to be the objects of a knower's knowledge. I will concentrate, instead, on the processes whereby knowledge is generated by a knower. Thinking is, after all, an activity.

I propose an analysis of thinking that considers its structure to be that of an interactive relationship between a knower and his or her world. Since Aristotle's time, at least two ways of coming to have knowledge have been acknowledged. Aristotle distinguished between these two methods of knowledge acquisition in the *Posterior Analytics*, when he discussed the types of 'pre-existent' knowledge that one had to have if one was to learn anything.

> The pre-existent knowledge required is of two kinds. In some cases admission of the fact must be assumed, in others comprehension of the term used, and sometimes both assumptions are essential . . . as regards 'unit' we have to make the double assumption of the meaning of the word and the existence of the thing. The reason is that these several objects are not equally obvious to us. Recognition of a truth may in some cases contain as factors both previous knowledge and also knowledge acquired simultaneously with that recognition — knowledge, this latter, of the particulars actually falling under the universal and therein already virtually known.[2]

In this passage Aristotle claims that gaining knowledge requires both a recognition of the 'meaning of the word', which he allies with 'falling under a universal' and the recognition of the 'existence of a thing', which he allies with 'knowledge . . . of the particulars.'

Following Aristotle's distinction, I will claim that the process by which one acquires knowledge of particular existent things is quite different from the process by which one acquires knowledge of concepts and universals. Propositions combine these processes into products, as Aristotle himself does when he declares that all basic knowledge is of the form 'x is y'. In this formula, the 'x' represents some subject, and the 'y', some property or concept being attributed to the subject. I adopt Aristotle's formula for basic knowledge, and his distinction between the two types of knowledge in this book in order to adapt his insights to my analysis of the structure of thinking.

---

[2]   Aristotle, *The Basic Works of Aristotle*, ed. Richard McKeon, 'Posterior Analytics', 71a, 11–19, p. 110.

People, I claim, perform two types of thinking processes. One corresponds to the generation of the 'x' in the Aristotelian formula, so I will call it 'object positing' loosely adapting Quine's use of that concept. The other, corresponding to the 'y', I will call 'property attributing.' The names imply only that different methods for mental processing are involved in thinking of the relationship between oneself and some understood item of knowledge as a relationship to an object, than are involved in thinking of the relationship between oneself and some understood item as a relationship to a property or set of properties. Nothing else about properties or objects is implied by the choice of names.

My reason for distinguishing between these processes in this way is to point out how each can be separately analyzed, even if they rarely operate independently of one another. The type of analysis that I intend to give of each will be the interpretive kind of psychological explanation advocated and defended by Robert Cummins in *The Nature of Psychological Explanation*.[3] The object-positing capacity of mind is an identifying and recognizing capacity, that deals with particulars in thought.

Cases of immediate perception or direct experience are the chief types of knower-known relationships in which we would find the object-positing capacity operating relatively independently. It is an empiricist's direct hold on experience as reality; Aristotle's hedonistic devil. The property-attributing capacity of mind is a sorting, qualifying and quantifying capacity, which deals mainly with universals in thinking. Apprehension of second or third order relations might rate as the types of knower-known relationships in which we would find the property-attributing capacity operating relatively independently.

Here is an argument for the need to make this distinction in this way and to analyze each capacity in its own terms, in order to understand thinking.

Is the Basic 'Stuff' of the Universe Properties or Objects?

If, on the one hand, one asks the metaphysical question, 'What exists?', or 'What things are there?', the natural response is 'objects' or 'matter'. Metaphysical questions most frequently yield universe inventories in response. Once one has compiled a list of objects or components of objects in one's universe inventory, analysis of the list can go several ways. One could be impressed with the unity of

[3]   Robert Cummins, *The Nature of Psychological Explanation*, Bradford Books, M.I.T. Press, Cambridge Mass., 1983.

the list, and insist with Parmenides[4] and Spinoza[5] that there is really only one, very complex substance, here. Or one might be impressed with the diversity of the list, and defend some form of atomism to explain recurrent patterns across differing items in the list. One could claim that modern chemistry and physics have united the primitive, natural answers to the metaphysical question by offering a table of elements, together with an account of bonding principles for intermediate composites of elements, plus an account of the relationship of all material diversity to one thing, energy, in $E = mc^2$. But, however one analyses one's object lists, the lists themselves will contain only particular things. Concepts, relations, and other platonic entities would seem to be ruled out by an enterprise aimed at compiling a universe inventory. Mental phenomena of any kind make very questionable objects.

If, on the other hand, one starts one's inquiry with questions about knowledge, such as 'What do we know?' or 'What can be known?', the natural answers to these questions seem to be 'properties' or 'universals'. Plato and Berkeley both start their investigations with epistemological questions, and both ultimately have trouble with particular, material objects. For, once the properties and universals have been established as prior, objects become reducible to sets of properties. The third man argument exhibits the chief weakness of a property-oriented account of the nature of the world. Properties and relations are too variable to rate as the basic content of a recalcitrantly solid reality.

Aristotle tried to resolve this dilemma by arguing extensively for the integrity of mid-sized objects in his works. Substances were both properties and matter, combined in specific ways. In Aristotle's arguments, the chief enemy was relativity[6] and relativity's most prominent guises were elements,[7] universals,[8] and lack of specificity or 'thisness'.[9] Obviously, the 'elements' arise as a relativity problem in an objects- or matter-oriented universe inventory, while the 'universals' and lack of 'thisness' arise as relativity problems with a property-oriented account of the world. We might put the relativity

---

[4]   See J. Burnet, *Early Greek Philosophy*, London, 1920, for an account of Parmenides' one-substance world.

[5]   See B. Spinoza, *Ethics*, trans. by R.H.M. Elwes, Bell, London 1919, for Spinoza's account of the universe as consisting of one substance.

[6]   Aristotle, *The Basic Works of Aristotle*, ed. Richard McKeon, 'Categories', 8a, p. 22.

[7]   *Ibid.*, 'Metaphysics', 1041b, p. 811.

[8]   *Ibid.*

[9]   *Ibid.*, 'Metaphysics', 1038b–1039a, p. 805.

problem with which Aristotle was grappling this way. Once the intellectual principles that initially motivate a property theory are allowed to develop, they tend to drift in the direction of the realm of the forms. And once the intellectual principles that initially motivate an objects or matter theory are allowed free reign, they drift in the directions of progressively more minute elements, or progressively more all-encompassing wholes.

Aristotle's solution to this dilemma, of course, was the four causes. Four types of principles had to be evoked to account for the existence of any substance. Of the four, the formal cause insured that properties were considered, while the material cause insured that objects were not neglected. Two of the causes were straight-forwardly physical; the material and efficient causes. The other two, we might say, were 'mental' and anthropomorphic. The formal and material involved the basic 'stuff' of the universe, while the efficient and final involved relationships in which that 'stuff' might be encountered.

Since the scientific revolution, Aristotle has been much abused for the anthropomorphism of his formal and final causes. But perhaps if I recast his insights as a discussion of mental interpretation by intellectual processes, rather than as a discussion of the physical nature of matter, his anthropomorphism won't seem quite so objectionable. The problem of reconciling the tendency of property theories to drift in the direction of the realm of the forms with the tendency of object theories to drift into elements and all-encompassing wholes is not, after all, a problem for scientists to resolve in laboratories. These are problems of intellectual synthesis, philosopher's problems, par excellence. And the solution to these problems is to be found, not in some supposedly patent structure of the natural world, but rather, in the processes by which people think. Rather than four causes, I'm offering two types of mental process by which people generate for themselves mental interpretations of the way the world is; object positing, and property attributing. I'm claiming only that humans have two distinct methods by which they characterize their experience for themselves, and therefore, two quite differently organized types of experiences of mental data can be presented to the mind for thought. The end products of the processes will be objects and properties. These, in turn, in combination, will yield facts, expressible as Fregian propositions. Once full-blown propositions are in place, computational processes may operate on them, as I see the situation. But this occurs many steps beyond the basic operations of the mind that I am arguing are the ground-floor operations.

As I am presenting the situation, the dispute between Plato and Parmenides, or between Quine and Goodman, is a question of preference for method of thinking. Whether by nature or nurture, I don't wish to argue here. But, it seems to me rather apparent that some people are property-thinkers and others are object-thinkers, to a greater extent.

This analysis is not a proposal that there is no external world, or that there are no objects or properties. It is only a proposal that more productive results might be accomplished in philosophical inquiry by examining mental processes, first.

The Integrity of Mid-Sized Objects

Aristotle was particularly concerned, as I have pointed out, with establishing the integrity of mid-sized objects. For it would typically be the tables, chairs, trees and pencils of common experience that would be lost in the metaphysical drift to atoms, property-instantiations, or all-of-space. Stable objects are not good candidates for intellectual primitives, whatever one's prejudice in primitives might favor. For, as Aristotle rightly saw, we only mark out substantial objects in virtue of some properties that we attribute to them, but, contra Plato, we would have no access to the properties were they not instantiated in some particular, sensory or intellectual item, occupying some specific place.

Mid-sized objects are also lost in a Russell-like logical system, in which they become reducible to sets of properties.[10] Problems like the sling-shot argument accent how much of the integrity of the particular has been lost in the abstraction from things to sets. Logical systems, like Russell's or Quine's,[11] are exclusively property-oriented systems. Even in an existentially quantified statement, the 'x' is a mere place holder, which may be substitutionally construed. Identity and uniqueness quantifiers have been devised as attempts at circumventing the tendency of a logical system to wipe out the particularity of particulars. But from my perspective, such attempts to save objects within property-oriented systems are just new ways for property-systems to chase a third man. For within an exclusively property-oriented system, any index element that could be introduced would have to be introduced as a new property of the 'x', which would simply, again, retreat to the status of a place-holder.

---

[10] Bertrand Russell, *The Principles of Mathematics*, Cambridge University Press, New York, 1938.
[11] W.V.O. Quine, *Mathematical Logic*, Harvard University Press, Cambridge, Mass. revised ed. 1981.

This is my objection, ultimately, to strong AI's proposal that a unitary symbolic language can account for all mental activity. As Jerry Fodor originally described this language,[12] it's essential features are those of a logical computer programming system, like Russell's or Quine's. While Fodor has since clarified his position on the computational nature of thinking,[13] other philosophers are continuing to insist on a computational account of all mental processes. I think that the philosophical tradition to which Russell and Quine belong has done an impressive job of analyzing the property-attributing capacity of mind in the twentieth century. But I think that this has been done at the expense of the object-positing capacity, and hence, at the expense of the integrity of mid-sized objects. In proposing a two-part analysis of mental processes, I am proposing that another type of study has to be done, in addition to the study of logical systems, to fully account for the capacities of mind.

Again, in the spirit of Aristotle, we could examine the problem of how the 'x' in knowledge and the 'y' in knowledge come to be joined to each other as a puzzle about giving the persistence conditions for stable objects. Only the concrete individual, as composite of matter and form, has the necessary stability to hold its own against the tides of metaphysical drift. A substance must be an individual, but all of its true characterizations will be of it as a member of a class. So, the integrity of the substance, even if it is only temporary, will be the product of the intersection of some logical considerations and some empirical considerations. The empirical considerations will deal with particulars in experience, indexically notable singular items, which are temporally bound as a 'this x'; vignettes in the passing show generated by the Heraclitean flux.[14] The logical considerations will deal with the structure that thought unites with some bit of the flux, forming the composite stable substance.

The Tension between Platonic 'Technical Definitions' and Empirical Evidence in the Growth of a Science

Consider a case in which the see-saw of logical and empirical considerations actually causes a practical dilemma. I ask about a very ill medical patient, 'Is P still alive?' When the empirical evidence is unclear or inconclusive, a definition of the word 'alive' might substi-

---

[12] Jerry Fodor, *The Language of Thought,* Harvard University Press, Cambridge, MA, 1975.

[13] Jerry Fodor, *The Mind Doesn't Work That Way,* Bradford Books, MIT Press, Cambridge, MA 2000.

[14] See an account of Heraclitus' belief that all things are in a constant state of 'flux' or change, in *Early Greek Philosophy,* trans. by J. Burnet, Black, London, 1920.

tute for an investigation. For instance, 'alive' might be defined as meaning 'having brain wave activity, as measured by an encephalogram.' Sometimes, in scientific investigations, such definitions are substituted, across the board, for empirical evidence. It could be established by rule that all and only things causing encephalogram activity rate as alive, even in spite of counterintuitive instances. On the empirical side, however, ability to register on an encephalogram is only one indicator of the presence of life. Exchanging oxygen, being part of a food chain, being composed of hydrocarbons, having a heartbeat, or Aristotelian locomotion, might all equally well be used as criteria for life, for purposes other than establishing criteria for medical malpractice. These empirical considerations, dealing with the data of experience, as presented, are hardly irrelevant to the stability in thought of the 'substancehood' of live things. Indeed, considerations about his or her range of experiences of living things would be the considerations that would lead a thinker to believe that the consequences of one definition or another were counterintuitive.

Hence, to analyze thought properly, one must attend to two types of processes; the process in which one incorporates the passing show into thought, and the one in which one computationally structures the raw data incorporated by experience. The language of thought, as a computational structuring system, will not do alone, because its substitutionality deprives it of substantive content; it lacks the raw data of experience, as it exists, unincorporated into a structured system like a language. And the passing show is inconclusively determinate without the organization imposed by the structuring system. This is not a claim that 'the passing show' is unknowable, but only that it does not arrive in conscious experience equipped with a program. So, only an analysis of the union of the two can 1) give an adequate account of stable objects, 2) give an adequate account of causation, and 3) give an adequate account of how the mind uses mental data.

In what follows, I will develop arguments for independent theories of the 'x' and the 'y' in thought, together with proposals for constructing those theories and suggestions for ways to construe the composite.

Syntax and Logical Structures are Platonic, but Semantics belongs to Aristotle's 'x'

In some respects, my distinction between a process yielding knowledge by acquaintance and a process yielding knowledge by chains of reasoning or 'meanings of terms' is not new in the history of philosophy. But recent philosophical work, especially in the analytic school and among cognitive scientists like Stalnaker, has concentrated on developing theories about the 'y' process in thought, at the expense of the 'x'. First, let me sketch the line between the two types of theory where I think it should go, using the terms of the contemporary debate on issues related to thought. Then I will argue that the contemporary platonism of Quine, Stalnaker and kindred thinkers is inadequate to deal with the data that I have segregated as being properly analyzed as x-type data.

As I am analyzing these processes, a theory about the y-process would give analyses of truth conditions for statements, entailment relations among propositions, concatenation rules for languages, and accounts of the computational properties of mental reasoning. Logical or necessary truths, kinds, whether natural or otherwise, *de dicto* truths and syntactical analyses would also be included in the theory about y-processes in thought. Possible-world semantics is also an analysis of how thoughts concatenate, not of what their content is.

A theory of the role of the 'x' in thought, however, will be perceptually or sensorily based, dealing with singular items, and related to the existence or appearance of the data involved in the thinking process, rather than to generalizations about that data. *De re* truths, indexicals, names, and singular referring expressions will be analyzed under these auspices.

This theory will analyze the way that we use perceptual input to image objects, and how, conversely, our conceptualization about the data generates selectivity in perception. One of the most central features of this data will be its intentionality. Logically intensional and opaque expressions will belong here as well. Semantics is amenable to an analysis in truth-functional terms when construed linguistically, but is also notoriously infected with Gricean intentionality, which, I think must be analyzed in an Aristotelian way as some 'x', some 'this', playing the role of 'matter' for a 'substance-making' process in thought. Cognition has no content without experiential interaction.

Platonic Cognition is Vacuous Without Aristotelian Perception

Quine rejected most of the data that I have placed in the theory of the x in thought as too unruly to be handled according to his principles, and hence, too unruly to countenance, period. In so distinguishing fields of study, I will argue that the principles of a theory of truth conditions are certainly not the ones that one ought to use to tackle the topics that I have characterized as x-type topics. But these topics must be tackled, even if new principles must be devised for the job. I consider Kripke's possible world semantics,[15] as well as adaptations on Kripke's analysis by authors like Stalnaker,[16] attempts at reducing the data that I am distinguishing to something analyzable in terms of truth functions. But, I think that these authors have butchered the data to make it fit, and lost, not gained, intellectual clarity in the effort. I share Quine's lack of sympathy with the enterprise. The effect of concentrating inquiry on the platonic entities, and despising or underrating the perceptual, ephemeral, 'x' side of my distinction, as Quine clearly does, is to discard as 'rationally irrelevant' all that passes in time. The platonic universe is, banally, eternal, as are eternal sentences and propositions. But, regrettably, we — poor shadows of our platonic selves — are mortal and transitory, as are most of the objects and events that we experience and discuss. Although some fields of human endeavor, such as mathematics, may be able to get by without the 'x', one field that most certainly can't make do without the hedonistic devil is theories about causation. Banally, again, theories of causation are not about eternal truths, but rather are about how transition takes place in time. I will argue in this book that the notion of a stable object depends on the notion of causation that one is using, and so, without a clear notion of causation, one's analysis of a stable object is bound to be badly skewed. Existence, I shall argue, belongs to stable objects.

Three Specific Areas of Mental Activity that are Butchered by Reducing x-Type Phenomena to y-type Phenomena: Causation, Stable Mid-Sized Objects and Existence

Some Skewed Accounts of Causation

Hume's[17] critique of causation assigns causation to the domain of the transitory in order to argue against its alleged law-likeness. Remember, no causation is observed when the stone hits the glass because the event is a series of momentary 'ideas', each of which is a particular, unique 'x' in thought. In so analyzing the situation, Hume consciously and deliberately rejects the persistence through time of any stable object. In his discussion of personal identity,[18] even the series of perceptual ideas that constitute his own identity

---

[15] See Saul Kripke, *Naming and Necessity,* Harvard University Press, Cambridge, Mass., 1980.

[16] Robert Stalnaker, *Inquiry,* Bradford Books, M.I.T. Press, Cambridge, Mass. 1984.

[17] David Hume, *A Treatise of Human Nature,* ed. L.A. Selby-Bigge and P.H. Nidditch, Clarendon Press, Oxford, 1978, Book I, sec. xii - xv, pp. 130–176.

[18] *Ibid.,* p. 252.

turns out to be insufficient to yield even himself as a stable object over time.

Hume's problem with stable objects focuses particularly sharply on the conceptual interdependence of the roles of the 'x' and the 'y' in thought. Hume says a series of unconceptualized sensory 'hits' will not yield even oneself as a stable object. And, it is because no causation is observed that no stable object can be generated. Of course, without stable objects, any discussion of universal laws covering stable objects is going to be moot. Anyway that we construe this observation, it is bad news for philosophers like Kripke, who think that a mere, indiscriminate pointing is going to yield not only causation, but also a full blown natural kind, genetics, chemical elements, and all. If I am right, a pointing yields nothing but a completely unique sensory experience. From this, one cannot even presume that causation connects experiences or events, much less that the same objects are featured in various events.

From the point of view of the analysis that I am offering, Hume is right to look for causation and for the stability of objects in the realm of experience of particulars and the transitory, but by concentrating on products of mental operation, rather than processes used for mental operation, he cut his materials too thin. He is even indecisive about whether his 'objects' are ideas, as mental percepts, or events, such as stones hitting windows. What he needed was the process by which an active mind makes a stone hitting a window its own thought.

Hume could then have said, as I do, that causation was experienced as *the process* by which a mind incorporates an experience into thought. Via this process, a mind identifies the mental idea with the experienced, physical event, attributing substantiality to the stable aspects of the experience, and causation to the transitory aspects of it. More on this when I explain my own account of causation.

At the opposite end of the causation debate from Hume are theorists who offer patently platonic accounts of the nature of causation, such as Hector-Neri Castaneda,[19] or David Sanford.[20] Castaneda, for instance, says the following things in delineating his account of 'causity'.

> Causity is partly transferred in causation across a time, 'T' by continuing to be attached to the objects that undergo the relevant causal changes at

[19]   H. Neri-Castaneda, 'Causes, Causity, and Energy', in *Midwest Studies in Philosophy IX*, Minnesota University Press, 1984.

[20]   David Sanford, 'Direction of Causation and the Direction of Time', in *Midwest Studies in Philosophy IX*, op. cit.

> time 'T' as the totality of the causal powers . . . of the objects involved in
> the causal reaction. Causity is not a part of an object, but migrates from
> object to object riding on the backs of the objects that abide in the causal
> transaction. Causity, like space, time and motion, remains an abstract
> quantifiable structure that unifies sets of objects into tightly organized
> systems.[21]

I find this migratory non-entity, that really isn't a property, either,
extremely peculiar. Suppose we could describe an 'abstract quantifiable structure' that tied a collection of objects together in a system.
Would that describe what happens when a rock breaks a window?
Most relationships, whether real, fictitious, imaginary, or abstract,
and whether between points, lines, objects, or impossible topologies,
are quantifiable. And anything quantifiable can be described as
determining an abstract system of some kind. But it does not follow
at all from the fact that this intellectual exercise can be performed
that this is what causation is. For one thing, Castaneda's abstract system would be no more observable in experience than Hume's
object-to-object transitions were. For another, it would be of no more
assistance in practical cases, such as deciding how nicotine causes
cancer, than plain old statistical co-relation is.

Interestingly enough, in the above cited article, Castaneda actually raises the question that I'm asking about the relationship of rules
of transition to the nature of objects, only to decide not to deal with it.
There, he says;

> Causity is so intimately bound up with transfer and preservation across
> time that one cannot help asking whether the postulation of enduring
> objects involves the postulation of causity, whether substance and cau-
> sation go conceptually hand in hand. The correct answer to this question
> seems to me to be emphatically affirmative. But we will not explore the
> connections between causity and substance here.[22]

But Castaneda hasn't just shelved the issue, he has left himself completely without adequate materials with which to deal with it.

David Sanford, in 'The Direction of Causation and the Direction of
Time', struggles to give an account of temporal order for Mackie's
theory of causation. Banally, again, in the platonic universe there is
no passage of time. Sanford replaces Mackie's notion of 'fixity' with
his own account of 'conditionship',[23] which he argues does not have
the property of reflexivity. But reflexive or not, a logical,
substitutional mathematical structure has no inherent ties to exis-

---

[21]   *Ibid.*, Castaneda, p. 24.

[22]   *Ibid.*, p. 25.

[23]   *Op. cit.*, p. 73.

tence, and hence, no inherent ties to causation. Aristotle's devil 'x' has not been given his due in either Mackie's or Sanford's account of causation.

Judea Pearl[24] has come much closer to giving an account of causation that respects both the 'x' and the 'y' sides of the issue. Pearl uses explicitly intentional and perceptually oriented DAG's (Directed Acyclic Graphs) to describe the x side of the problem and statistical and algebraic formulas to describe the y side of the problem. I will invoke Pearl as an ally when I give my own account of what is needed for causation in a later chapter of this book. For now, I will turn to the relationship between causation and stable objects.

Some Skewed Accounts of Objects

Now, I will describe, in very quick overview, three accounts of what a stable object is that I believe miss the mark because they rely too heavily on a platonic, property-oriented view of an object. None of these accounts yields an actual thing, present to consciousness in experience. None describes the 'that' of a pointing or the index element in a 'one of these'. So, none of these accounts has given my devil 'x' her due. The views I will examine are a) Russell's view that an object is a set of properties, b) Kripke's view that an object is an instantiation of a natural kind, and c) Quine's view of an object as a posit of a world-view. (With a brief addendum on Putnam's pre-pragmatism sociological variant of the Quine view.)

An Object is a Set of Properties

The program that Bertrand Russell[25] entered with Alfred White-head, to describe the logic of mathematics and the logic of language in terms of one another, made it necessary for Russell to explain how grammatical structures that seem to express equivalent relations can nevertheless be logically quite different from each other. For instance, 'I see John', 'I see a man' and 'I see a unicorn' all look like

[24] Judea Pearl, *Causality, Models, Reasoning and Inference*, Cambridge, UK, 2000.

[25] As W.T. Jones points out in his *History of Western Philosophy*, pp. 158–159, Russell changed his account of what an object is at least four or five times over the course of his long and productive career. Jones characterizes the 'object is a set of properties' view as Russell, stage four, or so. Russell's view of objects as the denizens of acquaintance, was stage one or two. He discarded the earlier view to be consistent in his view of logic. I deal with the Russell view of knowledge by acquaintance later, when I discuss objects and perception. This 'divide and conquer' technique may be unfair to Russell, the individual. But I am out to show the shortcomings of certain arguments, here, not to tar and feather Russell.

they logically commit a speaker to the existence of a particular thing. To circumvent this difficulty, Russell distinguishes between names, which he says directly denote particular things so named, and definite descriptions, which have to be qualified as denoting, in case there is something to be so denoted. But even names, to be marked as unique and as denoting, sometimes require uniqueness indicators, to prevent names like 'Hamlet' from becoming confused with 'real' names.[26] This is a problem, for Russell, because in his logical system, the concatenation rules are the rules of set theory, from which it follows that individuals are sets of elements, and in the case of language, the elements are properties. Certain properties may truly be said to belong to Hamlet or a unicorn, even though neither exists.

Of course, as a practical matter, one could always follow Russell's advice, marking only 'real' things with constants and uniqueness indicators, and leaving fictions and 'empty' sets of properties as mere empty property sets. But, it seems to me that the uniqueness indicator, itself, stands in no better position with respect to the 'real' John than the original description did. The question we were really asking when we asked for the uniqueness indicator was '*What* makes the real John set real?' If the answer is a set qualifier, it seems to me that we are stuck with a third man, here, as much as Plato was. For, the claim of uniqueness is, itself, either another element in a set or another set. If another element, it is only another property, and is, itself, a description of the object, not the object as it would exist independently of description. If another set, it, itself, requires a uniqueness qualifier to make it 'real'.

In the above argument, I granted practical applicability to Russell, even though I think that his account of the objecthood of a set of descriptions describing 'John' chases a third man. But the practical applicability comes about, because people, in sensation and perception, have causal interaction with the things for which they would decide to use constants and uniqueness indicators. Russell cannot accept my reason for the applicability of his constants and uniqueness qualifiers because it is anthropomorphic, intentional, and temporal. My explanation is not amenable to conversion into set theoretic terms. But his explanation of denotation simply doesn't work in his own terms. No concrete, real thing is a retreat through a series of progressively more amorphous sets, nor can any real thing be successfully denoted in this way.

---

[26]   Bertrand Russell, 'Descriptions', in *Readings in the Philosophy of Language*, ed. by Jay F. Rosenberg and Charles Travis, Prentice Hall Inc., Englewood Cliffs, New Jersey, 1971.

My conclusion on Russell is, thus, that an object cannot be a set of properties. This form of Platonism is as mired in third man regressions as Plato's was.

An Object is a Member of a Natural Kind

Saul Kripke, of course, was the initiator of the point of view that holds that contact with an object, whether by naming or by pointing, is contact with a natural kind that can be described as a scientific type. 'Water, ' for instance, is a rigid designator for a natural kind, consisting of all and only items composed of H_2O. Things get their names at initial baptisms, which establish the name as connected to the thing by *de re* necessity. Kripke argues that *de re* necessities of this type yield analytic *a posteriori* statements. He explains as follows:

> Now imagine an object occupying this very position in the room which *was* an ethereal entelechy. Would it be this very object here? . . . it seems to me that it could not ever be *this thing* . . . whatever we imagine counterfactually having happened to it other than what actually did, the one thing that we cannot imagine happening to this thing is that *it*, given that it is composed of molecules, should still have existed and not have been composed of molecules. We can imagine having discovered that it wasn't composed of molecules. But once we know that this is a thing composed of molecules — that this is the very nature of the substance of which it is made — we can't then, at least if the way I see it is correct, imagine that this thing might have failed to have been composed of molecules.[27]

Obviously, Kripke was out to try to fix the problems I cited in Russell's and like-minded descriptions of property-oriented views of an object. I think that he has part of the solution to the problem I cited with Russell's view in his initial baptisms. But I think that Kripke is incorrect about what the baptism picks out. I will later argue for a notion of a stable object that indexes an act of naming to a point of view. Kripke has his baptism indexed to the point of view of molecular biology and chemistry. Certainly, the point of view of science is a fine, reputable point of view to select, and I agree that that point of view is often the one that a thinker would choose to mark or name a bit of her experience. However, I disagree with Kripke that it is the only one 'we can imagine', or the only one that can be correct. To start with, the people who first named water had no access at all to that point of view. If they thought of water's structure at all, they were more likely to have thought of it as 'holy nectar of the stars', or 'tears of the clouds' than as composed of molecules. Furthermore, no

---

[27] Saul Kripke, *Naming and Necessity, op. cit.* pp. 126–127.

two-year-old, learning the word now, has any notion at all of the molecular structure of water. In addition, I think that it is twentieth-century chauvinism of a very arrogant sort to suppose that even science cannot, ever, develop a substantially different view of the composition of water. And it is scientific chauvinism with a vengeance to suppose that only the points of view of biology and chemistry uniquely and rigidly designate.

Certainly, the point of view of science is the most universal one that people have access to today. But it does not follow from the universality of science that the point of view of science is the only one that might conceivably interest a thinker. For example, someone who is concerned about the 'stuff' that is leaking into his basement is a lot less concerned with whether it is H_2O than he is with the fact that it is leaking into his basement. Location is far more important than molecular structure, in this case of picking out a substance.

In addition to the unnecessary and scientific-myopic restriction that Kripke imposes on the point of view from which an initial baptism can take place, he also explains the necessity of the *de re* connection between a thing and its name by a completely unhelpful account of 'possible worlds' in which the thing does or does not have certain properties. 'Possible worlds' talk puts Kripke right back in the third man fix that he was trying to evade in Russell's work. For, whatever protests Kripke may raise about the simplicity of his possible worlds, [28]they will still be sets of properties or sets of descriptions. And, again, if we need a 'possible world' set of descriptions to verify the set of real world descriptions, don't we also need a possible-possible world set of descriptions to verify the reality of the possible world set? The problem, again, is that a y-type, property oriented, logically structured explanation is being offered for an x-type sensory, experiential, indexical, existence-related problem. Kripke, like Russell, is looking in the wrong place for an account of a stable object. He is trying to reduce my Aristotelian devil to a platonic set of properties. I insist, again, that the attempt fails.

An Object is a Posit of a Theory

W.V.O. Quine is more consistent and deliberate about his platonism on objects than are many other twenty-first-century philosophers, so I will spend a little time arguing against some of his objections to a point of view like mine, next.

---

[28]   Kripke says, 'A possible world is given by the descriptive conditions we associate with it.' *Ibid.*, p. 44.

Quine's view of the nature of an object is that an object is a posit of a theory, or world-view.[29] Quine knows that he has to give an account of a stable object to even lay the groundwork for a broadly-based theory of the nature of reality. Also, he acknowledges the role played by sensory data in establishing that groundwork. But having acknowledged the existence of 'sensory hits', or what he calls 'the fanciful fanciless medium of unvarnished news',[30] he then dismisses the importance of direct contact with experience to accentuate the uniformity of language in communication.

> The uniformity that unites us in communication and belief is a uniformity of resultant patterns overlying a chaotic subjective diversity of connections between words and experience. Uniformity comes where it matters socially; hence rather in point of intersubjectively conspicuous circumstances of utterance than in point of privately conspicuous ones.[31]

Quine's commitment to behaviorism plays an important role in his insistence that publicly conspicuous circumstances are prior to privately conspicuous ones. Quine maintains that if publicly observable performances of speakers can be made uniform, this entails that there *are* no significant differences in the private arenas. He claims that no matter how different the experience of 'redness' might be for a normal person than it is for a colorblind person, if both respond 'red' only in appropriate circumstances, no important difference exists. He explains this claim as follows.

> Different persons growing up in the same language are like different bushes trimmed and trained to take the shape of identical elephants. The anatomical details of twigs and branches will fulfill the elephantine form differently from bush to bush, but the overall outward results are alike.[32]

Of course, the restrictions imposed on psychological investigations by methodological behaviorism are therapeutic. But my contention is that if one is to give an account of how minds or thinking operate, or of how language acquires meaning, or of what a stable object is, or how transition takes place in time, one cannot be so disdainful of the 'chaotically subjective' arena of experiential thinking processes.

---

[29] See W.V.O. Quine, *Word and Object*, M.I.T. Press, Cambridge Mass. 1960.

[30] *Ibid*,. p. 2.

[31] *Ibid.*, p. 8.

[32] *Ibid.*, p. 8.

Quine, of course, also discards beliefs, intentions, *de re* predication, modal contexts and Donnellan-type[33] reference. His reasons for discarding all of these items are the same as his reasons for discarding sense-data and idiolects: a nice, neat, behavioristically constrained account of their operation cannot be given. This insistence on following a certain scientific methodology so slavishly despite its obvious inadequacy to deal with certain common human experiences seems perverse. To me, hitting such a 'brick wall' in inquiry signals a need to restructure our thinking on methodology, not a need to deny the data.

Even if we do currently lack the knowledge of neurophysiology that would be needed to describe how photoelectric stimulation does or does not conjure up sensations of redness, we can still give another kind of account of what it is to see or fail to see red. We can do the type of psychological analysis that Robert Cummins[34] describes in the absence of any knowledge of brain chemistry.

Quine would still object, however, as follows;

> But this is a misleading way of depicting matters, even when the idea of a sense-datum language is counted frankly as metaphor. For the trouble is that immediate experience simply will not, of itself, cohere as an autonomous domain. References to physical things are largely what hold it together. These references are not just inessential vestiges of the initially inter-subjective character of language, capable of being weeded out by devising an artificially subjective language for sense data. Rather, they give us our main continuing access to past sense data themselves; for past sense data are mostly gone for good except as commemorated in physical posits.[35]

Quine is surely right about two aspects of the situation, as he describes it above. First, he is right about the murkiness of the subjective sense-data domain. And second, he is right to say that the invention of an 'artificial sense-data language' will not help. But I think that he is wrong about *why* the mire will not cohere of itself, and about the role played by physical objects in giving us access to the domain.

As I have previously pointed out, the murkiness of the sense data domain comes about for two reasons. One, syntax is not being used to sort and categorize experience at this stage in the process of coming to understand experience. Two, the domain is essentially inten-

---

[33]   Keith S. Donnellan gives examples of strangely successful cases of reference in 'Reference and Definite Descriptions' in *Readings in the Philosophy of Language, op. cit.*, pp. 195 ff.

[34]   *Op. cit.*

[35]   *Word and Object*, pp. 2-3.

tional, and hence, essentially personal and private. There could be no 'artificial sense-data language' only for Wittgenstein's[36] reasons that there can be no private language.

Quine *thinks* that the mire will not cohere of itself because a) it needs to borrow objects from elsewhere to make it cohere and b) it is inaccessible to behavioristically constrained investigations. On point a), I would counter that objects *come from* this domain, they are not borrowed from elsewhere to be used here. The notion of an object just *is* the notion of some *this* impinging upon my personal experience. On point b), Quine's dogmatic behaviorism is, again, playing a definitive role, and, again, I would cite Cummins to argue that the restriction is both extreme and unproductive.

John Searle has argued[37] that we must concede that there are events in the universe, namely, some brain events in autonomous creatures, that are not accessible to objective investigation, whatever one's methodological preferences might be. This inherent privacy will remain as a practical matter, barring grossly immoral intrusions (no vats, please!) even in the presence of a completely detailed neurophysiology of brain events.

I agree with Searle that even if we had knowledge of biochemical events that always and everywhere accompanied sonnet-writing, still the experience of writing a sonnet would remain, like the bat's radar experience, an intentional, private experience. The domain of object-positing will remain analytically independent of brain events even if those brain events can be biologically or neurologically described. Cartesian dualism is just the wrong way to think about this distinction. The difference between a brain involved in sonnet composing and a sonnet writing experience is one of point of view, or methodology of approach, not the traditional difference between types of substances. I will still claim that a substance distinction can be made, here, but it is based on difference of point of view, not difference of class of thing.

One final comment on Quine's objections to a position like mine about objects: Quine defends his notion of a material, scientific, object as a posit of a theory as follows.

> To call a posit a posit is not to patronize it. A posit can be unavoidable except at the cost of other, no less artificial expedients. Everything to

---

[36] Wittgenstein's famous 'What we cannot speak about we must pass over in silence.' is the final statement of the *Tractatus Logico-Philosophicus*, Routledge and Kegan Paul, London, 1961, p. 74. He argues more extensively for the impossibility of a private language in *The Philosophical Investigations*, trans. G.E.M. Anscombe, MacMillan, New York 1953.

[37] In a lecture at Syracuse University, 1986.

which we concede existence is a posit from the standpoint of the theory-building process, and simultaneously real from the standpoint of the theory that is being built. Nor let us look down at the standpoint of the theory as make-believe; for we can never do better than occupy the standpoint of some theory or other, the best we can muster at the time.[38]

In this passage Quine is claiming to be simultaneously a scientific realist and an empiricist by equating Johnson's rock *qua* posit of geological science with Johnson's rock *qua* pain in Johnson's toe.[39] He thinks he can hold the two together via his 'self-rebuilding ship' metaphor. But I don't think that any intellectual clarity is gained by allowing Quine to get away with this.

Rather, I think that we should distinguish as best we can between sensory contact with reality in its unsystematic, singular, imagistic, sensory and essentially private nature, and the theory-laden domain of platonic concepts and universals. Johnson's rock, qua geological item, is a platonic construct. Qua pain in Johnson's toe, however, it is a piece of data for a theory of object positing, in Aristotelian terms, an 'x' for predication of which nothing has yet been predicated. Contra Quine, I would insist that Johnson's 'Ouch!' is an indexical, not a predicate; not even a predicate of a very degenerate sort.

En route to becoming a pragmatist, Hilary Putnam passed through a functionalist stage that proved to be very influential in late twentieth-century thinking on the nature of objects. One might also say that Putnam's functionalism held that objects are posits of theories. But the Putnam version of this view makes the theories in question more broadly sociological than Quine's strictly science-oriented view.[40] In Putnam's version of this story, a language is a community effort, and the meanings of its expressions are determined through a 'division of labor' in which experts know the 'real' meanings of words that everyone else uses. Putnam claimed that it is not possible for an individual to mean something different by his or her words than other members of the community do.

Putnam, however, in his move towards pragmatism, rejected his sociological view of meaning and object-positing, citing reasons such as the following for doing so.

[38] *Ibid.*, p. 22.

[39] Samuel Johnson, compiler of the first English Dictionary, is said to have claimed to have disproved Berkeley's idealism by kicking a rock and declaring, 'There, I've proven that it exists.' Quine discusses Johnson's rock in *Word & Object*, p. 3.

[40] Hilary Putnam, 'The Meaning of 'Meaning' ', in *Language, Mind and Knowledge*, ed. K. Gunderson, Minnesota Studies in the Philosophy of Science, vol.7, Minneapolis, University of Minnesota Press, 1975.

There is a common sense way of clearing up the [Humean] puzzle about how many objects there are in the room, and that is to say, 'It depends upon what you mean by 'object'.' This common sense remark is perfectly right, but deeper than may appear to the common sense mind, itself.

As we say, there are many ways of *using* the notion of an object — even the so called 'logical notion' of an object — or the existential quantifier. And depending on how we use the notion, the answer to the question 'How many objects are in the room?' can be 'Five', 'seven', '2^n' — and there are many more possibilities.[41]

Putnam is explaining, in this passage, that the grounding of the notion of an object cannot come from any theory, whether scientific, sociological, or otherwise. I would insist that there are many possible sources for structuring the notion of an object, but ultimately there is only one place from which the grounding under any structured notion can come: first person singular human experience.

A Skewed Account of Existence and Categorization

Since I will, in a later chapter, argue at length for the position that existential quantification in a symbolic logic does not adequately capture the general notion of existence, I will here give only a brief overview of what that argument will look like, in order to indicate why I believe that ideas about existence in general are skewed by inattention to my Aristotelian 'x', as badly as notions of causation and stable objects are skewed by this slight.

In this area, as well as in the area of discussion of stable objects, Quine saw, and argued against, many of the difficulties that I believe are fatal to an exclusively platonic view of reality. Quine's theses on 'Ontological Relativity' and the 'indeterminacy of translation' both point out what I have called 'metaphysical drift' problems with property-oriented views of the nature of existence. Quine discusses substitutionality problems with the existential quantifier when he discusses the slingshot argument, the Lowenheim-Skolem theorem, and Gödel's proof of the impossibility of a simultaneously consistent and complete system. But Quine believes that he has these difficulties under control when he describes a 'proxy function' from one theory to a background theory, or metatheory, in which he believes he can specify the truth conditions of the described theory. I will claim that Quine has failed to prevent metaphysical drift by retreating through a proxy function to a background theory to describe the truth of symbolic logic. Again, my claim will be that Quine is not drawing closer to truth and reality by his 'semantic ascent' to a back-

---

[41] Hilary Putnam, *Representation and Reality*, M.I.T. Press, Bradford Books, Cambridge, Mass. 1988, p. 113.

ground theory; rather he is just, through another means, chasing a third man.

In contrast, I will claim that any theory that purports to discuss reality must be grounded in human experience. For experience is the only contact with reality that we humans have. This, I hope, has been a sufficient argument for the need for a new look at Aristotle's devil x.

Summary

In this chapter, I have argued that there are non-computational mental processes that must be considered if one is to understand thinking. I have argued that, in addition to the computationally based platonic mental processes, there are also experientially based, object-positing processes. The object-positing processes deal with data of an unclassified sort which may be sensory or perceptual and is always intentional, private, singular, immediate and indexical. The object-positing process produces knowledge by acquaintance or recognition, and produces the 'x' that occurs in propositions as a 'this something'.

By contrast, the computational property-attributing process is a quantifying and qualifying process, used by the mind to sort and classify data offered by the object-positing process for classification. The distinctive marks of this process are syntactic order, and use of concepts or categories. Property-attributing produces eternal, truth-functional propositions, and well-structured concepts. Computers, as syntactic engines, can mimic most of the mind's property-attributing processes. But as John Searle has argued, in the case of human thinking, this is only part of the story.

The two processes are interactive, both with each other and with the thinker's environment. Replacing the current static view of knowledge, that represents knowledge of a proposition as a mind having apprehended an isomorphic structure of the world, with this, more dynamic view of thinking, will open new doors for research on the mind. This dynamic, interactive, operational view of mental processes provides an inherently more complex view of human thinking, that does a better job of accounting for the range and subtlety of thinking that humans actually do. On this view, an active human mind interacts constantly with a dynamic environment, both manipulating it through thought, and manipulated by it in sensation and experience.

I think that a lot of good academic effort has been wasted in the twentieth century by philosophers like Russell, Ryle and Quine, and by psychologists of a Skinnerian bent, on trying to disprove either the existence or the significance of the elements of thought that I have characterized as belonging in a theory of object-positing. I propose that we abandon the denial approach, and deal with the phenomena in their own terms.

Further, the project of analyzing human thinking *ha*s to be done in this way, because several of the most basic aspects of human thinking are badly misunderstood unless the interactive character of these two processes is recognized. For a stable object is the result of the object-positing process, causation is the experience of world-to-mind and mind-to-world manipulation encountered in the object-positing process, and existence is a generalization on stable objects and causation.

In the next few chapters, I will give my account of what causation, stable objects, and existence are.

Chapter 2

Causation

A Formal, Semantic Account

What Causation (Kausation) is NOT

The notion of causation that I will develop in the ensuing few chapters of this book is new in the philosophical literature, although there are some approximate predecessors. So, to forestall confusion for readers who have their own notions of what causation is, I will preface this discussion of causation with a short chapter of disclaimers, specifying what my notion of causation is *not*. In addition, I will spell my notion with a 'k', as 'kausation', to distinguish it from other concepts of causal transfer that might be around.

Kausation isn't Efficient Causation as Described by Dretske, Kripke, or Mackie

Each of the above authors supposes that causation is a brute fact about the external world. A billiard-ball case is a classic example of this type of causation. Aristotle called the Mackie et. al., notion of causation efficient causation, while the scholastics called it transuent causation. But there is a big difference between Aristotle and the scholastics on one hand, and Dretske, Kripke and Mackie, on the other, on this issue. That is, the old-timers thought of efficient causation as only one of several types of explanation of transition, whereas the contemporaries think that efficient causation is all there is. Indeed, a lot of the projects of Dretske, Kripke and Mackie can be viewed as attempts at reducing other types of explanation of transition to this one.

Kausation isn't Agent Causation , as Described by Searle

John Searle argues in *Intentionality* that the ability to make one's own body move is the basic notion of causation. He thinks that efficient notions of causation are projected agency. Berkeley argued for a similar notion of causation, ultimately claiming as a result of his position that only minds can really cause motion. But Searle ultimately commits himself to a more Kantian notion of causation, which is both more flexible and less idealistic than Berkeley's view. In his 1990 Presidential Address to the Pacific Division of the A.P.A., Searle argued that even syntax and computational structure are not brute facts about the external world, but rather, are interpretations of experience by an active mind.[1] This Searle position is very Kantian, very sensitive to Hume's critique of induction, and not at all projected agency.

Kausation isn't what's Left Over after Hume's Critique of Induction. But we're getting Warmer.

I'll say that Hume's[2] critique reduces the common notion of causation to the following remnants:

   a. An observation is made of spatial and/or temporal contiguity between two objects or impressions.

   b. An observation is made that similar objects or impressions are often contiguous in experience.

   c. A lazy habit of expecting the future to resemble the past is superimposed on (a) and (b).

Hume hasn't completely gutted the notion of causation, here, although he has discarded efficient causation and projected agency. But, he has left statistical co-relation in (b). That is an important remnant.

The difference between my notion of kausation, and Hume's causation arises over (a) above. Hume either doesn't care or claims to not know whether the relata of the spatial or temporal contiguity relationship are two objects or two impressions. But he does suppose that causal transition is *either* object to object transition *or* impression to impression transition. Kausation, however, occurs between *one* object and *one* impression. The kausal relationship can only occur from a specific point of view because it relates an observer to an observed object. The primary role of this relationship is identification of objects and understanding of experience, from the observer's point of view. Once this co-relation is established, statistical co-relation among large numbers of observed occurrences is all that is needed to extend the understanding gained to agency and pro-

---

[1]   John Searle, "Is the Brain a Digital Computer?", Presidential Address to the Pacific Division of the American Philosophical Assn., in *The Proceedings and Addresses of the American Philosophical Association*, Vol. 64 No. 3, November, 1990 University of Delaware, Newark, Delaware, 1990.

[2]   Hume's *Treatise*, op. cit.

jected agency. And, as Hume rightly pointed out, statistical probability is as close to certainty as anyone will ever get in this area.

Kausation isn't really a Kantian Category of Apperception, but we're Getting Still Warmer

For one thing, a tendency to relate to one's world as a manipulated
experiencer and a manipulating namer and identifier has to be at
least endemic in the human condition if not outright innate. I am less
concerned than Kant was with demonstrating that the capacity to
interpret experience kausally is synthetic rather than analytic. In
fact, I think that the point of view chosen analytically selects the
nature of the relationship. But I will discuss this point more later. My
version of this story will contain elements that might be termed
either analytic or synthetic, in the traditional senses of those words.

For another thing, I need something like Kant's distinction
between phenomena and noumena. Kant didn't think that this distinction made him an idealist, and I don't think that I need to be committed to idealism for adopting the distinction, either. In the kausal
relationship, an observer is in direct contact with an external world,
on the world-to-mind side of the relationship, where the observer is
being manipulated by the real world. And, on the mind-to-world
side of the relationship, wherein the observer is identifying and
naming various aspects of his or her experience, the observer is also
relating directly to the real, external world. (I will now stop using the
common external-internal metaphor because I believe it badly misrepresents the nature of experience.)

The gap between phenomena and noumena arises from a combination of the intentions and ignorance of the observer. Kausal
observers see, feel, taste, smell and are subject to the real things of the
world, but they sometimes fail to understand what they experience.
If they did completely understand what they experience, they
would be omniscient, within the range of their experience. But, even
if they had achieved omniscience within the range of their experience, they couldn't know that they had achieved it. This impossibility occurs because of the practical impossibility of comparing the
two ends of the kausal relationship for accuracy, because the two
ends of the relationship are mutually determining of each other.[3]

[3]   Kant, in *The Critique of Pure Reason*, distinguishes two senses of the word
       'noumenon'. The negative sense means '..a thing so far as it is not an object of our
       sensible intuition, and so [is] abstract from our mode of intuiting it.' The positive
       sense means 'we understand by it an object of a non-sensible intuition.' Kant
       emphatically denies that the positive sense identifies a form of thought for he
       says of it, 'we thereby presuppose a special mode of intuition, namely the

I differ from Kant, however, on the relationship between phenomena and noumena. Kant thinks that there are two classes of things here: phenomena, which are intuited sensorily, and noumena, which are the 'objects' of ' . . . a mere limiting concept, the function of which is to curb the pretensions of sensibility; . . . '[4] Kant claims that the concept of a class of noumena is necessary;

> to prevent sensible intuition from being extended to things in themselves, and thus, to limit the objective validity of sensible knowledge.[5]

While I think that Kant's cautionary warnings are important to curb excessive knowledge claims, which seems to be his chief goal in the above passages, I think that they may be more than one needs to understand objects.

That is, I think that it is possible to heed Kant's warnings, and still be a direct realist. I do this by taking seriously the identification of a thing with the intention that names it. The thing does not, in Kantian terms, transcend its identifying point of view, because the point of view is exhausted by the identification; there is nothing more to it than the identification of the thing. And, conversely, there is nothing more to the identification of the thing than the point of view that names it. Kant's caution, in my terms, is a reminder of the very redundancy of this relationship. A universe inventory can, thus, be compiled in terms of lists of points of view, but not in terms of lists of transcendental noumena. And, we don't need to postulate the existence of transcendental classes of things, because we already have the things, as identified in the respective points of view.

To put Putnam's observation about object counts (see p. 25) in perspective, if one doesn't count the 'transcendental' objects, but only the phenomenal ones, count conflicts will not be a problem. Count conflicts can only arise if a point of view inventory list is compared to some, supposed 'objective', in Kantian terms, transcendental, inventory list. Kant and I agree that the comparison cannot be made. He thinks that it can't be made because knowledge does not extend to the things to which it would have to extend in order to make the comparison, or because the things-in-themselves are property-less. I think that it can't be made because the knowledge that we do have is of the thing, but is redundantly self-limiting. Humans directly expe-

---

intellectual, which is not that which we possess, and of which we cannot comprehend even the possibility.' Thus, the thing-in-itself is only a limiting concept for Kant. Platonism is side-railed by being declared, 'empty'. *Critique,* trans. Norman Kemp Smith, St.Martin's Press, New York 1965, p. 268.

[4]   *Ibid.* p. 272.

[5]   *Ibid.* p. 272.

rience reality, but often project mistaken or overly limited precon-
ceived ideas of what reality is on their experience, perpetuating their
own ignorance. The marine biologist and the four-year-old seaside
bather both know seaweed, and both experience the real thing. The
fact that neither is omniscient about seaweed is a comment on their
respective states of ignorance, not a comment on the inherent tran-
scendence of seaweed.

Kausality also differs from a Kantian Category of Apperception in
that the Kantian Category is something of a static sorting box. Experiences come in to a somewhat passive observer, who tosses them in
the 'causal' box because this is where they fit, in Kant's picture of
thought. My picture of how thinking occurs replaces the passive
observer with an active mind reaching out to understand an
ever-changing onslaught of data. Manipulation and creative
construal are continually taking place on both sides of the relationship. In my view, what rates as a 'fit' is always negotiable. Only a
dull-witted person would undergo a static, sorting-box thinking
process, in which new points of view did not continually develop.

What Causation Is

Kausation is a Semantic, Object-Positing Process

I have been arguing that kausation and objecthood are inextricable,
and so neither concept can be used to account for the other in a way
that fails to recognize their interrelatedness. Both objecthood and
kausation are parts of the process that I have called object-positing.
In this process, a mind picks out an aspect of its experience and
names or identifies it. The 'x' that I have been discussing up to this
point ambiguously denotes the process, and its two 'sides', the identification of the thing in a mind, and the thing in experience that is
identified by the mind.

For purposes of my discussion of kausation, I have to disambigu-
ate the two sides of the relationship. I will, thus, adopt John Searle's
terminology for his similar discussion of thinking, and call the
'mind' side of the relationship the 'x' in thought, and the 'world' or
'reality' side of the relationship the 'r' side of kausation. Because I
consider this relationship to be semantic and redundant, and perhaps even analytic, in Kant's sense of 'analytic', I will say that the
ambiguity does not in fact mark a real difference. In fact, I will claim
that the 'x' ultimately equals the 'r'. They are separable only for purposes of discussion.

The Incoherence of the Received View

First, let me point out how different my notion of kausation is from the causal intuitions that seem to motivate the large number of 'causal' theories of mental representation that are in the recent literature. The motivation behind theories like Dretske's seems to be roughly the following.

 a. We have a very clear idea of what causation is in cases in which one billiard ball knocks into another one and makes it move, or a tiger passes on stripes to her cubs.

 b. That's what happens when things cause our perceptions of them — things pass something into our brains the same way that balls pass motion to other balls and tigers pass genes to other tigers.

I find this picture of perception, causation, transition, and understanding incoherent. Let me explain why.

Suppose that something 'genetic' or 'motile' about a pencil stimulated my various sensing devices to pass pencil 'g'(for genetic) or 'm'(for motile) messages into my brain. These variously specific stimulus messages would have to somehow unite in my brain to form a unitary 'object message' for me to recognize a pencil as a unitary object. On the causal view, the unrelated but concurrent synaptic events that are triggered by the 'm' or 'g' stimuli, and united in my polyglot representation of the pencil, are highly unlikely to have anything at all to do with the unit object in space, the pencil, that I take the synaptic events to be representing. Nothing like a recognizably continuous chain of motile or genetic code markers is likely to be preserved across this biochemical chain of events. Even if some motile or genetic marker were to be preserved down the chain of events, it would be impossible to know that it had been preserved, because no 'resemblance check' could ever be performed between the pencil and the representation of it in the mind or brain.

The problem with the above story of mental representation is not that the biochemical chain of events in perception is unimportant. Obviously, those events are a necessary condition for the occurrence of perceptual experience. The problem is rather that the biochemistry of the situation is uninformative. The relationship between a pencil and a person's experience of a pencil is not a genetic transfer or motile transfer relationship. Rather, it is a semantic relationship, of an object-positing kind. For, only an explanation of the relationship between 'x', taken to be someone's experience of a pencil, and 'r', taken to be the pencil as a unit object in space, that claims that x = r can explain why both genetic or motile markers and resemblance

checks at the two ends of the relationship are irrelevant to the identification of the thought with the pencil. And obviously, they are irrelevant. Even Dretske winds up having to admit the irrelevance of
these factors in a paper with Berent Enc, that I will discuss later in
this chapter.

The Semantic Character of Causation

However, if one admits the irrelevance of the so-called causal factors
in perception and experience, the nature of the semantic relationship
between the x and the r becomes apparent.

The x is an experience 'of' the pencil. 'Ofness' is a semantic relationship that is possible only for a creature with a point of view. For
one thing, ofness is an identity relationship of just the kind that
Hume argued that causal relationships can't be. The object is picked
out, identified, distinguished from the rest of someone's experience
and named by the point of view in the experience. And, conversely,
the point of view is determined by the impinging kausal impression
of the unit object in space.

To explain the character of this relationship, I will borrow terminology from John Searle's description of the relationship in his book
Intentionality. There, Searle argued that thinking should be understood as the basic human activity of which speech acts are a specific
type. There will be some differences between my account and
Searle's, but I believe that our views largely complement and rein-
force one another. So, using similar terminology seems appropriate.

The Structure of Causation

The relationship between the experience of a pencil and the pencil,
taken as the source of the experience, requires a reciprocal, interactive process between some 'x' taken as someone's experience of a
pencil, and some 'r' taken as the unit object in space, the pencil. The
semantic, object-positing relationship takes place as a perceptual
process between someone's impressionistic 'hit' in experience and
the aspect of reality that that person identifies as the kause of the hit.
The relationship has to work two ways, as represented by the chart
on the next page.

If this analysis of the relationship between x and r looks redundant
and circular, that is exactly as it should be. The relationship between
x and r is what Searle calls 'causally self-referential'.[6] But Searle presumes in his account that the basic notion of causation is agent-cau-

---

[6]   *Intentionality*, p.53.

sation, and that he is importing agency into perception to explain perception. On the contrary, I believe that the analysis in the chart gives the most basic notion of kausation, and it must be *exported* to agency in order to give a coherent account of agency.

	world-to-mind	mind-to-world
1.	An aspect of reality 'r', impinges on a person 'p' kausing the occurrence of an experience, 'x'.	A person 'p' takes an aspect of her experience 'x' to be kaused.
2.	P recognizes 'x' as an experience of r.	X becomes the basis for P's notion of r.
3.	P individuates and names r as the kause of x.	P identifies r with her notion of x.

Kausation is part of the object-positing process, directly experienced in perception and other types of direct recognition. Kausation is not *observed* in perception because it is a part of the observation process, not an extrinsic, autonomous thing. Further, kausation can only occur from a specific point of view, and the identification on the mind-to-world side of the process always involves a judgment about the experience being marked. The options for kause or source of an 'x' in thought range from one's internal states, including items as diverse as dreams, thoughts, memories and indigestion, through variously construable objects or events in the so-called 'external' world. The judgment that a person makes about the kause of his or her 'x' in thought involves induction of a Humean sort, in this way.

a) P establishes experiences x_1, x_2, x_3, and x_4 as discreet mental impressions.

b) Over time, P notices lack of constancy in her experience of those impressions.

c) P is confronted with several options concerning x_1 through x_4.
   i) She may persist in taking all four impressions as kaused by objects,
   ii) She may decide that some of them are adjectival, either as properties of an object or background for the object(s), which are taken as figure against a ground.

iii) Or, She may decide that all of them are adjectival on some, further, unobserved, object.

d) To judge among the available options, P analyses which, if any of them, is most stable through time.

e) P assigns status as 'r', known as 'x', to her most stable x_ns, status as kause to 'r', and status as transitional property to all xs not consistent with r's role as kause of x.

In saying that this world-to-mind and mind-to-world reciprocal interaction is the most basic notion of kausation, I am claiming that kausation is the mutual ability of experience to manipulate thinking, and conversely, of thinking to manipulate experience. The type of mutual manipulation here *can not* be efficient causation because it is wholly intentional. Whether P is effected by r depends *completely* on whether P is paying attention to r and has r fixed in consciousness as a 'this thing' to index. No matter how persistently r may be impinging on P, if P does not focus attention, and intentionally index r, r does not become a point of view for P.

I will show how other notions of causation can be understood in terms of this mutually manipulative relationship later in the next chapter. For now, I want to explain the roles of the observer and of the judgment in the structure of kausation that I have just presented.

The Roles of the Observer and Judgment in Causation

My structure for kausation requires a point of view, and hence, an observer who is capable of having a point of view. But this role will not turn out to be a homunculus in this account of kausation. For, the described relationship is semantic, rather than being patterned on agent causation. In agent causation, the point of view is limited to that of the agent; the 'push' that starts the ball rolling must originate with a specific agent. A semantic relationship of the kind that I am describing, however, is generalizable. P may, of course, take his own point of view towards some aspect of his experience. In that case, his semantic relationship with 'r' will parallel his teleological relationship with it. But, people can be disinterested, or variously interested observers or namers in ways that they can't be disinterested or variously interested doers.

So, while putting P into a teleological account of causation has the effect of requiring that there must always be a person-surrogate in all cases of causation, putting P in my kausal account only has the result of requiring that there be a point of view from which the kausal story is being told.

Point of view, unlike agency, can be 'behind the scenes' in a semantic relationship in much the way that it is behind the scenes in ordinary observation of the passing show. If one is absorbed in watching the parade before one, the point of view can fade to insignificance in apprehension of the events. Scientific disciplines specifically espouse particular points of view. For instance, physics requires that all data be construed as matter in motion, biology, that data be viewed as organic systems. The point of view adopted can be God's eye, fish eye, microscopic, macroscopic, social, political, or of any other kind conceivable, as long as the two way relationship between x and r can be maintained from that point of view. The objects posited and the capacity of experience to kause impressions will be mutually determined by the point of view adopted, in any scenario involving understanding experience.

Thus, the homunculus evaporates from this account of kausation, but intentionality and judgment do not. Again, this is as things should be for an account of causation.[7] D. S. Shwayder argues for the opacity of contexts containing ' . . . . causes___' on the grounds, also cited by Davidson, that what rates as a cause depends very much on what it is that one wants explained. In discussing what rates as cause or effect in a billiard-balls type case, Shwayder comments,

> . . . the assignment of an impact as cause or as effect depends on whether it is 'taken' as the end of one movement or the start of another.[8]

Movement, taken as a conserved quantity in nature, is continuous and uninterrupted. Any interruption in movement is somewhat artificial and is imposed by a point of view more limited than all-of-motion through all-of-time. Shwayder proposes later,

> . . . a perfect intellect who perceived the cosmos for what it is, in all of its continuances and connections and who accordingly never suffered the need for explanations, would never perceive causes.[9]

Let me add to Schwayder's observation that the point of view required to perceive causes must be rooted in time, as well as short of omniscience. For if the time across which a transition takes place is too long, the object positing process would yield a single, stable object as an analysis of the relationship of xs and rs, not a cause-effect

---

[7]   Follesdal points out how context-dependent causation is in 'Quantifying into Causal Contexts', in *Reference and Modality*, ed. by Linsky, Oxford University Press, England, 1971.

[8]   D.S. Shwayder, 'Hume Was Right, Almost; And Where he Wasn't, Kant Was', in *Midwest Studies in Philosophy*, University of Minnesota Press, Minneapolis, Minn. 1984, p. 145.

[9]   *Ibid.*

pair. The removal of all time would give a Spinozistic one-substance world.

In addition to the intentionality needed for a point of view, there is also further intentionality in the kausal relationship, resulting from the status judgments on x and r that are made as part of the object-positing process. Since these judgments can be made in a variety of ways, the process is both intensional in the sense of logically opaque and more generally intentional, in the way that agent causation is. Even in the most simple and straight-forward cases of a person interpreting his or her experience, a judgment must be made about what is kausing the experience, and whether the experience is being kaused in the ordinary way.

We do in fact make this kind of judgment all the time, with relatively little difficulty. It is a strength of my account that the account clarifies what is happening in these cases. Consider an x that I might be experiencing of a colleague. I can judge the x kaused by him and consistent with what I know of him (veridical perception), or kaused by him but inconsistent with what I know of him, in which case I will wonder if he's been ill, or has some serious problem. I can also judge the x to be not kaused by him, but consistent with what I know of him. This might occur if I had a dream in which he was interrogating me on some fine point of logic, and I woke thinking, 'I'd better straighten that out, or he will take me to task for it.' I could also judge an x of a colleague neither kaused by him nor consistent with him, for example, if I dreamed he was a wild boar attacking me, when I know he is a gentle and reasonable person.

On my account of the relationship between x and r it is easy to see how these judgments are made. We can either manipulate the object-positing process or be manipulated by it. Most sensory data, as well as great ideas, flashes of insight, and dreams 'burst' on consciousness unsolicited. And, the character of the experiences, alone, if viewed statically, would not enable us to tell dream xs from veridical perception. But, we do in fact, make these distinctions, and we can teach children to make them, as parents do when children wake up with nightmares. The way that we do this is very similar to the way we learn to distinguish homonyms in language. We analyze the kause, the context, and the way in which we are using the name to identify the experience. We clearly do have access to the kause, the context and the experience when we make these judgments, and are not relying exclusively on a static, picture-like impression, as Descartes presumed.

Since the mind-to-world part of the x=r relationship is intentional and semantic, mistakes of equivocation can occur in these judgments. Good perceptual illusions such as mirages are examples of truly equivocal or ambiguous sensory data that make kausal judgments very difficult. But I think that the fact that we do regularly make these judgments, and that the mistakes that we do make can be understood as mistakes of equivocation, indicates that I have rightly described this judgment as a semantic judgment. The possibility of mistaken identifications does not pose a general epistemological problem in this area any more than homonyms pose a general meaning problem in language. But further intentionality is added to the object-positing process by the judgments involved in kausation.

Michael Tooley attributes what he calls a 'singularist' view of causation to C.J. Ducasse and G. E. Anscombe.[10] The singularist view claims that the primary model for causation is single-event causation, and the systems of causal laws that we construct in the sciences are generalizations over the various single cases. A proponent of this view would typically claim that the universal laws articulated by the sciences are artificial constructs. They only really apply to ideal cases or to artificially controlled laboratory situations. Although they can be used to explain natural occurrences, their explanatory power in the natural world never matches their elegance in dealing with ideal cases.

I agree with these authors that single case causation is the primary type of kausation. But I think that there is a systematic relationship between singularist accounts of causation and all other accounts of what a cause is. My distinction between object positing and property attributing can help to clarify respects in which the scientific causal laws are built up from a formal cause base, which means they are not completely 'artificial'.

In my view, a large percentage of the work done by scientists involves studying the interrelationships of concepts, and no object positing is taking place. Since this type of work is mostly property-attributing, y-type work, it follows that it will be abstract, quantificational, and not related to particular objects of any kind. Scientific laws can be artificial in the same way that mathematical laws are. Once progress in math has been made beyond the postulation of a unit and a recursive sequence, the need for objects drops out all together. The laws thus developed are 'artificial' only because they are syntactical and quantificational.

---

[10] Michael Tooley, 'Laws and Causal Relations', in *Midwest Studies in Philos.*, *op. cit.* p.93 ff.

In the case of science, sometimes the object-positing process re-enters the scene at another level, postulating the existence of theoretical entities to unify some of the syntactical and quantificational y-type data. From the point of view of my analysis of object-positing and thought, these theoretical entities are playing the same role at higher levels in a scientific analysis that grapefruits, tables and shoelaces play at the perceptual level. And, the theoretical entities don't need to apologize for themselves any more than their perceptual cousins do, either.

So, for me, kausation is a singularist concept at its basis, but when projected into agency, probability, deductive nomological, and retroductive types of causation, it becomes progressively more and more y-type, until the edges of the scientific body of knowledge are reached. There, retroductive causes re-apply the object-positing process to the y-type causal laws, themselves, at the highest level of scientific thought. I will explain this more fully in a later chapter, when I show how to develop the more sophisticated concepts of kausation out of the basic concept of a kause that I have been developing, here.

My description of the content of my notion of kausation is now finished. In the next chapter, I will defend this position from some likely objections.

Chapter 3

Objections and Replies

How Can X = R?

Both Stewart Thau and José Benardete have objected to my claim that x=r in my formula for kausation. The intuition behind the objection seems to be that a thought in a mind (the x) is one kind of thing, and a physical object in the 'external' world (the r) is quite another, and to put an equals sign between them is a misuse of an equals sign. It is the same type of consideration that leads Kant to make more heavy weather than I am inclined to make of noumena, and transcendental objects.

Let me talk first about the equals sign. As I understand the equals sign, the identity expressed by it is a semantic identity. That is, if Samuel Clemens = Mark Twain, the name on the left of the sign and the name on the right of the sign mark the same thing. Also, when it is asserted that 1+1=2, what is being asserted is that the expression on the right marks another way of saying the same thing that the expression on the left says. Thus, in this context, semantic identity means that x and r are alternate ways of picking out the same thing.

My claim as a direct realist is that an x in thought and an r, taken to be an aspect of reality encountered in experience, are different ways of marking one thing, which typically will be an object. Direct perception is grounded in immediate experience, and is an identity relationship in a very redundant sense. A person who identifies a grayish, fuzzy, scampering form as a mouse is not naming her experience 'mouse', she is naming a mouse 'mouse'. Unless they are doing sense datum philosophy, most people don't bother naming the experience, at all. All that the 'x' in the formula really marks is the point of view of the namer. It is important to mark the point of view of the namer because without it, the r would not be characterized in the way it is, and thus would not be the object it is. But, having marked the point of view as identified with the 'that', marked by the r, the point of view becomes, as it were, transparent to it, or interdefinable with it. To give the point of view is just to give the character of the r from the point of view, and to specify the nature of the point of view is just to characterize the r. The point of view is intellectually 'buried' in the r in the same sense in which 1+1 is buried in 2.

Apparently, seeing poses a problem for this identity relationship because it has been maintained in the philosophical tradition that since there is a spatial distance between a percipient and a mouse, something must carry 'mouselikeness' to a percipient's brain before a percipient could notice a mouse. I have two objections to this analysis of the situation. First, it presumes that a percipient is not an active participant in his or her own perceptual experience. Second, it espouses a notion of action that should have gone out with the discovery of gravity.

On my first objection, the notion that some unexplained thing must carry mouselikeness to a percipient presumes that perceivers play a completely passive role in perception. I believe that this is untrue. Perceivers actively solicit sensory experience from their surroundings through curiosity and focusing of attention. Perceivers use object-positing to actively engage their surroundings, thereby constructing scenarios for themselves about their environment. Nothing has to bring 'mouselikeness' to a consciousness, because it is the nature of consciousness to reach out into its environs to latch on to a mouse.

My second objection to the passive picture of perception is related to the first. If someone finds the notion that a perceiver can actively attend to and interact with his or her environment implausible, chances are good that the objector is thinking of action at a distance as implausible. Since there is a spatial distance between that perceiver and the mouse, conscious interaction across the space is deemed impossible.

I think that all I have to do to argue against this objection is to point out how ridiculous it is when applied to cases of recognition that do not occur across distances. Would anyone have trouble with an assertion that an experience of lightheadedness + an experience of stomach rumbles = hunger? Certainly, hunger can also be defined in other ways, such as low blood sugar level, reduced fat content in the blood, reduced metabolic rate, etc. But none of these cases of object-positing, initiated from a medical point of view, vitiates a claim of being hungry, presented as an individual case of direct sensory awareness.

Or, consider an Eureka! type intellectual insight. All that the person is doing is thinking. She may be thinking about propositions, equations, experiments, observations, diagrams, pictures, metaphors or gadgets. All of a sudden, a connection clicks. The disjoined factors are arranged in thought in a new pattern or relationship. This type of insight, like the hunger case, is a case of completely unmediated direct awareness. To call the result a proposition badly obfuscates its nature. It may be describable through propositions or by diagrams, metaphors, equations or pictures. But as a case of direct awareness it is not any of those things, and has no need to be mediated by any of them.

Let's return to sight. Why does recognition of a mouse have to be any more mediated than recognition of hunger or intellectual insight? Sight and hearing are just two types of sensory awareness that operate at a distance. It is the nature of visual and auditory sensory organs to be keyed to environmental cues, rather than to intestines or a brain. I think that denial that awareness can operate in this way is a recycling of the ancient objection to action at a distance, coupled with a mistaken priority on the 'external' cases, which are wrongly taken as paradigmatic. It is an inadequate account of action that is at fault in this mistake, not the impossibility of direct awareness across a space. The misleading internal/external distinction that I have been trying to get rid of throughout this book may also be doing some dirty work, here. The intellectual insight case should be taken as the paradigm, and extended to recognition across a space, not vice versa.

Sensory awareness is no less direct because it is of things deemed 'external', rather than 'internal'. Indeed, the deeming of the kause of an 'x', itself, is part of the judgment included in object-positing.

So, I claim that the x=r relationship is an identity relationship, by which I mean that it is redundant, or analytic in the sense that its terms are interdefinable. It is the relationship that some perceiver has with some aspect of his or her environment, some idea, or some state of him or herself, when the perceiver recognizes something with sufficient clarity to mark it as a subject matter and think about it indexically as a 'that'. This is strong numerical identity between the subject matter and the conscious point of view that characterizes it as a subject matter. There aren't two things; an object and an awareness of it. There is only one thing; the object. The point of view in the mental process defines the character of the object, but then becomes transparent to it, or buried in it.

It is important to notice that the identity of the x and the r does not imply that perceivers are automatically omniscient about the nature of the environment that they perceive. Indeed, saying that there is a 'nature' that the environment 'has' implies that there is something transcendent above and beyond the knowledge of all perceivers to which the limited point of view of a perceiver could be compared for accuracy. Part of my motivation for separating object-positing from property-attributing is to argue that the types of inference that would have to be used to make this comparison are property-attributing type inferences, and they cannot be used on logically opaque and intensional object-positing type phenomena.

Property-attributing processes are syntactical and logical. They involve propositions, and describe truth-functional relations among their propositions. If we were capable of doing truth-functional inferences on the positing of objects, we could do an inference like the following.

> P's x contains r_1 and r_2
> N's x contains r_1, r_3, and r_4, but not r_2 (N's=nature's)
> therefore, P's x $\neq$ N's x,

from which it follows that nature's knowledge of x is accurate, and P has it wrong.

But the intentionality and opacity of object-positing make the above type of inference a platonic fairy-tale of certainty and truth. For, though each side of the mind-to-world and world-to-mind relationship is an identity of a redundant sort, the two sides can be blinded to each other by the intentions or ignorance of the observer.

Pylyshyn, for instance, discusses the 'cognitive penetrability' of perception.[1] When undergraduates are asked to analyze a scene that depicts impossible fluid constancy levels, it turns out that only the students who have studied fluid mechanics 'see' the scene accurately. The students who have not studied fluid mechanics are 'blinded' by their ignorance, and misdescribe the picture that they have right in front of them.

To combine my insight with Pylyshyn's; The students who have not studied fluid mechanics are making a stab at doing 'visual physics', and, as it turns out, not doing a very good job of it. They really see the scene on the world-to-mind side of the relationship, but because of their ignorance of physics, they fail to understand what

---

[1]   see Zenon Pylyshyn, *Computation and Cognition*, Bradford Books, M.I.T. Press, Cambridge Mass. 1986, pp. 130 ff.

they see, and so it plays no role on the mind-to-world side of their perceptual experience. The physics students, however, have played with some straightforwardly platonic equations and concepts in class, and have these concepts at their disposal to apply to the mind-to-world side of their perceptual experience. Their perception of the scene, itself, is altered by what they know, on the mind-to-world side.

A reader might ask at this point, 'So, if perception is this intentional and opaque from side to side, how would even the 'A' physics student, or for that matter, the Ph.D in fluid mechanics, know when he or she had gotten it right?' My answer to this is that no one ever really does. Platonic certainty may apply to the relationships between equations worked out by the master physicist on her computer, but once she is applying a concept to her experience, the certainty is lost. The only source of verification for immediate experience is more immediate experience. And, as we have already seen, that will give an observer back exactly what she's put there.

Concepts acquired in this way can, of course, be checked socially, against what other people know or believe, or against ways in which other people use language. In property-attributing, people compare concepts, models, and equations to each others' for consistency, and to what other people in the scientific community think, for social acceptability. But once one is dealing with the platonic constructs of logic and math and the social roles of language in a community, one is no longer dealing with object-positing or the level of immediate experience, at all. Reality, objects, kausation, and semantic denotation, all become reduced to placeholders for predication or social roles in these discussions.

I hope that this discussion has better explained why I believe that it is reasonable to call the $x = r$ relationship an identity relationship. I think that unwillingness to see it this way might stem from one of two beliefs that have been common in turn of the twenty-first-century philosophy, both of which I consider false.

1. A belief that perception and denotation are physical, mechanical relationships between perceivers or namers and things, such as the Dretske claim that information is mechanically passed through efficient causal chains from things to perceivers. This belief is false. I have demonstrated that the relationship between perceivers and the objects that they name or perceive is an intentional co-relation, in which the object-positing process redundantly or analytically identifies a subject matter.

2. A belief that there is some kind of logical isomorphism or necessary connection between some aspect of reality and a proposition

> that describes it. Jay F. Rosenberg explicitly prescribes to this point
> of view when he says; ' . . . How [is it] that language represents a
> non-linguistic world . . . The answer which I propose is that the one
> represents the other by being *structurally* a system of objects in the
> natural order (natural linguistic objects) *protocorrelated* with the
> system of non-linguistic objects represented and (ideally)
> extentionally isomorphic to that system of non-linguistic objects.'[2]

This belief is also implicit in David Lewis' version of possible worlds
semantics, according to which a logical isomorphism exists between
'the world' and the complete set of true propositions.[3] This belief is
also false. The relationship between propositions and things presented in the 'isomorphism' view is a mechanical mirroring relationship, which would be, in Gricean terms, a conception of 'meaning' in
the natural sense. The intentionality required for communication
and understanding, in contrast, implies that Gricean 'non-natural
meaning'[4] is what is needed. For understanding and communication depend on a far stronger relationship on the mind-to-world side
of the relationship, identifying the thing in experience, and a far
weaker co-relation on the side of the experience being of the thing.
All that is needed on the world-to-mind side is that the thing be
co-related to the experience, however that co-relation may have
been achieved.

Didn't Kripke and Dretske have Semantics Right?

Kripke's Historical Causal Chains are Pre-semantic[5]

Joseph Almog has argued persuasively that Kripke's historical
chains of communication are pre-semantic, and so they cannot be
used, as Kripke tries to use them, to give an account of semantics.
Almog observes, '[The chain] preserves the *linguistic meaning* of any
expression. In the case of names, all there is to this meaning is to
stand for the given referent. Ergo, the chain preserves the fact that
the name stands for the referent.' Almog explains 'The chain assigns

[2]   Jay F. Rosenberg, *Linguistic Representation*, D. Reidel Publishing Co., Dordrecht,
       Holland, 1974, p. 118.
[3]   David Lewis, 'Possible Worlds', in *Meaning and Truth, the Essential Readings in
       Modern Semantics*, eds. Jay L. Garfield and Murray Kitely, Paragon Press, New
       York 1991, pp. 478–484.
[4]   H.P. Grice, Meaning, in *Philosophy of Language*, ed. Andrea Nye, Blackwell
       Publishers, Oxford, UK, 1998, p. 119.
[5]   see Saul Krippe, *Naming and Necessity, op. cit.*

a rule of reference to a syntactic shape; it is not mentioned in the rule of reference itself.'[6]

Even Kripke's initial pointings do not give him the fixing of denotation that he thinks they do, and they certainly don't give a mechanical transfer chain that could carry the established reference abroad, even if the fixing had worked at home.

First, as I have already argued, the initial baptisms do not do what Kripke thinks they do. For, a pointing person cannot denote something of which he has absolutely no conception whatsoever to use to mark a point of view. The person who named 'water' for English-speaking people may have thought of it as 'the washing stuff', but almost certainly could not have thought of it as H_2O. No one was to think of the chemical composition of water until chemistry emerged as a possible point of view — centuries later. Drawing a line from the tip of someone's finger to a lake simply does not rate as convicting him of prescient intuitive knowledge of twentieth and twenty-first century chemistry. And, in the absence of such a conviction, he has not tied the word 'water' to the chemical formula. The entire story is, as Almog points out, pre-semantic. Of course, it follows that if the initial baptism did not stick the namer of water with Kripke's full-blown natural kind, the corresponding social chain from the namer to us is not going to pass the natural kind along, either. For Helen Keller, the word was just a game played in hands with a teacher for a long time. When it finally clicked with her that the shape being pressed in her hand *meant* something, what she did was connect the game to a common experience, washing. The semantic relationship, for her, linked an 'x' that was a socially learned arrangement of hand-pressing symbols, to an 'r', the experience of washing. It is the indexing of the shape to the experience that rates as learning the meaning of a word. A thing that did not have experience, such as a computer, could not perform this indexing operation. No causal chains to it from anywhere, or lines drawn from it to any lake, would constitute giving it semantic capability to mean 'water.' As Searle also argues in his 'Chinese room' example, symbol crunching does not constitute passing on meaning.[7]

So, as an account of semantics, Kripke's story can't work. At the outset, his baptisms aren't correctly indexed to experience. And, his historical chains, in the absence of individual indexing experience by everyone in the chain, are pre-semantic, as well.

[6]   Joseph Almog, 'Semantical Anthropology', in *Midwest Studies vol.IX, op. cit.* pp. 482–483.

[7]   John Searle, *Minds, Brains, and Science,* Harvard University Press, Cambridge, Mass. 1984, pp. 32–35.

Dretske's Conclusions on Semantics Admit that his Account of them is Unhelpful

In *Knowledge and the Flow of Information*, Fred Dretske argued that physical causal chains of a roughly Kripkean sort pass 'information' from transmitter-like objects to receiver-like minds. But, in a later paper, he expressed doubts that a causal theory of this type can do justice to the type of data that I am discussing as object-positing type data. In 'Causal Theories of Knowledge', with Berent Enc, he imposes a series of qualifications and conditions on his causal theory of knowledge, until he winds up with the following limiting condition:

> C_3 S knows of a that it is F only if S's belief of a that it is F is caused by (a) a's being F or (b) a causal surrogate of a's being F, or (c) some condition (b's being G) whose effective property's (i.e. G's) correlation with F has produced in S the disposition S manifests in acquiring this belief.[8]

In this passage, Dretske and Enc are discussing beliefs and knowledge, which they claim are limited to full propositional structure. I think that their failure to connect their propositions to their F things is a good indicator that, for one thing, propositions are too complicated to have on the 'x' side of a discussion of perception. My object-positing process does a far better job of explaining what occurs in a mind in a direct case of recognition. For another thing, the relationship between what is occurring in the mind and what is stimulating that experience cannot be a physical transfer relationship. The (c) condition in the above formula simply isn't describing a physical transfer relationship, at all.

Dretske and Enc aren't happy with condition (c), either. They observe;

> We are, however, very reluctant to propose this as even a partial analysis of knowledge. The whole structure is getting too creaky and unwieldy . . . Furthermore, the suggested change [the addition of condition (c)] departs significantly from the kind of intuitions that motivated a causal theory of knowledge. If this is *a* causal theory of knowledge it certainly isn't what most philosophers will recognize as *the* causal theory of knowledge.[9]

The problem that they have discovered is that condition (c) gives a correlation condition, and one that resembles Grice's non-natural meaning much more than it resembles a transfer condition. And the fact that this condition can work in the case they discuss points out that, even in cases in which they do believe that a transfer of some-

---

[8]   Fred Dretske and Berent Enc, 'Causal Theories of Knowledge', in *Midwest Studies in Philosophy IX, op.cit.*, p. 525.

[9]   *Ibid.*, p. 525.

thing has occurred, the transfer is irrelevant to the acquisition of knowledge. They articulate the general problem that this discovery raises for a causal theorist in these words.

> ... the causal connection [expressed in clauses (a) and (b) above {in C_3}] between individual beliefs and their satisfaction conditions, turns out to be irrelevant. The relevant question is whether the correlations that make a belief reliable were themselves instrumental in shaping the cognitive mechanisms that determine what and when an organism believes.[10]

But even in admitting defeat on causal transfer of information, Dretske and Enc are still looking for 'cognitive mechanisms that determine' beliefs. From my point of view, they are still adopting a passive, mechanical, view of thinking and object positing, that simply doesn't capture the nature of the beast. For one thing, simple correlation on the mind-to-world side of the relationship is not strong enough to establish a semantic identity. For semantic identity, the perceiver must be applying an attentive point of view to the object selected. For another, on the world-to-mind side of the relationship, their notion of correlation will not do the job of seeing to it that the experience in question is *of* the thing. The 'ofness' relationship must be kausal, with the understanding that not mechanical transfer but awareness of experiential impact is implied by 'kausal'.

How Can Sense Perception Get By Without Sense Data and Inferences from Sense-Data to Physical Objects?

Discussing Berkeley's idealism, Russell made the following distinctions.

> It will help us in considering these questions to have a few simple terms of which the meaning is definite and clear. Let us give the name of 'sense-data' to the things that are immediately known in sensation: such things as colours, sounds, smells, hardness, roughness, and so on. We shall give the name 'sensation' to the experience of being immediately aware of these things. Thus, whenever we see a colour, we have a sensation *of* the colour, but the colour itself is a sense-datum, not a sensation. The colour is that *of* which we are immediately aware, and the awareness, itself, is the sensation. It is plain that if we are to know anything about the table, it must be by means of the sense-data — brown colour, oblong shape, smoothness, etc. — which we associate with the table; but, for the reasons which have been given [divergence between appearance and reality] we cannot say that the table *is* the sense data, or even that the sense-data are directly properties of the table. Thus a problem arises as to the relation of the sense-data to the real table, supposing there is such a thing.

---

[10] *Ibid.*, p. 526.

> The real table, if it exists, we will call a 'physical object'. Thus, we have to consider the relation of sense-data to physical objects. The collection of all physical objects is called 'matter'. Thus, our two questions may be restated as follows: (1) Is there any such thing as matter? (2) If so, what is its nature?[11]

Russell believes that the territory must be thus split into sensations, sense-data, and physical objects to resolve issues concerning at least two aspects of perception that he would otherwise find worrisome. For one, he believes he needs the sensation/sense-data split to explain the difference between the act and the object of apprehension. He says,

> Acquaintance with objects essentially consists in a relation between the mind and something other than the mind; it is this that constitutes the mind's power of knowing things.[12]

For another, Russell believes that he needs the sense-data/physical object split to account for the difference between reality and dreams or imagination. In discussing this issue he asks, 'Is there a table which has a certain intrinsic nature, and continues to exist when I am not looking, or is the table merely a product of my imagination, a dream-table in a very prolonged dream?'[13]

In what follows, I will argue that Russell's way of splitting up the territory is not the most simple, definite, and clear way of doing it, as he supposes. In addition, I will argue that, when the territory is better defined, his worrisome issues are not problematic. Let's start by asking what matter, or 'the total of all physical objects' is.

What is Matter?

For Locke, matter was 'the minute parts' of things, or the inert causes of sensations. For Russell, matter is wave motion, having position in space and 'the power of motion according to the laws of motion'.[14] For either of them, thus, a mind-independent physical object, such as a table, rates as mind-independent because it is *really* a scientifically described occupant of space or collection of atoms *rather than* a table. The table is an appearance superimposed on atoms or space. Let's analyze this notion of a mind-independent physical object a bit, from an Aristotelian or Kantian perspective.

---

[11]   Bertrand Russell, *The Problems of Philosophy*, Oxford University Press, London, UK, 1912, p. 12.

[12]   *Ibid.*, p. 42.

[13]   *Ibid.*, p. 17.

[14]   *Ibid.*, p. 28.

In Aristotle's case, there has been considerable intellectual debate on the question of whether he believed in 'prime matter', and what prime matter was, if he believed in it. The issue arises because Aristotle allows room for relativity in substances. Matter is relative, in Aristotle's notion of a substance, in the sense that a phoneme can be matter for a syllable, which can be matter for a word, which can be matter for a sentence. Now, if we ask, 'But what is the matter for the phoneme?', any answer that we give will be strange. We might say 'sound', in some generic and non-specific sense is the matter for the phoneme. Or, we might cite some sub-atomic division of a tone, if we could find one. The phoneme must be a composite of matter and essence if it is to be a substance, but what is its matter?

The situation will be no better with a more properly substantial item like a table. The wood may be matter for the table, and cellulose fibers, matter for the wood, and molecules matter for the cellulose fibers, and atoms matter for the molecules and electrons and neutrons matter for the atoms, and quarks matter for the electrons and neutrons . . . But what have we arrived at when we hit the quarks? Are quarks prime matter? Or, will they, too, turn out to have a sub-quarkian structure once we develop the theory and technology in terms of which to describe the quark's composition?

Even if one were to concede status as 'prime matter' to the quarks in the last paragraph, there would still be a question about which, if any, of the structures listed in the last paragraph is the 'real' physical object. Locke says the atoms are the real physical object. Russell says the space is the real physical object. Aristotle says it depends on what you want to know. Usually, for Aristotle, the table will turn out to be the real physical object because it is mid-sized, and most useful to people. Notice, the objecthood of the table does not rule out the objecthood of atoms for Aristotle. But they are posited from a different, microscopic and scientific point of view, when one's intention is to discuss chemical and electrical bonding forces rather than locations for placing books and packages.

Notice, also, that this discussion of objects does not deny the existence of mind-independent reality, if what one means by mind-independent reality is amorphous 'prime matter'. The discussion *does* deny that the real physical object *is* the atoms and *is not* the table. Tables are objects and atoms are objects; they are different objects from each other. Their existence and their capacity to kausally impinge on human experience are mind independent. But their respective characters, as specified by book-placing or chemical-analyzing points of view, are not mind-independent. Without a specific point of view from which to object-posit, we would have no reason to call whatever is recalcitrantly impinging on us a table, or a block of wood, or atoms, or quarks, or space.

Aristotle said very little about prime matter, probably because there is very little that can be said about it, once it has been described as I have described it. Kant makes this point more explicitly when he calls the thing-in-itself, independent of any phenomena, a noumena or transcendental object. Something is there. And, the something that is there recalcitrantly determines human experience of it; it kauses the experience. When someone calls an impinging experience of hardness a table, it is that something, not 'hardness' that he experiences. And he experiences the table with the same immediacy with which he experiences hunger, or dream-tables. But, because he is awake, he knows that the experience is kaused by a table, not a dream.

So, my conclusion on physical objects is that their existence is mind-independent but any knowledge that we have of them is not. If one is discussing the prime matter or transcendental noumena that kause sensory experience, and that we index with points of view and intentions when we choose to pay attention to it, it is clear that something other than oneself is this kause. Human history shows that the more we humans pay attention to this kause of our experience, the more we can learn about it. Most major advances in human knowledge have come from the development of new points of view from which to index and discuss our impinging environment.

But, it seems to me that we have good reasons to suppose that there are sensory or psychological, and perhaps also logical limits on the number of points of view or intentions that humans could use to index and characterize the nature of this transcendental world. It further seems to me that we have *no* reason to presume that these human limits on characterization also limit the nature of this mind-independent world. Consider Locke's questions about creatures with radically different sensory apparatus from ours. Why should we suppose that our range of intellectual and sensory capabilities coincides with the full range of possible 'objects' in transcendental reality? I consider such a supposition blatant arrogance; hubris of an inevitably self-destructive sort. I think that we have every reason to suppose that the limits on our access to prime matter are our own sensory and cognitive capacities; and no reason to suppose that our capacities and limitations dictate the character or extent of the real.

So, any name or object that we posit arises from some human experiential or cognitive point of view. In this sense, nothing that we can discuss is mind-independent.

Since we don't kause our own experience, however, we do have a reason to believe that prime matter is out there. And, as a direct realist, I insist that the table is one of the things that prime matter is. In all probability the table is also a large number of other objects for which I have no concepts or points of view. But, at least one of the things that it is *is* a table. I know that because I can consistently maintain my kausal and semantic relationship to it as a book and package holder, and wildly inconsistent experiences do not interfere with this relationship.

Let's return to Russell's sensation/sense-data/physical object distinction to see what the preceding discussion of a physical object has done to that distinction. Obviously, the need for a sense-datum drops out. I'm not inferring space or atoms from brownish shapes, for the experience, itself, is directly table kaused and table indexed. And there is no more to being a table than being whatever is thus kaused and indexed in experience. Russell's act–object distinction is not violated because the kausal side of the experience guarantees the independence of the table from my mind, while the naming side of the experience represents the 'act' of paying attention to the kause and indexing it by the mind. Qua transcendental prime matter, the physical object's independence is assured by the fact that I did not kause my experience of the table. As such, the object is a table, but possibly also a large number of other things that people don't and possibly can't conceive or perceive. Qua table, however, it is an 'act' of human object-positing, initiated by humans who call it a table, write letters on it, eat on it, and put books and packages on it.

Further, Russell's concern that real tables and dream tables would be regularly confused with one another proves unfounded, because in both the awake table case and the dream table case, we also have access to the kause and the context. We know that when we sleep we have dream-induced experience, and the kause of this experience is our own biological or psychological condition. Dream tables have different practical and symbolic meanings for us than tables experienced when awake do, and they behave differently from the tables of waking experience. Only extreme trauma or severe disorientation would seriously confuse a normal adult about the kause of a table experience.

What's Wrong with the Dogmas of Sense-data theory?

My position rejects several presuppositions or dogmas of sense-data theory that have remained unquestioned throughout the twentieth century and into the twenty-first. First I will list them, and then I will argue against the suppositions underlying them.

1. The mind, or cognitive apparatus of the body, is hooked up directly to body parts, like intestines and toes. So, feelings like pain and hunger have a direct, 'internal' effect on the mind of their percipient. This is not the case with objects that are not body parts, such as tables. They are 'external', and their ability to affect the mind of a percipient is seriously problematic. In these cases, inferences are necessary.

2. Our sensory contact with 'the world' clearly and emphatically distinguishes between the unproblematic 'internal', uninferred cases and the fraught, 'external' inferred cases. The distinction is that a sense-datum is present in the external case, and one must concentrate on it intently to make the necessary inference, whereas there is no such thing in the internal case, and no such concentration of attention is necessary to experience toe tingles or hunger.

3. Inferred though they are, (or perhaps, *because* they are inferred) the 'external' cases are cases of sensing objective reality, whereas the fuzzy, uninferred, 'internal' cases are personal and subjective, and do not represent access to the 'real' world.

I think that a little reflection on Russell's description of the role of sense data will reveal that he is presuming the truth of these three dogmas. In what follows I will argue that there are several presuppositions imbedded here that are false.

i Sensing objects is not more 'problematic' than sensing pains.

ii No inference is used or needed to identify an object.

iii 'External' cases are not clearly distinguished from 'internal' cases by the presence of a sense-datum.

iv The difference between sensory kauses and memory, dream or bodily-induced kauses is not the difference between 'fuzzy and personal' as opposed to 'objective and real.'

Sensing Objects is not more Problematic than Sensing Pains

For one thing, I believe that a fair appraisal of the psychological literature on sensory perception will indicate that humans are as well equipped by their sensory apparatus to detect objects in the environment as they are to detect problems with their own bodies. It is the same process, object-positing, by which a human learns that she has a blister on her toe or a mouse in her cabinet. There is not a substantial philosophical difference between positing a mouse in the cabinet as the kause of a sound and positing a blister on a toe as a kause of an ache. She could miss either experience (scuffle or ache) if she were not paying attention to it, and could mis-identify either object (mouse or blister) through lack of attention or lack of an appropriate point of view from which to object-posit. If there is an inference in the mouse case, there is every bit as much an inference in the blister case. And, if the feeling of a blister is not inferred (as I believe it is not) from a pain, no more is the presence of a mouse inferred from hearing a scuffling sound.

To support my claim that experience of pains is no more or less problematic than experience of a mouse, I will cite some of the psychological research that has been done on sense perception. This short digression will show that sensory organs and developmental repertoires in humans are attuned to object-positing, as I have described it, and not to making propositional inferences from sense data to anything. I will briefly comment on the established constancies in visual and auditory perception, repertoires of interpretation cited by Gestalt psychologists, and the consequences of developmental disabilities, to show that sensory capacities are directly attuned to object- positing.

Constancies in Visual and Auditory Perception

Psychologists who study visual and auditory perception have shown that there are certain constancies built into the operation of our visual and auditory systems. That is, there are certain operations performed by eyes and ears and sections of the brain that interpret visual and auditory data that are performed all the time in the same way by humans with functional visual and auditory organs. In animals who have similar visual and auditory systems the same or analogous operations function. These basic operations are called *segregation, determining distance, and determining motion,* in texts on perception. Segregation is described as a process that finds objects by distinguishing figure from ground in a perceptual scene, in this way.

> The image projected on our retina is a mosaic of varying brightnesses and colors. Somehow, our perceptual system organizes the mosaic into a set of discrete objects projected against a background . . .
>
> If a stimulus contains two or more distinct regions, we usually see part of it as a *figure,* and the rest as *ground.* The regions seen as a figure contain the objects of interest — they appear more solid than the ground, and they appear in front of the ground. This is the most elementary form of

perceptual organization. Figure 5-1 [vase/faces picture] illustrates that figure–ground organization can be reversible. The fact that either region can be recognized as a figure indicates that figure–ground organization is not part of the physical stimulus, but rather is an accomplishment of the perceptual system . . .

Interestingly, a stimulus need not contain identifiable objects in order for a person to organize it into figure and ground. (Note that we can perceive figure–ground relations in senses other than vision. For example, we may hear the song of a bird against the background of outdoor noises, or the melody played by the violin against the harmonies of the rest of the orchestra).[15]

I believe that my description of the mechanics of object-positing, as a type of Humean inductive reasoning, explains the 'somehow' by which people sort figure from ground. This passage also stresses some of the other essential aspects of the object-positing process that I have cited; the importance of 'interest', which corresponds to my intentional focusing of attention, and of 'judgments' made in reversible or non-determinate cases.

Some of the cues that people use to make these perceptual judgments, according to Atkinson et al., are proximity of forms, closure of shapes, good continuation or uninterrupted contours, relative distance, and relative motion. These would be the cues used to judge some aspect of a scene 'object' and other aspects 'adjectival' or transitional, relative to the thing judged object.[16] From the universality of these principles of perceptual judgment, Atkinson et al. presume that these are built-in functions of human and some animal perceptual systems.

Some of these operations are imitated by robotic scanners, which also operate by detecting the intensity of color at edges, interruptions in contours and closure in shapes, for instance. The operations that are unlikely to be simulate-able in a robot are the ones that involve judgment and 'interest'. A robot can be programmed to perform a task, such as removing widgets that deviate from listed specifications. And when the task at hand is that specific and mechanical, robots can perform it better than humans, whose attention and perceptual acuity tend to be less focused. But there is still no sense in which the robot sees that widget x is defective. The robot has no concept of use for widgets, no point of view from which to posit widgets as objects, and is not capable of interest or intention-forming with

[15]   Rita L. Atkinson, Richard C. Atkinson, Edward E. Smith, and Daryl J. Bem, *Introduction to Psychology*, 10th ed., Harcourt, Brace, Jovanovich, San Diego, 1990, pp. 158–159.
[16]   *Ibid.*, pp. 159–160.

respect to widgets. This disability of robots will remain, no matter how superior their widget sorting abilities may become.

In addition, people use built-in perceptual system features, such as binocular parallax, binocular disparity, superposition, relative size, relative height, and texture gradients to judge distance in a visual scene. Similar cues help us to make distance judgments in sounds. Psychologists have found that some of these cues are directly activated in the nervous system. For instance, binocular disparity operates this way;

> Binocular disparity is a particularly powerful cue. It leads to a vivid impression of depth, even with completely meaningless stimuli, such as a random pattern of dots that contains no other depth cues (Julesz, 1971).[17]

Furthermore, binocular disparity seems to be coded directly by the visual system. Researchers have found single neurons in the visual cortex of cats that respond best to particular disparities. Thus, some of these cells respond most to one particular degree of disparity, while other cells are most responsive to another degree of disparity.[18] Binocular disparity, then, is treated by the nervous system in the same manner as the wavelength of light or the frequency of sounds.[19]

The obvious conclusion to be drawn from this type of research is that no inference is needed to perceive an object. The perceptual act is as directly tied to the nervous system of the perceiver in a case of seeing a mouse as it is in the case of feeling a pain. To the degree that this process is, thus, mechanically tied in to the nervous system, robots will be able to simulate the operation. It is likely that engineers will design robots that can make distinctions based on visual or auditory parallax. This is the direct, and non-inferential aspect of perception.However, as I pointed out above, judgment and intentionality do not drop out of this story because the process is direct and mechanical. On the contrary, it is judgment and intentionality, not inferences, that make the meaningless dots/running mouse distinction that Atkinson et al. presume in this passage.

Further, the notions of relative size and relative shape, which Gestalt psychologists have cited as central to figure–ground judgments are straightforwardly judgmental, and intentional. The following experiment by Frank showed that object-constancy judgments are

---

[17]   Quoted in Atkinson, et al., op. cit.

[18]   Barlow, Blakemore, & Pettigrew, 1967. Quoted in Atkinson, et al., *op. cit.*

[19]   *Ibid.*, p. 161.

based on interpretations of a field, analyzed in a Humean way, as I have described it.

> Thirty children, ranging from eleven months to seven years of age, were trained to go to the larger or smaller (depending on the group) of two boxes: correct choices contained chocolate, fruit or a toy hidden beneath. In the critical test situations which followed, the boxes were so placed that the remote larger box cast a much smaller image on the retina than the nearer smaller one. In some instances, the retinal image of the larger box had only 1% of the real size of the smaller. Nevertheless, 23 out of 30 children made no errors at all on this basis and four made but one. Even the little youngsters, who were unable to walk, crawled a good distance to the objectively correct box.[20]

This experiment clearly indicates that the spatial and distance judgments made in perception are based on an analysis of a field that presumes that space is perspectival, not Euclidian. Judgment does not consider the golfer on the green to be one-eighth the size of the golfer standing next to the judge at the club house, even though the visual datum presents the distant golfer as that much smaller. If Euclidean space were presumed in this judgment, as Russell's claim that the space is objective and real implies, the distant golfer would be judged leprechaunesque. But judgment presumes relative size constancy for postulated objects, and attributes radical size differences to distance, directly, without inference. It is the Euclidean postulates that require inferences, not the perspectival judgments. Consider the fact that Euclidean, inferential geometry developed along with math and logic in the Egyptian and Greek worlds, while the non-inferential rules of perspective had to await the visually-immersed world view of the renaissance: Fra Angelico and Masacchio. To learn Euclidean geometry is to learn a set of postulates and rules for deriving one from another. To learn perspective is to learn to draw what one sees, *and not* what one believes or thinks is there. Learning perspective is learning to judgmentally de-compose a gestalten or field, a natural whole, not to infer anything. In perception, the perspectival whole is given, undecomposed. Intentions, points of view and judgment decompose it into objects.

Consider further, that the children in the above experiment were mostly younger than the age that Piaget considers the age at which formal operations first become possible. Yet these children, without any capacity for formal inferences or derivations, could judge relative size and distance accurately.

_____
[20]   Hartmann, *op. cit.*, p. 129.

The conclusion from these considerations is, thus, that there is no sense-data in perception, nor is there any inference from a sense datum to anything. What is given in perception is an experiential 'field', from which one sorts objects, using sensory apparatus that is attuned to just that task. The sense organs are not disadvantaged by distance. Rather, seeing and hearing are modes of perceptual understanding that operate by taking a percipient and his environment as a perspectival gestalten out of which self and other than self, near and far are to be sorted.

Repertoires of Interpretation

Gestalt psychologists demonstrated that the perspectival wholes that I have described in the last section fit into gestalten, or what I will loosely call repertoires of interpretation. What gestalten have in common is the fact that the whole structural or configurational organization of the gestalten is not a function of, and is not reducible to, the sum of atomistic subunits of the whole, no matter how they may be construed. Thus, the criteria of compositionality, presumed by both Russell and (early) Fodor to apply to all mental operations, is violated by gestalten.

Candidates for gestalten are soap bubbles, which require a specific organization in addition to the presence of a certain amount of liquid and soap, ocean waves, which possess capacities that exceed anything calculatable from the net capacities of all drops of water in them, all organic and ecological systems which produce what they need out of what they have, altering elements to fit structure, rather than vice versa,[21] and perceptual interaction with one's environment, in which as much is regularly attributed to a stimulus by a perceiver as is present in it.[22]

---

[21] Early Gestalt experimenters demonstrated that a lizard's right front paw, when amputated and reattached to the lizard's left, rear hip socket, backwards, assumed the function of a left rear leg when healed. Certain fish change sex to compensate for deficiencies in numbers of fish of one sex or the other. See George W. Hartmann, *Gestalt Psychology*, reprint by Greenwood Press, Westport Conn. 1974, pp. 60–61.

[22] Experiments by Wulf (1922) indicate that people produce accounts or reproductions of what they have seen that accent symmetry, normalcy or anomalies of a figure, rather than accurate reproduction of it. Wulf called these tendencies, leveling, assimilation and sharpening, respectively. These tendencies indicate that the parts are being generated out of a conception of the whole, rather than the whole being constructed as a composition of the parts. Cited in Lyle E. Bourne, Roger L. Dominowski, Elizabeth F. Loftus, And Alice F. Healy, *Cognitive Processes,* 2nd ed., Prentice Hall, Inc., Englewood Cliffs, New Jersey, 1986, p. 26.

In general, I think that some conclusions reached by gestalt psychologists rely on presumptions made by Husserl, that I think are false. For instance, the gestalt principle of isomorphism presumes that an iconic resemblance of some sort obtains between a perceived gestalten and a mental operation that comprehends it.[23] I think that this claim is a variant on the Husserlian notion of 'abstraction' for logical principles that Frege abused in his review of *Principles of Arithmetic.*

Further, I think that this abstraction/isomorphism mistake is a result of following Hume's assumption that the relata of causation must be two objects, or (preferred) two impressions. Something has to tie these objects to the impressions, and it is presumed that causation, having been usurped to do another task, cannot perform this one. So, abstraction or isomorphism is dragged in as a *deus ex machina* to perform this 'tying' task. If, however, one sees that the proper relata of kausation are *one* object and *one* impression, which is transparently *of* the object, the gestalten is freed to be the total or whole of the kausal-naming process.

Gestalten are often described by Gestalt psychologists as wholes, whose total structural content exceeds the sum of their composing parts. Hartmann quotes Dilthey on the subject as follows.

> 'The whole is more than the sum of its parts' — that all psychic processes are characterized by the fact that *the apprehension of the total is a condition precedent to the adequate interpretation of the 'item'.* The full import of this suggestion is not developed at length but the following suggestion has a programmatic ring, 'In psychology, all functional connections in experience are intrinsically given. Our knowledge of individual facts is simply a dismemberment of this union. Herein is manifested a firm structure, immediately and objectively present.'[24]

As I said, I think that some Husserl-like abstraction and isomorphism is imbedded in this view of Gestalten. But, if those metaphysical presumptions are removed, what is left is a notion that you can't have objects unless you have a point of view from which to posit them. Further, the 'items' and 'functional connections' encountered in experience are interpretations of some structural configuration or repertoire, without which, the figure/ground distinctions would not be made in the ways in which they are being made.

The conclusion to be drawn from these considerations is that neither sense data nor inferences are needed to perceive objects. A point of view from which to object-posit is needed, or perhaps a configura-

---

[23]   Hartmann, *op. cit.*, p. 210.

[24]   Hartmann, *op. cit.*, p. 14.

tional repertoire into which to set a structure is needed, but these intellectual 'placings' are not, in any sense, inferences.

Consequences of Disabilities

Experiments performed with cats have indicated that perceptual-motor coordination, unlike ability to judge size constancy in objects, is learned. Cats that are prevented from seeing at crucial points in their development, never learn to see, even though their visual systems are intact. If they are prevented from seeing their limbs, they do not learn sensory-motor coordination. If cats or people are prevented from engaging in self-produced movement, they do not learn to move. For example, a kitten that was experimentally prevented from moving its limbs did not learn to put a paw forward to prevent a collision.[25]

The fact that the aspects of kinesthesis in this experiment are *learned* supports my claim that 'internal' sensory knowledge is not less problematic than 'external' sensory knowledge. Indeed, it may be more problematic. This experimental evidence indicates that a mouse sighting may be more straightforward and direct, more attuned to innate sensory capacities, than a kinesthetic response to collision, which must be learned.

Hartmann, further, cites Gestalt evidence to argue that self consciousness does not have the kind of isolated privilege that Russell's sensation/sense-data distinction affords to self.

> Should one claim that self-consciousness and consciousness of external objects are mediated by different agencies, one will find that the Gestalt position has been well fortified at that point. Despite Descartes' famous dictum, the fact that 'I think' or 'I doubt' is no surer foundation for reality than 'I see' or 'I feel'. Kohler justly observes that no one marvels that the concrete object 'pencil' lies outside the equally concrete object 'inkwell', and that there is just as little reason for being astounded over the fact that one's hand is a third object *beside* the other two. Awareness of one's physical frame must involve the same brain processes as awareness of extra-cutaneous data. This unquestionably occurs in special laboratory situations when a pronounced turning of the visual field leads to a convincing impression that the self is moving in a direction opposed thereto, despite the stability of one's physical organism upon a chair. If the observed ego is based upon one such set of processes, the physical environment on another *like* it, and the relative localization of both is based upon the same functional disparateness found in distinguishing one outer object from another, then this old pseudo-problem disappears. All

---

[25]   Atkinson et al., *op. cit.*, pp. 190-191.

> phenomena which is the common frame of reference for all events have
> equal standing within the brain-field experience.[26]

Hence, no inference takes place in any 'external' case that does not
also take place in an 'internal' case of perception, no extra sense
datum is present in the 'external' case, and indeed, the distinction
between 'internal' and 'external' is not as neat and clear as Russell
supposes it is.

No Inference is Used or Needed to Identify an Object

For another thing, the notion of 'inference' in the dogmatic sense
data account is very peculiar. Inferences, properly speaking, are logical transitions made from one proposition to another in a piece of
discourse. If I believe that all basketball players are tall, and I learn
that Gwen plays basketball, I might infer that Gwen is tall. That is an
inference. The same type of reasoning process might apply in either
a case in which I surmise that I have a mouse in my cabinet or a blister on my toe. The inferences would go, in those cases, like this. In the
toe case, a) I have a belief that my shoes are not a good fit, b) I believe
that ill-fitting shoes cause blisters. I infer, on the basis of beliefs a)
and b) that the shoe has given me a blister. Or in the mouse case a) I
have evicted mice from the cabinet before, b) I hear a sound that I
believe is little claws scuffling in my cabinet, c) I reason that little
scuffling noises signal the presence of a mouse, and I infer that there
is a mouse in my cabinet, again. However, what is being described
by these inferences is *not* sense experiences. Each is a bit of logical
reasoning that is almost completely independent of sensory experience. I could symbolically represent the inferences above as
instances of reasoning from Universal Generalization to Existential
Instantiation, that would bear the same degree of validity regardless
of content inserted in them. To conflate these logical inferences with
what occurs in sense perception is to misunderstand both the logical
inferences and sense perception.

In sense experience, unlike in logical reasoning, propositions are
not necessary. The role of sense experience, whether the experience
is of pains in toes or mice in cabinets, is identification of objects, not
inferences of any kind.

Irvin Rock tries to analyse perceptual judgments into propositionally based logical arguments, but he clearly overloads the content of
what is done in a case of recognition. He describes the processes
inherent in many examples similar to the ones that I have given as
involving hypothesis testing or deductions based on rules, which

[26]   Hartmann, *op. cit.*, p. 249.

generate very complex descriptions of an object, from which phenomenal effects, such as seeing a car, are then deduced. But his rules of inference all involve principles of physics or optics that are not based on perspectival space, but on Euclidean space. And his propositional descriptions, that he believes play a role in these deductions are all far too complicated to be entertained by children or animals, who clearly make perceptual judgments prior to and independently of any extensive mastery of even language, much less physics, optics or Euclidean geometry.[27]

No currently articulated rule of inference would cross the transition between a sound heard and an object named, or a pain felt and a problem named. If we tried to articulate such a rule, it would have to be formulated in such a way that it was redundant or misrepresented the nature of identification. For one thing, the inference rule would have to operate on perspectival space. For another, it would have to include stimulation, and naming as an analysis of its process. What would such a rule look like?

Stimulation implies stimulant, therefore, name it?
(S → So) .:. N ?

If that is a logical inference, it is a very strange one, indeed. There are no propositions involved, the inference proceeds from an experience to a name, and the relationship between the premises and the conclusion is identity. Furthermore, it does not have the level of generality that is usually required of logical inferences. We have no reason to assume that this silly 'inference' would hold true of anything that did not have a sensory system very much like ours, and semantic capacity to isolate and name aspects of that sensory experience. I can't see that anything is gained for logic or for sense experience by attempting to force this unproductive conflation of experiential identification with logical inference making.

No Sense-Datum is Present in the 'External' Cases, and Missing in the 'Internal' Cases

In addition, the so-called 'internal' cases are not clearly and emphatically distinguished from the 'external' by the presence or absence of a sense-datum. In both cases, a person posits an object on the basis of a kause. We learn, through experience, to distinguish between kauses for experience that are rooted in our own bodies, such as pains, or that are more generally self-kaused, such as dreams and

---

[27]   Irvin Rock, *The Logic of Perception*, MIT Press, Cambridge Mass, 1983, especially p. 18.

memories, or that are kaused by objects that are not part of our bodies, such as tables and mice. A concept of 'self' and a concept of 'other than self' are constructed out of the manner in which such kauses are attributed. There is a considerable degree of flexibility in the way that people can and do attribute these kauses and construct these concepts.

Hartmann quotes Bleuler and Schulte to explain how paranoia can be analyzed as 'hypertrophy of the ego'. When a person finds him or herself in a situation in which 'we' consciousness is necessary to perform a task, but the social conditions for identifying with the group are not realizable, paranoia results.

> Where the 'we' is not realizable, a gap appears between the individual and his group, and a new relation results: I am no longer 'with' the others in a community, but am now *between* them or *beside* them . . .
> One reason why the prognoses for paranoid conditions have usually been bad is that they have been explained too much on an individual and not enough on a social basis . . . Schulte cites a number of cases which conform to the etiology which his theory of a 'we-sickness' demands . . . The persecutory delusions of prisoners follow from the mechanically enforced isolation, and generally disappear with a change of milieu. Even the paranoid maladies of senescence may be traced to arteriosclerotic changes evoking new peripheral sensations which are not understood. Finally, the reason this form of insanity does not develop until maturity is that a really isolated ego does not occur in early childhood, hence, paranoid mechanisms are excluded.[28]

First, Hartmann is pointing out that what rates as 'self' or 'other' is negotiable, both in the case of individuals, who do not develop a notion of complete autonomy until adulthood, if at all, and in the case of groups, which individuals can choose to see themselves as part of or separate from. Second, the Cartesian isolated doubter, far from being normative of self-identity, is an isolated paranoic. Third, the late-blooming and negotiable distinction between 'self' and 'other' is based on understanding of sensory data, as the senescent cases indicate, and on social expectations, as the paranoia of the 'unwelcome' group member indicates.

All of the above considerations clearly indicate that the distinction between self and other is not as readily available, clear-cut and present to sensation as Russell's sensation/sense-data/physical thing distinction requires it to be. No sense-datum pops up like a little flag on any experience to announce 'I'm internal, I'm part of your body, and so no information about me has any real objective significance.' or 'I'm external, I'm objective and real.'

---

[28] Hartmann, *op. cit.*, pp. 247–248.

The 'External' Cases are not 'Objective and Real' in Contrast with the 'Internal', which are 'Subjective and Personal'

Any act of object-positing takes place from the point of view and intentions of a person. So, in the most general sense, all object-positing is personal, and idiosyncratic. 'Objectivity' is a blessing that is bestowed on a point of view, when the point of view is sufficiently well established in a linguistic community that it is well documented by that community's conceptual system. So, by adopting a point of view that has been blessed as 'objective' by one's community, anyone can, in those blessed respects, transcend the idiosyncratic and personal basis of object-positing. The difference between what is 'personal' and what is 'objective' is not the difference between what is sensed 'internally' and what is sensed 'externally'. I have demonstrated at length, here, that no such distinction can correctly be maintained. Rather, the difference between what is 'personal' and what is 'objective' is a difference in point of view adopted for object-positing and the degree of conceptual sophistication that one's community bestows on the adopted point of view. In our society, for instance, the point of view of chemistry is a well blessed and heavily conceptually (and financially) endowed point of view. Hence, object-positing done from that point of view rates as objective. In contrast, the point of view of a parent is, in our society, denigrated as having no conceptual consequences, and no value. So, it is not studied, not respected, no theorizing is done about it, no money supports it, and object-positing done from the point of view of someone who loves a child does not receive the blessing of 'objectivity.' Yet there is nothing 'external' about the perception of a chemical that is 'internal' about the perception of a child. There is no sense-data from which the character of a chemical is inferred that is missing in a parent's claims about a child. And the parent is not relying on 'unreal' 'internal' feelings to any greater extent than is the chemist, who also object-posits based on experience when naming or describing chemicals. If there were an equally conceptually-laden and socially funded and blessed point of view for parenting in our society there would be no reason to call a parent's claims about a child 'less objective' than a chemist's claims about his chemicals. It is social refusal to take one subject seriously, not 'internality' of perception, or 'lack of objectivity' that differentiates the two points of view.

Summary; There are No Sense Data

I think that it should be apparent that Russell's need for sense data and inferences from sense data to objects relied very heavily on the three dogmas listed at the beginning of this section, and on the pre-suppositions of these dogmas that I have just argued against. With the foundation dissolved from under them, the dogmas don't stand. And without them, it becomes apparent that there are more productive and more accurate ways of understanding perception.

Isn't This Position Just Idealism Revisited?

Berkeley's version of Idealism analyses the thing-in-itself, the noumena or prime matter as mind-dependent. I don't do that. Berkeley infers from his claim that to be is to be perceived, that nothing non-perceptual can exist. My much more moderate claim is only that there isn't much point in discussing a noumena because there isn't anything non-mind-dependent that we could say about it. Mind and world represent loci in an uninterrupted continuum, but mind neither causes nor controls the continuum. Rather, mind depends on experience received, recalcitrantly, and as often as not independently of the will of the thinker, to object posit.

G.E. Moore is credited with having refuted idealism of the Berkeleyan variety, by distinguishing between consciousness and objects of consciousness, in this way.

> We all know that the sensation of blue differs from that of green. But it is plain that if both are *sensations* they also have some point in common. What is it that they have in common? And how is this common element related to the points in which they differ?
> I will call the common element 'consciousness' without yet attempting to say what the thing I call so *is*. We have, then, in every sensation, two distinct terms, (1) 'consciousness', in respect of which all sensations are alike; and (2) something else, in respect of which one sensation differs from another. It will be convenient if I may be allowed to call this second term the 'object' of a sensation . . .
> Accordingly to identify either 'blue' or any other of what I have called 'objects' of sensation with the corresponding sensation is in every case a self-contradictory error. It is to identify a part either with the whole of which it is a part or else with the other part of the same whole.[29]

Moore is subscribing in this passage to the sensations/sense-data/physical things distinction as made by Russell. With that as his starting ground, he then attacks Berkeley for letting

---

[29] G.E. Moore, 'A Reply to My Critics', in *The Philosophy of G.E. Moore*, ed. P.A. Schlipp, Tudor Publishing, New York 1952, p. 546.

the physical things drop out. As I have argued extensively against Russell, this is not the most productive way to understand the territory. Research on sensations indicates that we directly see things, not blue sense-data from which we infer the existence of things. In ordinary perception, the percipient is not aware of the act of consciousness at all. So, although Moore can point to the act of consciousness as if it were a separate thing from the object apprehended, he has not, thereby isolated a distinct entity, 'Consciousness'. Moore realizes this, himself, and comments on it as follows.

> ... the element which I have called 'consciousness' ... is extremely difficult to fix ... It seems, if I may use a metaphor, to be transparent— we look through it and see nothing but the blue ... The moment we try to fix our attention upon consciousness and to see *what*, distinctly, it is, it seems to vanish: it seems as if we had before us a mere emptiness. When we try to introspect the sensation of blue, all we can see is the blue: the other element is as if it were diaphanous. Yet it can be distinguished if we look attentively enough, and we know that there is something to look for.[30]

This concession on Moore's part is no different from what I have said in claiming that the 'x' and the 'r' in object positing can only be distinguished for purposes of analysis. Ultimately, the 'x' is transparent to the 'r'. All that the 'x' really marks is the intentionality and point of view from which the 'r' is being marked. But, beyond that, Moore is losing his own analysis by waxing vague and poetical about the 'emptiness' and 'diaphanousness' of consciousness. If he were clear about it, he would see that there is reason to mark the 'x'; to discuss the point of view and the intentions of the perceiver. But this does not give us a distinct entity, an objectified act of consciousness, to set in opposition against a thing perceived.

Furthermore, he is waxing vague and poetical about the thing perceived because he thinks that it is a sense-datum; 'the blue'. According to my analysis of the situation, unless they are lying flat on their backs on a mountaintop staring at the sky on a clear day, people rarely see 'the blue'. Someone looking at a blue dress, or book, or carpet, would see a dress, book or carpet, not 'blue'. The color of the item would, in context, not normally be objectified. When aviators talk of 'the blue', of course, they are objectifying the color, as I will later in discussing my magenta-thing.

So, Moore's concession on the transparency of consciousness means that his position on the nature of consciousness is really not <u>different from</u> mine. He and I differ most on what he thinks the

[30] *Ibid.*, pp. 544–545.

object of consciousness is. For him, it is a sense-datum, while for me it is a posited object. Moore further explains why he believes he needs sense-data as follows.

> What my analysis of sensation has been designed to show is that whenever I have a mere sensation or idea, the fact is that I am then aware of something which is equally and in the same sense *not* an inseparable aspect of my experience. The awareness which I have maintained to be included in sensation is the very unique fact which constitutes every kind of knowledge: 'blue' is as much an object, and as little a mere content, of my experience, when I experience it, as the most exalted and independent real thing of which I am ever aware. There is, therefore, no question of how we are to 'Get outside the circle of our own ideas and sensations.' Merely to have a sensation is already to be outside that circle. It is to know something which is as truly and really *not* a part of *my* experience, as anything which I can ever know.[31]

Here, Moore is using his notion of a sense-datum to fudge a number of substantive issues that I believe have been made much more explicit in my analysis of sensation. For one thing, his concern to 'get outside the circle of our own ideas and sensations,' is a reaction to philosophers like Descartes, who thought that his ideas were real but his sensations weren't, and Berkeley, who thought that only perceptions and minds are real. Since my view of perception includes kauses, gestalten, points of view, intentions and posited objects, it is a direct realism, and so, there is no closed circle to worry about. One of my major motivations for arguing for this form of direct realism is to insist that people should pay more attention to experience and less attention to the closed and stagnant circle of their own ideas. If my analysis of perception is adopted, thus, it will immediately become clear in what sense people do merely posit what they want to see, and in what sense they really attend to the kauses that impinge on them, bringing them data concerning their environment. For me, the environment and the range of experience are already quite a bit broader than Descartes' solipsistic realm of ideas.

But Moore fudges about *how* he thinks he gets out of the circle. He thinks that he can get out of it by making the sense-datum an intermediary that runs back and forth from a sensation, in which it appears as a content, to a physical thing, in which it appears as a mind-independent surface. When he says, ' 'blue' is as much an object, and as little a mere content of my experience, when I experience it, as the most exalted and independent real thing of which I am ever aware,' he is really saying no more than I said when I claimed

---

[31] G.E. Moore, *Some Main Problems of Philosophy*, Macmillan Publishing, New York, 1953, pp. 132, 134–135.

that awareness is directly of objects. But his analysis of the way this happens via a sense-datum intermediary and a detached 'exalted and independent real thing' misrepresents both the nature of the experience (as restricted to single-property, i.e., 'blue', qualia) and the nature of the 'exalted and independent real thing,' (as mind-independent even as characterized, and yet, simultaneously, 'external', as an object of no intentions or points of view).

In addition, Moore fudges about the relationship between 'the real' and 'the known' in the above passage. He qualifies his two most trenchantly realistic statements in this passage with the modifiers, 'of which I am ever aware' and 'as anything that I can ever know.' As so modified, there is no disagreement between Moore's realism and my position. I agree that the closest that one can get to reality is experience, and that what one can know about reality is what kausally impinges on experience. But, despite tagging his realism claims with these qualifiers, Moore really is using his sense-datum/physical object distinction to claim that on the basis of the blue, he knows all kinds of things that have *nothing* to do with his experience, intentions, consciousness, or points of view *about* the blue book. It is this version of realism that I am out to block. I insist that unless I object-posit the book, blue prime matter would fade to background in my experience, unnamed and unattended.

So, to conclude my discussion of Moore's refutation of idealism, I need only to point out 1) that he is relying on an unproductive analysis of perception. When the territory is better analyzed, the 'closed circle of ideas' is not a problem. 2) that the sense-datum/physical object distinction does not help him, and it actually gets in his way when he tries to explain how we get outside the circle of ideas, and 3) that his qualifications and fudges on the issue of the relationship between knowledge and reality conceal a real confusion about what 'reality' is and how we know it. I don't mean this to sound glib. Most of the intelligent people of the twentieth century thought of these issues more or less as Moore did. But, I do think that there is a better way to think of them, and it is time to attend to the better way.

My position is not idealism because I believe that kauses of sensations are mind-independent, and human thinking does not dictate the character of the real.

Having answered these objections, I will now turn my attention to showing how my account of kausation can be supported by some contemporary research in cognitive science.

Chapter 4

Cognitive Science on Kausation Rather Than Causation

Some recent work in Cognitive Science and Consciousness Studies describes mental operations in ways that indicate that experience is a very complex matter, which favors my account of kausation over more naturalistic logical (Quinean) or mechanical (Dretskian) reductivist accounts. In this chapter of this book I will cite some recent work that collaborates my claim that human connections with the perceptual world are more complex, and more driven by intentionality, than current naturalistic accounts of perception would indicate, whether the naturalistic accounts are logically or mechanically oriented. I will start with a demonstration, from the work of Francisco Varela, and some of his colleagues, that human thinking operates from a base of conscious experience that has more in common with a Jamesian stream of consciousness, or a gestalt of the type discussed in the last chapter, than it has in common with a computational system, such as a logic system or a mathematical system. Next, I will highlight Andy Clark's claims that mind cannot be separated from body and world. After that, I will present Walter J. Freeman's analysis of causality as intentional and circular, which parallels my analysis in several ways. I will then argue, using some arguments from the work of Lakoff and Johnson, that mathematical logicians have overestimated the scope and range of the application of their Platonism. Some recent work in independence-friendly logic by Jaakko Hintikka will conclude this chapter on why humans need kausation rather than causation to apprehend reality.

Varela and Mangan on Mental Duration and the Fringe in Consciousness

Francisco J. Varela and Bruce Mangan have been doing research on temporal duration in phenomenal consciousness and the experience of conscious states 'between' the consciousness of objects or events, that they refer to as fringe consciousness.[1] Unlike reductivists, such as Daniel Dennett and Patricia and Paul Churchland, who argue that all consciousness is reducible to neurological functioning which is ultimately describable in objective, third-person, scientific or syntactical language, Varela and Mangan argue that time, as experienced by humans, is deeply, pragmatically rooted in the intentionality, the emotional tone, and the dynamics of a lived life. Unlike logical reductivists, such as Quine and Russell, Varela and his colleagues argue that many aspects of conscious thinking processes are non-linear and non-computational. The very conception of an object is a result of the interaction of sensations, intentions and emotions within a flow of experiential time, primed by dispositions to action.[2] Varela's studies have demonstrated that the flow of time in phenomenal consciousness is complex and non-linear, and not reducible to physical-computational temporal elapse.[3] Varela explains phenomenal time as follows:

> Even under a cursory reduction, already provided by reflections such as those of Augustine and James, time in experience is quite a different story from a clock in linear time. To start with, it does not present itself as a linear sequence, but as having a complex *texture* (whence James' 'specious present' is not a 'knife-edge' present), and its fullness is so outstanding that it dominates our existence to an important degree. In a first approximation this texture can be described as follows: There is always a centre, a now moment with a focused intentional content (say, this room with my computer in front of me on which the letters I am typing are highlighted.) This centre is bounded by a horizon or fringe that is already past. (I still hold the beginning of the sentence I just wrote) and it projects towards an intended next moment (this writing session is still unfinished.) These horizons are mobile: this very moment which was present (and hence, was not merely described but lived as such) slips towards an immediately past present. Then it plunges further out of

[1] Francisco J. Varela, 'Present Time Consciousness', in *The View From Within, First Person Approaches to the Study of Consciousness,* ed. Francisco J. Varela and Jonathan Shear, Imprint Academic, Exeter, UK, 1999, pp. 11–140.

[2] Varela, p. 25.

[3] *Ibid..* p. 112.

view: I do not hold it just as immediately and I need an added depth to keep it at hand.[4]

What Varela calls object-events are the experience of an intentional focusing within this Jamesian 'specious present', and they produce what Varela calls a non-isomorphic neurophenomenology. A triple-braid of neuro-biological events, formal descriptive tools derived from nonlinear dynamics, and lived temporal experience, in combination, constitute his new way to describe human thinking.[5] In the terms that I have been presenting in this book, Varela is pointing out that sensory, kinesthetic and other types of experience, especially of the type that that is rooted in time, are not characterizable as formal operations on computational systems. Rather, they are only characterizable in their own terms, which, as I have argued, are x-type,object-positing terms.

For issues related to truth, the new approach indicates that any propositional analysis, given in terms of linear mathematical or logical functions, such as Tarski's or Quine's, must be mistaken. The locus for the representation that will be judged true or false is not specific enough to be restricted to a propositional form. Further, the dynamic process involved in sensory and motor thinking is too complex and multi-faceted as an experience for a redundancy theory of truth, such as Tarski's, to truly represent it. The very complex texture of thought rules out a simplistic, isomorphism of proposition in mind and fact in reality. In addition, the logical opacity generated by the affective and intentional aspects of thought rule out a redundancy theory as inadequate to discuss the nuances of thinking.

But, because thinking involves specific processes rooted in brain chemistry, and designed to do representative tasks directed at intentional goals, the relationship between language and reality is not a deconstructible or idealistic free-floater, either. Someone's thoughts and feelings must be tied to their biochemistry, representational capacity, experience, and motives, in important, specific ways.

Mangan explains that the various threads of Varela's braid can be thought of as various types of restraints and limits on what consciousness can do to focus intentionality. He discusses these constraints and limitations in the following terms:

> What then is the operative limitation on the trade-offs in consciousness? At this point the answer should be evident: Articulation capacity. *At the deepest level consciousness IS the limited but infinitely plastic capacity to articulate experience.* This overall capacity is conserved during a large number

[4] *Ibid.*, p. 112–113.

[5] *Ibid.*, p. 137.

of phenomenological transformations. Normally, when something becomes clear, something else becomes vague – the sum of total articulation remains more or less constant.[6]

So, intentionality, biology and representational capacity all aim in a specific direction; that is, the direction of articulating experience. This is not a simply free-floating imaginative capacity, but a multiply constrained set of processes directed at articulating the experiences from which they arose. So, in this sense, the relationship between language and reality is first-person personal, and a product of consciousness. The first-person singular perspective of object-positing, featuring as it does a dynamic interaction between a conscious thinker and his or her world, is essential to access the articulation capacity of a human being.

Varela et al., do not discuss the processes in the world that would provide the context for mind-independent truth. But since the Platonic metaphysics of spiritual minds seeking abstract spiritual forms presumed by exclusively y-oriented accounts of truth and language use is so thoroughly undermined by their research, we might presume that platonic metaphysics will be banished from the context and environment of thought, as well.

And indeed, Andy Clark argues that articulation capacity requires not just a triple braid of neuro-biological events, non-linear formal processes and lived experience, but also a dynamic relationship among a nervous system, a body and an environment. I will now highlight some of Clark's claims about perception, to point out how they parallel my analysis.

Andy Clark's Ventral and Dorsal Perceptual Streams

Andy Clark has been arguing that perception requires a two-part analysis that parallels my analysis of perception into world-to-mind and mind-to-world streams. Clark claims that the mind-to-world, or dorsal stream, is an embodied physiological reaching out to the environment to apprehend it through motor processes such as kinesthetic awareness. Clark points out that:

> There is now a large and compelling literature that shows how such activity arises from the complex interactions of neural resources, bodily bio-mechanics, and (sometimes) external environmental structure. Such

---

[6]   Bruce Mangan, 'The Fringe: a Case Study in Explanatory Phenomenology', in Varela and Shear, op. cit. p. 251, Mangan's emphasis.

accounts reject the once popular . . . view of centralized control or centralized pattern recognition . . .'[7]

For Clark, as for me, perception covers a broader range of types of access to reality through experience than the standard empiricist's list of five senses. And reality, or the environment, has direct kausal effects on a person who intentionally interacts with it. Clark calls this aspect of perception efficient causation, and insists that a 'larger autonomous dynamical system' than a formally structured and materialistically reduced brain is required to account for how it works. [8]

In contrast, the visual or ventral stream in Clark's analysis parallels my world-to-mind side of the perceptual equation. Clark cites the research of Milner and Goodale, to argue that visual processing involves a recognition capacity, a formal kause apprehension of something as a such-and-such, occupying a time and place.[9] Clark argues for the need to make the distinction between the dorsal (mind-to-world) and ventral (world-to-mind) aspects of the x-type reasoning process based on several considerations.

First, Clark argues that there are two classes of patients who suffer from deficits in one stream or the other. People who suffer from visual form agnosis, on the one hand, report no visual experience of a presented object, but retain sufficient visuomotor skills to catch a ball or stick. Optic ataxics, on the other hand, can clearly see a presented object, but cannot grasp or reach for it.[10]

Next, Clark points out that research by Milner and Goodale shows why the two streams of perceptual processing must be relatively independent of one another. Clark observes:

> The deep reason for such functional compartmentalization, Milner and Goodale conjecture, involves the very different computational demands of visuomotor guidance and object recognition. The former requires precise knowledge of spatial location and orientation, and must be constantly and egocentrically updated to reflect real world motion and relative location. The latter requires us to identify something as the same thing, irrespective of motion and current spatial orientation, and demands only as much spatial sensitivity as is necessary to support conscious object recognition and reasoning.[11]

[7]   Andy Clark, 'Visual Awareness and Visuomotor Action', in *Reclaiming Cognition, the primacy of action, intention and emotion*, Raphael Núñez and Walter J. Freeman, eds., Imprint Academic, Exeter, UK, 1999, p. 2.

[8]   *Ibid.*, p. 3.

[9]   *Ibid.*, p. 5.

[10]   *Ibid.*, p. 6.

[11]   *Ibid.*, p. 7.

But, in a normal thinking person, the world-to-mind visuomotor skills and mind-to-world ventral skills have to be coordinated to each other to a very high degree, as well. Clark describes the relationship between the ventral and dorsal perceptual processes as a feed-back loop, in which information from each side of the process fully informs what happens on the other side. He describes this relationship as follows.

> It is thus the putative involvement of the motor output signal itself (and not its effects on subsequent worldly input) in determining the contents of our perceptual experience that makes for the non-instrumental dependence of perception on motor output and that allows, more generally, for a genuinely deep . . . dependence of perceptual content upon 'feedback loops with orbits of varying sizes . . . that can . . . in principle spread across internal and external boundaries.[12]

Such complexities in my devil x indicate that ignoring this entire area of intellectual life is a highly counter-productive methodology for understanding thinking. But Clark proceeds to point out that not only is perception this internally complex in its own terms, but its relationship to abstract thought is also far more complex than Quine's[13] observation sentences or Hempel's 'something with which we are already acquainted'[14] would allow. Again, citing Milner and Goodale, Clark points out that the activities involved in planning, choice and reason are distinct from the activities involved in fine motor control.[15] I take this point a bit farther than Clark does, to insist that even the visual aspects of the x-type reasoning process are not sufficiently systematic and organized to give complex planning activities. For that we need the y-type reasoning processes.

Clark's feedback loops are explicitly called intentional causation by Walter J. Freeman. I will now turn to a comparison of Freeman's work on causation with my similar approach.

Freeman on Consciousness and Causality

Freeman, like Clark, argues that intentionality and action are central in perceptual and linguistic thinking. Freeman says of Clark's feedback loops:

[12]   *Ibid.*, p. 10.

[13]   W.V.O. Quine, *Word and Object*, MIT Press, Cambridge, MA, 1960, p. 42.

[14]   Carl Hempel, *Philosophy of Natural Science*, Prentice Hall, Englewood Cliffs, NJ, 1966, p. 51.

[15]   Andy Clark, 'Visual Awareness and Visuomotor Action', p. 11.

Circular causality explains intentionality in terms of action–perception cycles (Merleau Ponty, 1942), and affordances (Gibson, 1979), in which each perception comcomitantly is the outcome of a preceeding action and the condition for a following action. Dewey (1914) phrased the idea in different words: an organism does not react to a stimulus but acts into it and incorporates it. That which is perceived already exists in the perceiver, because it is posited by the action of search and is actualized in the fulfillment of expectation.[16]

So, intentionality plays the essential role that I claimed for it in the feedback loops described by Clark. Further, Freeman argues that the concept of causation that he develops in analyzing how the brain uses these feedback loops is not efficient causation. For, the system of dynamical interaction that he is describing is non-linear, as Varela pointed out, and operates using self-organizing attractors, of the type that develop in other non-linear systems in physics, such as a pot of boiling water. Chaotic attractors, such as the location and coil of a row of boiling bubbles in a pot of boiling water, develop within a system, and pull the momentum of the system off equilibrium, changing the direction of the system. In the case of the brain, Freeman claims that each sensory and motor modality operates by producing patterns of neuronal populations that serve as attractors for new incoming stimuli. But, because the attractors operate in a self-organizing and non-linear way, they can undergo state transitions, and new attractors can determine the future states of the neuronal patterns. Freeman describes the effect his analysis of non-linear causation in the brain has on determinism and its behavioristic co-relates in these words.

> The attractor determines the response, not the particular stimulus. Unlike the view proposed by stimulus-response reflex determinism, the dynamics gives no linear chain of cause and effect from stimulus to response that can lead to the necessity of environmental determinism. An equally compelling reason is the requirement that all sensory patterns have the same basic non-linear dynamics, so that they can be combined into gestalts in conformance with the unity of intentionality, once they are converged and integrated over time.[17]

Freeman, hence, agrees that the formal kause, as I have described it, is a perceptually rooted, world-to-mind and mind-to-world process of forming *gestalten* and making judgments for the sake of understanding. His research points out that the brain does, in fact,

[16] Walter J. Freeman, 'Consciousness, Intentionality and Causality' in *Reclaiming Cognition, the primacy of action, intention and emotion*, Raphael Núñez and Walter J. Freeman, eds., Imprint Academic, Exeter, UK, 1999, p. 147–148.

[17] *Ibid.*. pp. 154–155.

operate in this way, and not through mechanical efficient causes. Freeman differentiates his notion of causation from the more prevalent, efficient notions by pointing out:

> Circular causality departs so strongly from the classical tenets of necessity, invariance and precise temporal order that the only reason to call it a 'cause' is to satisfy the human habitual need for causes. The most subtle shift is the disappearance of agency, which is equivalent to loss of Aristotle's efficient cause . . . [I]nteractions across hierarchical levels [of the brain] do not make sense in [efficient cause or agency] terms. Molecules that cooperate in a hurricane can not be regarded as the agents that cause the storm. Neurons cannot be viewed as the agents that make consciousness by their firing.[18]

So, Freeman's analysis of causality as a non-linear dynamical system, as intentional, as operating with what Clark called a feed-back loop of world-to-mind and mind-to-world interaction, and as operating on *gestalten*, parallels my account in many ways. Freeman adds the analysis of non-linear dynamics to the account, which might be regarded as an analysis of why certainty and isomorphism must be removed from an account of how mind relates to world, as I have already argued.

So, one might ask if determinism or Platonic certainty could still be expected to apply to the world, if it so utterly fails to apply to the mind. And, indeed, Lakoff and Johnson argue that the computational hypothesis about thinking is as misrepresentative of reality, the environment, and the contexts in which thought occurs, as it is misrepresentative of thought. A comparison of the position that I have been developing in this book, to Lakoff and Johnson's observations on this issue, follows.

Lakoff and Johnson on Embodied Thinking

George Lakoff and Mark Johnson have recently pointed out that the analytical notion of truth as correspondence between a proposition and an externally existing, independent reality depends heavily on the Cartesian conception of a mind as a disembodied entity. Descartes, of course, was recycling some very Platonic ideas of pure spirit or form, polluted matter, and mechanical causation. Since contemporary cognitive science is discovering the very high degree to which our knowledge is dependent on the structure and function of our brains and the structure and function of processes in the world, Lakoff and Johnson argue that both the scientific realism and the log-

[18] *Ibid.*, p. 159.

ical reductivism of some twentieth century philosophy have been empirically discredited. They present their view of embodied realism, in this way:

> Since embodied realism denies, on empirical grounds, that there exists one and only one correct description of the world, it may appear to some to be a form of relativism. However, while it does treat knowledge as relative – relative to the nature of our bodies, brains and interactions with our environment – it is not a form of extreme relativism because it has an account of how real, stable knowledge, both in science and in the everyday world, is possible. That account has two aspects. First there are the directly embodied concepts such as basic level concepts, spatial relation concepts and event-structure concepts. These concepts have an evolutionary origin and enable us to function extremely successfully in our everyday interactions with the world. They also form the basis for our stable scientific knowledge.
>
> Second, primary metaphors make possible the extension of these embodied concepts into abstract theoretical domains. The primary metaphors are anything but arbitrary social constructs, since they are highly constrained both by the nature of our bodies and brains and by the reality of our daily interactions.[19]

In the Lakoff and Johnson view of knowledge, conscious processes in an active, dynamic mind interact with a dynamic and changing environment, so there is nothing static on either end of the knower–known relationship that could be the terminal points for a correspondence relationship between a proposition in a mind and a state of affairs in reality. Their 'basic level' concepts correspond to the object-positing processes of concept formation, kausation, and knowledge of existence that I have identified as the experiential basis for knowledge. Since they claim that truth is situational, and depends on a person's understanding of the situation,[20] there is a strong need for understanding of the perspectives of various individuals and groups to understand what is true, paralleling my claim that object-positing is rooted in a point of view.

It is important to specify that many of the processes that drive embodied metaphors for Lakoff and Johnson are sub-conscious physiological processes. Research work on blindsight indicates that there are subjects who seem to have some form of cognitive access to perceptual data to which the subjects consciously deny that they

[19] George Lakoff and Mark Johnson, *Philosophy in the Flesh, The Embodied Mind and its Challenge to Western Thought,* Basic Books, Perseus Books Group, New York, NY, 1999, p. 96.

[20] *Ibid.,* p. 102.

have access.[21] Also, the results of split-brain experiments indicate that people can have abilities that they are unaware that they have.[22] So, the perspectives, kausal processes and points of view involved in object positing need not be fully introspectively accessible, and in many cases may not be introspectively accessible at all. But intentionality does not generally entail introspectibility in ordinary cases, either. Animals act on intentions and perceptions, even in cases in which higher levels of self-conscious introspective ability would be highly suspect.

For Lakoff and Johnson, embodied metaphors, many of which operate at a sub-conscious level, drive the perspectives or points of view in thinking. These authors argue that metaphorical thinking is basic in reasoning, and most abstract thought is built on these basic, embodied metaphors. They concur with my claim that logic is wholly inadequate to capture the embodied nature of thought. But, Lakoff and Johnson argue that this is true because logic rejects the basic metaphorical structure on which most thought is built. They argue, more radically than I do, that even logic is ultimately based on embodied metaphors, thereby reducing even the y-type reasoning processes to x-type ones. Their conclusions from their reversal of the logical reductivist argument concludes:

> Reason and our conceptual structure are shaped by our bodies, brains, and modes of functioning in the world. Reason and concepts are there-fore, not transcendent . . . Much of everyday metaphysics arises from metaphor.[23]

So, these authors support my contentions on a number of issues, such as, that a substantial part of language is its use as a tool for understanding that emerges from human experience and is characterizable as having certain functional, psychological constraints. Lakoff and Johnson also agree with my claim that the relationship of language to the world is that processes in the world seem describable by certain apt metaphors and projections of psychological processes, (my world-to-mind and mind-to-world kausal processes.) In addition they agree that empirical reiteration and study of these relations over time reinforces the value of some, which become established as scientific truths, while discounting the aptness or usefulness of other metaphorical or projected understandings, which

[21] See Lawrence Weiskrantz, *Blindsight: a case study and implications*, Oxford University Press, Oxford, UK, 1986.

[22] See Michael S. Gazzaniga, "Consciousness and the cerebral hemispheres" in *The Cognitive Neurosciences*, MIT Press, Cambridge, MA, 1995.

[23] Lakoff and Johnson, p. 128.

are then discarded as counter-productive. Both individuals and society as a whole go through these learning processes, and the fund of human knowledge builds over time because of the reiteration process.

I differ from Lakoff and Johnson, however, in taking the y-type reasoning processes more seriously than they do, and in considering the main relationship between mind and world and world and mind to be kausal rather than metaphorical. I think that the concept of metaphorical projection that they use is just too weak to explain either the relationship that ties our experience to a reality that is not of our creation, or the relationship that ties the intellectually compelling nature of mathematical and logical truths to a parallel reality that is not of our making. A more explicit analysis of contact with reality has to be made to prevent the collapse of the source of kausal impingements, whether prime matter, on the one hand, or platonic forms, on the other, into products of human metaphorical projections, which might be misread as products of human imagination in the Lakoff and Johnson view of things. On the issue of the recalcitrant reality of the world encountered in experience , my position is closer to that of Jaakko Hintikka, in his development of independence-friendly logic, which I will discuss next.

Independence Friendly Logic, Game-Theory Strategies and Kausation

Jaakko Hintikka has made a distinction that parallels my distinction between x-type, kausal, object-positing processes and y-type, abstract, property attributing processes in his recent work on independence-friendly logics. Hintikka points out, as I will in a later chapter, that even within mathematics and logic, a distinction must be made between what Hintikka calls 'interrogative games' and 'descriptive games.'[24] The interrogative games deal with proof procedures and inferences among logical claims, while the descriptive games relate to the representational and semantic functions of language.

Hintikka faults some of his fellow cognitive scientists for inadequate attention to the descriptive games and their value in seeking truth, in this passage.

> The neglect of the descriptive function of logic is especially striking in recent discussions of the philosophical problems of cognitive science. A

---

[24]   Jaakko Hintikka, *The Principles of Mathematics Revisited,* Cambridge University Press, Cambridge, UK 1998, pp. 6–7.

central role is played there by the notion of representation, especially mental, but also to some degree, linguistic.[25]

Hintikka argues that failure to distinguish between syntax, as an analysis of the functions of language as relations among properties, and semantics, as an analysis of the functions of language as related to truth, existence, causation and indexical reality has resulted in misunderstandings of how truth functions, even in logical systems. He criticizes Tarski's truth definition as follows.

> ... Tarski's undefinability result inevitably gives every model theorist and most semanticists a bad intellectual conscience. The explicit formal languages Tarski's result pertains to were not constructed to be mere logicians' playthings. They were to be better tools, better object languages for the scientific and mathematical enterprise. But if a model theorist decides to study one of them, he or she will then have either to use a stronger metalanguage for the purpose or else to leave the metalanguage informal. In the former case, we have the blind leading the blind, or, more specifically, the semantics of a language being studied by means of a more mysterious language, while in the latter case the semanticist has simply given up his or her professional responsibilities.[26]

Again, Hintikka is arguing that failure to give my devil x her due results in failure of ability to discuss semantics, truth, and existence. He further argues that we need to acknowledge:

> ... [H]ow to implement an idea that the received epistemic logic does not capture. This is the idea of *knowledge of entities* (objects, things) as opposed to *knowledge of facts* (propositions, truth of sentences.)[27]

The distinction between these two types of knowledge is essential for Hintikka because different types of knowledge games are involved in learning and verifying the two types of knowledge. He ties the conception of truth to the existence of a winning strategy in a language game, and conceives of a language game in the sense that the later Wittgenstein would have conceived of it.[28] The notion of semantics is tied to the expression 'one can find', which Hintikka says is a literal translation of the word used in some languages for the mathematical conception of the meaning of a logical constant.[29] Finding a thing, an object or a process is essential to knowledge in the semantic sense.

[25]   *Ibid.*, p. 11.

[26]   *Ibid.*, p. 16.

[27]   *Ibid.*, p. 240.

[28]   *Ibid.*, pp. 28–29.

[29]   *Ibid.*, p. 24.

Hintikka uses what he calls *Skolem functions* to connect game strategies to the finding of the objects denoted by logical constants, on the descriptive side of logical language. Also, in the spirit of the later Wittgenstein, he shows how the *Skolem functions* tie his game theoretical conception of truth to 'the activities (semantical games) by means of which the truth and falsity of our sentence is established.'[30]

I won't go into detail at this point about how Hintikka's game theoretical semantics work. At this point, I'm merely claiming empathy with his criticisms of the logical reductivism inherent in much of contemporary analytical philosophy and cognitive science, and with his claim that substitutional logic will not give one objects or existence. Hintikka sees, also, that a distinction must be made between syntax and semantics as distinct functions of language, rooted in different thinking processes, more clearly than most contemporary philosophers do. And he argues, as well, that relativism or idealism are not the only alternatives to logical rigor mortis. It is possible to retain the pragmatist conception that there are no correspondences between sentences and the states of affairs, without buying the relativism that pragmatism is sometimes faulted for.[31]

Now that I have marshaled some support for my positions expressed in the first three chapters of this book from Varela, Mangan, Clark, Freeman, Lakoff and Johnson, and Hintikka, I will proceed to tackle the issue of extending my formal-cause account of kausation to the more frequently acknowledged accounts of causation, such as agent causation, efficient causation, deductive-nomological causation, and statistical causation.

[30] *Ibid.*, p. 32.
[31] *Ibid.*, p. 44.

Chapter 5

Semantical Causation

Expanding the account to include Formal, Teleological, Probabalistic, Deductive-Nomological and Retroductive Causes

Formal Causation

It should be fairly obvious that the account of kausation that I have been offering in this book is a formal cause account of causation. Aristotle considered the form to be 'in the thing', and was much abused by the scientific revolution for this gross anthropomorphic blunder. My suggestion is that we agree with Aristotle that the form is in the thing, but, also concede to the scientific revolution that we put it there, by our semantic activity. This way, we can plead 'guilty' to the charge of anthropomorphism, and still insist that no harm has been done. Perhaps it is true that the scientific world of atoms, as conceived of from the perspective of a y-type, specifically mechanical conceptual point of view, is mechanical. But human thinking activity about the world is never completely free of intentions and judgment. And, to the extent that the humanly conceived world is a product of human thinking, it, too, is quite polluted with intentionality and judgment. In particular, the objects that we choose to acknowledge, and the names that we choose to impose upon them, are very much a product of human thinking and judgment.

I pointed out previously that science is largely a y-type, property-oriented activity. The sense of complete objectivity, and of 'rising above' the mundane and personal, that science has achieved is a direct consequence of the fact that it is y-type thinking activity. The ascent to platonic heaven brings the scientist or mathematician into the heady eternal realm of Forms and pure structures, where nothing polluted with individuality, emotions, matter, sensation, time or personality may dare intrude. Some scientists are sufficiently lost in their 'high', that like Plato, they scoff derisively at the mere mortal 'lovers of sights and sounds' that wallow in the pigsty of particularity below.

One of my major goals in arguing for this formal cause account of kausation is to point out the inappropriateness of this derisive attitude. Science does achieve a certain level of objectivity by retreating into platonic structures. But scientists should remember that the objectivity that they have achieved is achieved at the *cost* of a retreat away from experience, and hence, from reality. And, however intoxicated with pure structure a scientist may be, the objects he posits and the experience that he calls to witness his theories are still very much the products of a fallible human's mental activity. Platonic heaven may give him equations and relationships, but any objects that he thinks he sees there, he put there. And any experiences that he might call upon as evidence of the reality of his claims are intentional judgments, advanced from a human's point of view. In short, the pure objectivity of a scientific analysis is lost as soon as any attempt at using the theory is made.

Judea Pearl has offered a predominantly y-type analysis of causation, which very productively analyses the structures involved in terms of graphs, linear equations, Bayesian networks, and more general probabilistic methods. But interestingly, in a response to Bertrand Russell's objection that y-type structures are a-temporal while causation is always temporally directional, Pearl replies that we put the temporality and directionality in the causation. Pearl points out that it is the analyst's decision to determine that one set of equations, on which one is about to conduct 'surgery' is *in*, and another set is *out* for the sake of performing a 'surgical' operation. Pearl's explanation of what his causal graphs do appears similar to my formal cause account of causation in the following passage.

> Russell would probably stop us at this point and ask, 'How can you talk about two world models, when in fact there is only one world model given by all the equations of physics put together?' The answer is yes. If you wish to include the entire universe in the model, causality disappears because interventions disappear — the manipulator and the manipulated loose their distinction. However, scientists rarely consider the entirety of the universe as an object of investigation. In most cases the scientist carves a piece from the universe and proclaims that piece *in-*, namely, the *focus* of the investigation. The rest of the universe is then considered *out* or *background* and is summarized by what we call *boundary conditions*. This choice of *ins* and *outs* creates asymmetry in the way

we look at things and it is this asymmetry that permits us to talk about 'outside intervention' and hence about causality and cause-effect directionality.[1]

I will say more about Pearl's analysis when I discuss probability, more generally, but for now, it should be apparent that he has built his extremely useful analytical method on a basis that is a relationship between human minds and the world, that reflects intentionality, and is explicitly judgmental, i.e. formal kausation.

In defending Aristotle from the attack of the scientific revolution I am claiming that the scientific revolution 'went too far' in mechanizing reality. For measuring acceleration in ping pong and billiard balls the objectivity of platonic heaven may be an aid to understanding. But when human thoughts or naming activities, or kausal or temporal considerations are relevant in discussing an issue, mechanism is simply inadequate for the task. The reason for this, if I am right, is that a completely platonic, timeless, point-of-viewless world would not have any need for ways to explain experience, because it would have nothing that could count as experience.

For us poor lovers of sights and sounds, however, recognition occurs as I have described it; in the object-positing function. We put the form in the thing, then, recognize the thing for what we have marked it to be. Our idea of it can grow as our knowledge grows, but then, we are re-identifying and re-understanding the thing as well.

Aristotle called the mind 'The form of the body'.[2] Perhaps he wasn't too far off. The mind, as I have described it, is the net total of points-of-view, judgments and intentions entered into by a person, from the perspective of his or her body. That totality is also what a person would call 'myself'. To think of the mind as something separate from and added to the body is, thus, what Ryle[3] would rightly call a category mistake. But mechanism does not follow from a claim that the mind is the form of the body. On the contrary, what follows is that human judgments are rooted in a human point of view.

Aristotle never developed his notion of a formal cause to the extent that I have developed the notion of kausation in this book. And when he tried to account for perception, he slipped away to efficient causation. When he tried to develop a reason for the universe, as a whole, he slipped away to agent causation. Searle, too, slips away to agency when he tries to account for causation. Perhaps with

[1]   Judea Pearl, *Causality, Models, Reasoning and Inference*, Cambridge University Press, Cambridge, UK, 2000, pp. 349-350.

[2]   in 'De Anima' in *Basic Works of Aristotle, op. cit.*

[3]   Gilbert Ryle, *The Concept of Mind*, The University of Chicago Press, Chicago, 1949.

my more robust account of formal kausation articulated, some of the problems raised by these slips will be avoidable.

The formal kause, as I have described it, is not a static notion of a thing with its concept embedded in it. Rather it is a process, object-positing, by which an active, attentive and alert person reaches out to her experience in an attempt at understanding it. The process involves a two-way relationship between mind and world that is interactive and dynamic. The process is marked by intentionality and judgment at every step. It works as a kausal impacting relationship on the world-to-mind side, where some 'hit' in experience impinges on consciousness, and as a semantic relationship on the mind-to-world side. Its products are objects, names, and kausal relations. This, I have been arguing, is the most basic notion of a kause. A kause, is, most basically, whatever has the capacity to impinge on consciousness. I will now show how one generalizes this basic notion to explain agency.

Teleological Causation

Readers of John Searle will have recognized familiar ground in a lot of my arguments, already. Searle has argued that causation is part of the experience of perception, that law-like causal relations are cognitive constructs based on single case and experientially based knowledge of causation, and that the relationship between an intentional representation and its object is causal. For instance, Searle discusses the intentionality of the relationship between a description of a cause and a description of its effect in cases of perception or action this way.

> The reason that there is a logical or internal relation between the description of the cause and the description of the effect in our [perception] examples is that in every case there is a logical or internal relation between the cause and the effect themselves, since in every case there is an Intentional content that is causally related to its conditions of satisfaction.[4]

I have described the same relationship as a kausal relationship on the world-to-mind side, and a semantic identity relationship on the mind-to-world side, although the semantic relationship is also kausal, for the mind is manipulating the world on that side. But Searle's version of this relationship is obviously similar to mine in important respects.

---

[4]   John Searle, *Intentionality, op. cit.* p. 121.

However, Searle slips away from talk of 'logical or internal relations between causes and effects, themselves' when he characterizes the nature of causality, to discuss its role in agency. About his account of causation, Searle says:

> There are not two kinds of causation, regularity causation and intentional causation. There is just one kind of causation and that is efficient causation; causation is a matter of some things making other things happen.[5]

Here, I believe that Searle made a mistake. He had the basis for an account of formal kausation as understanding and recognition at his fingertips, and he let it escape. Then, he tried to drag efficient causation back into perception and agency, were they don't work, to try to plug in the deficit.

I will insist, rather, that kausation is primarily a matter of recognition and understanding, not of some things making other things happen. It is primarily a process whereby one divides one's experience up into discreet, understandable and nameable units. To have experience is to have one's consciousness impinged upon by some 'hit' in one's experience, and thus to suffer the impact of a kause. When one responds to the impact with a point-of-view, and a name that marks the 'impingement' as a kause, one has both manipulated, and been manipulated by some aspect of one's experience of reality. This notion of a kause is clearly present in agency, as well, although it is doing more and becoming efficient causation in agency. But, the agent-driven or efficient notion of a cause is not present in perception. Hence, Searle doesn't discuss causation much when he discusses perception. He acknowledges that perception is the more basic Intentional category, but he waits until his discussion of agency to mention causation.

Instead of doing things backwards, as I have claimed Searle does on this one point, we should take the kausal relationship as primarily a denoting and understanding relationship. This interpretation of kausation makes more sense for perception, in which we can describe the mind-to-world side of the Intentional relationship as denoting recognition. And understanding this relationship as denotative, rather than agent-propelled or efficient-cause propelled, will make better sense of agency as well.

For, if things are as I have described them for perception, it is easy to see what should be said about agency. A case in which someone wants, moves towards, pushes, or walks with Sally is a case in which someone has recognized several things, some of which are part of

[5] *Intentionality, op. cit.* p. 135.

himself and some of which are not, and has set out to rearrange the items in this recognition-inventory to make a preferred arrangement. Let me show how this comes about, in steps.

1. P remembers that John asked him to invite Sally to the party on Friday.

2. P enjoys Sally's company and looks forward to her presence at the party.

3. P spots Sally, having lunch in the cafeteria.

4. P moves towards Sally, intending to pass on John's party invitation.

Steps 1, 2, and 3 in this scenario are recognition, or formal kause steps. Step one is a bit of memory data that P could obviously have forgotten, or failed to recall at the cafeteria door. Step two is another bit of memory data, from past experiences of Sally, indexed to a current warm and fuzzy feeling about Sally. Step three is a current perceptual state, that obviously would not have occurred if something had been blocking P's view of the cafeteria, or P was preoccupied with deeper thoughts. But, obviously, unless they occurred, step 4 could not occur. Step 4 is an intentional, additive result of steps 1 through 3. Step 4 is also the only agent-propelled action in the list. Therefore, agency kausation is a complex type of kausation, which is the additive result of prior formal kause thinking.

I think that Searle's mistake, here, was in his definition of a cause as 'some things making other things happen'. That definition committed him to efficient causation as primary, and stuck him with little or nothing to say on perception. He was on the right track in calling intentional perceptual relations 'causally self-referential', but he slipped away to efficiency in discussing agency, abandoning rather than developing his earlier insight.

This formal kause account of agency also eliminates philosophical problems that have been raised about desires running efficient causation backwards from non-existent states of affairs like sloop ownership to present actions like saving money to buy a boat, or present intentions like wanting a boat. On this account, Quine's desire for relief from slooplessness would be an x in his consciousness, created by a variety of states of himself that we could characterize as a need for acceptance by his peers, a belief that all of his peers are at the yacht club, a love of sailing, an aesthetic appreciation for the appearance of sloops, a need for quietude, etc. These recognized 'deficiency states' in Quine additively produce an agent-propelled intention in him to save money to buy a boat.

Since judgment and intentionality are involved at every point in Quine's determination of his need, and what will satisfy it, he could at any point reevaluate his situation to form an alternate analysis of what he needs. Given a long enough famine at Harvard, Quine's need for relief from slooplessness would have been completely replaced by a need for a meal.

This analysis of the role of formal kausation in agency espouses a naturalistic approach to the entire genre encompassed by dreams, desire, imagination, hallucination and the like. In a nutritional condition known as pica, people are known to hallucinate, dream about and imagine foods which contain the vitamins, minerals, and proteins in which their bodies are deficient. Pickles are not the efficient cause of a pregnant woman's night time cravings. The cravings are formally kaused by a sudden deficiency of essential minerals absorbed out of her body by the fetus. Her recognition that pickles will resolve the deficit identifies the experiential 'hit' as a pickle-deficit, establishing a kausal, semantic, relationship between her recognition of the condition (an x) and the condition itself (an r). The condition, of course, might exist unrecognized and unidentified. In that case, her body would suffer the consequences of the mineral deficiency mechanically, without any semantic relationship developing between her and it. A hungry person who wakes up from a dream of a sumptuous meal, contra Descartes, knows very well that he hasn't seen a meal, he needs one.

Further support for my formal kause account of agency comes from the fact that people can, and sometimes do, misjudge their own needs, just as they sometimes misjudge what they are seeing or what the problem is with their own bodies. People think that they need self-destructive things like gambling, drugs, alcohol and tobacco, just as they misjudge conditions like indigestion for heart attacks.

A naturalistic account of agency like this presupposes that something like Abraham Maslow's hierarchy of needs[6] operates in people, and helps to explain how they behave as agents. The sources of perceived needs can be biological conditions of one's body, sociological or environmental conditions, collections of thoughts or memories, habits, delusions, etc. What must occur for an agent to act, however, is that he must be tying together the collection of items of data that he is considering relevant to the issue into a wish, motivation or desire, in a manner similar to the one that I described as motivating P to approach Sally in the cafeteria. Thus, in my account of

[6] see Abraham Maslow, 'Psychological Data and Value Theory', in *New Knowledge in Human Values*, ed. A. Maslow, Henry Regnery Co., Gateway edition, Chicago, 1970.

kausation, agency is an additive result of someone tying together an analysis of various x's in thought, which represent an understanding of the agent's present condition, with several more x's in thought, that represent the agent's preferred future condition. The agent, then, undertakes the action that he or she thinks will move the situation from the present condition to the preferred one. The agent's judgment could be mistaken, of course, at any point in his analysis, and then his behavior will seem inexplicable to someone who analyses the situation differently. But, in ordinary circumstances we do understand why people behave the way they do, because we are analyzing their situation in a manner similar to the way that they are analyzing it.

Thus, we might say that agency is projected understanding, but not vice versa. Formal kauses are built into teleological kausation, but teleological causation is not present in perception or understanding. When we turn to more systematic notions of causation, also, projected understanding will work better than projected agency as an account of what causation is. In the more systematic sciences, understanding remains the key concept in something making something else happen. And the homunculi stay in agency, where they belong. I will now turn to explaining how my account of kausation can better explain probability, deductive-nomological kausation, and retroductive kausation.

Probability and Statistics as Causes

Reasoning about probabilities was the only type of causal reasoning that Hume would accept. He was limited to this view by his restrictions on what could rate as causes and effects. Cause–effect pairs (c–e pairs) had to be either contiguous impressions in the stream of consciousness or (less preferred) contiguous pieces of matter that were causing those impressions. Matter-causing-matter c–e pairs were less preferred by Hume because, although he considered it likely that matter caused impressions, he considered this matter-causes-a-mental particular assumption a completely unanalyzed and unanalyzable guess. So, he preferred to discuss c–e pairs as impression-impression pairs. A result of this limit on what could count as a c–e pair was that his assumption of the existence of matter could not provide any more content to his analysis of causation than he could get just by counting c–e pairs in the stream of mental particulars.

Nevertheless, a simple count of c–e pairs in the stream of x's in thought does produce useful results often enough to make the procedure worth while. If we assume that statistical reasoning does just count c-e pairs among impressions in someone's stream of consciousness, we can still compile count samples that will enable us to do object-positing on the basis of the experiences and the counts. This process will involve Humean induction, and an object-positing judgment, in the following way;

1. P establishes discrete xs as experiences.

2. Over time, P sorts the xs as more or less constant in experience.

3. P judges some xs as constant and kausative, others as adjectival, background, or transitory.

4. P assigns status as r to the most constant and kausative xs; status as transitional property to all xs not consistent with r's kausative role.

Probabilistic kausation can be, as I have already explained in introducing my notion of kausation, a method of thinking that thinkers use to sort the barrage of sensory, imaginative, intellectual and generally experiential data that they experience into objects and kauses in this blind way. A conscious mind sorts experiences according to their frequency in occurring, declaring the most stable experiences object experiences, and judging less frequent impressions as adjectival on more stable ones.

First, notice that this procedure for counting c–e pairs in the stream of consciousness is somewhat 'dumb'. The person who is keeping track of the count need not know at the outset what it is that he or she is counting. Given a large enough sample of experience, the counting procedure will separate objects, kauses and adjectival properties into more or less appropriate figures and grounds. Actually, people do make judgments that are more sophisticated than this about kauses, showing, as well, a somewhat Kantian capacity to distinguish actual causal sequences from accidentally co-occurring perceptions.

Second, notice that my claim that an analysis of an experience of a mouse is as direct and immediate as an analysis of an experience of stomach rumbles, overcomes Hume's problem with unobserved causation and material objects. For, in my account, experiencing the kause is part of the experience of the thing. Kausation and material objects are not 'external' unexperienced hypotheses piled, ad hoc, on top of experienced impressions. Rather, they are part of the content of the experience, itself.

Judea Pearl argues for both kausal content in experience and the value of a blind statistical count when he distinguishes between statistical models, which he says are purely co-relational, and causal models which, he argues, have directionality.[7] He bases the distinction on the fact that people do, in fact, make the Kantian perceptual distinctions between correlated sets of experiences that they judge to be causal, and equally commonly correlated ones, in which they don't make the causal judgment. Pearl asks if there is a structural difference between probability judgments and causal ones that can be perceptually or observationally discerned, and concludes that there is such a difference. He explains it in these terms.

> The clues that we explore . . . come from certain patterns of statistical associations that are characteristic of causal organizations – patterns that, in fact, can be given meaningful interpretation only in terms of causal directionality.

Further, Pearl argues that these causal patterns are interpretive, rather than 'natural' or 'external' properties of events.

> . . . [C]ertain patterns of dependence, which are totally void of temporal information, are conceptually characteristic of certain causal directionalities and not others. Reichenbach (1956) suggested that this directionality is a characteristic of Nature, reflective of the temporal asymmetries associated with the second law of thermodynamics. ...We offer a more subjective explanation, attributing the directionality to choice of language and to certain assumptions, (e.g. Occam's razor) prevalent in scientific induction.[8]

Pearl later shows how heuristics that he develops using DAGs (Directed Acyclic Graphs) can be used to produce causal models that mimic the perceptual ability of people to distinguish between merely statistical and causal correlations.[9] Further, he shows how his combined methods of analysis, based on DAGs, can sort causal relations out of 'blind' statistical data, even when no apparent temporal difference between cause and effect is obvious in the data, and how his procedures can be used to detect unobserved latent causal structure 'behind' observed correlations.[10]

Stability, together with Occam's razor, are the major presumptions that Pearl includes in his methodology for distinguishing causes from spurious correlations. Clearly, what Pearl is doing, both in his presumptions and in his graphs, is giving an interpretation of statistics and probability that shows a way to provide a perceptual, intentional, formal kause basis for the y-type statistical reasoning that he intends to use later to sort and quantify his DAGs. It was just

---

[7]   Judea Pearl, *Causality, op. cit.* p. 40.

[8]   *Ibid,.* p. 43.

[9]   *Ibid.,* pp. 44 ff.

[10]   *Ibid.,* p. 45.

this that Hume saw no way to do, in part because he saw no connection between a thing and our perception of it.

Third, notice that status as an object can be awarded tentatively in a system based on formal cause perception joined to statistical analysis. Objects with little or no perceptual content can be postulated as underlying objects for cases that are consistently unstable at the perceptual or experiential level. Thus, statistical objects like 'the average American family' rate fine as objects, analyzed from a sociological point of view.

Of course, in the short term, accidental co-occurrences might become glorified as permanent structures. This is an unavoidable consequence of the fact that object-positing is a matter of intentions and judgment. It is just unreasonable to look for certainty or guarantees, here. The approximate degree of certainty that can be achieved by this process when it is viewed more formally as probability and statistics, comes from the size of count sample and the mathematical structure of the quantitative analysis used to compile the count. These factors are syntactical elements, and are more properly classified as ways in which minds use property-attributing abilities, rather than object-positing ones.

Probability theory is the favored scientific methodology of a large number of philosophers and scientists since Hume because its very dumbness gives it the potential to yield surprising new correlations, while its mathematical elements give it the power to distinguish between the more and less frequent of the correlations. The judgment that was a matter of discernment at the perceptual level, thus, becomes a matter of the count in systematic statistical studies. This is a disadvantage in the sense that statistical counts can be used to engage in deliberate deception, or can lead to perverse results, such as Simpson's paradox,[11] but an advantage in the y-type independence from theoretical prejudices that can be achieved by the blindness of the count.

So, probability procedures are rooted in the basic formal kause because a probability-like procedure is used when a person makes judgments about consistency and status as a stable object to perform object-positing, or naming. Someone isolates several xs in thought, and determines that some are stable, some transitional, and some adjectival on others. Systematic statistics and probability techniques transform this initially judgmental procedure into a method of quantitative analysis. Once transformed, the procedure becomes

---

[11] see numerous references in *Causality in Crisis?*, eds. Vaughn R. Mc Kim and Stephen P. Turner, University of Notre Dame Press, 1997.

less a matter of object-positing, and more a matter of functions and formulas. Reliability of analysis increases in the transformation, but relevance to experience decreases. The power of the procedure to increase knowledge is attributable to the fact that both object-positing and property-attributing mental abilities are being used in productive statistical analyses.

Hume was very concerned that the results weren't necessary, might yield random co-occurrences as c–e pairs, and relied always on past data to predict future events. In terms of the account of thinking that I am offering, Hume's fears can be somewhat mitigated on all counts except the uncertainty charge. And that charge will look less foreboding when one considers probability as only one of several available notions of kausation, rather than as the whole story.

To mitigate Hume's worries about probability; I can insist, with Pearl, that humans do distinguish more and less relevant cases of co-occurrence. There is no necessary connection in causation, but functional relationships are available, and are identified perceptually. Kausation doesn't even give a relationship of necessary connection in a case of direct sensory experience, so I consider the demand for certainty unreasonable, here. Random co-occurrences can be reduced by increasing the size of a count sample, and by increasing the level of analysis of the involved functions. But retreating to higher levels of analysis is not always desirable, either. For the potential for making more practically based judgments about relevance in data is lost with increasing quantification.

Another concern of Hume's was that the correlations discovered in probability thinking would be phantoms drawn from the past and used to predict the future. On my view, the role of the object-positing process is to understand the present, not to predict the future.

Two objections that someone might raise to my object-positing account of probability and statistics are the following, which I will call the billiard balls objection and the insurance company objection.

The Billiard Balls Objection

Common language and widespread opinion both claim that in a billiard balls case, ball A is *the cause* of ball B's motion. How can I say otherwise and claim to be discussing kausation? Causation cannot be in the mind of an experiencer because it is obviously in the balls. Ball A makes ball B move, not the mind of the observer. C–e pairs are always between things and other things. Even Hume was only being excessively fastidious when he implied that they might be impressions and other impressions.

My answer to this objection is that motion is not a part of either ball. A person who becomes aware of a series of experiences in which one ball rolls into another and makes it move has observed two objects, A ball and B ball, and is sorting the scene to determine what is happening there.

This is what I believe the observer does. The observer does a kausal probability count of the noticed aspects of the scene in which he rejects the motion of either ball as essential parts of the balls. This presumes prior experience of still balls, that is currently being used to evaluate this experience. The judgment of the observer, thus, analyses the motion of the balls as independent of the identity of either ball. In making that judgment, the observer has also concluded that the motion is not his kause, in the impingement sense, of his experience. That kause will rather be the balls that he has classed as the objects in the scene.

About the motion, the observer can still choose to objectify it, or to take it as a transitional property of the scene. In this perceptual context, from an amateur observer's point of view, motion would most likely be considered a transitional property of both balls. It would be left as unanalyzed and considered, in this context, as ephemeral as light flashes across the surfaces of the balls from an overhead lamp. But this is not the only option open to the observer. The motion could also be equated to kinesthetic sensation, or objectified, itself, as something like conserved force. Equating motion to kinesthetic sensation will have the effect of personifying A ball as an agent. By projecting agency into the scene, the observer will interpret the scene as having a homunculus jumping from ball A to ball B at point of contact.

If the observer objectified the motion as a thing itself, he might wind up with a Castaneda-like 'causity', that I argued is an incoherent migratory non-entity in the first chapter. A full-blown objectified notion of all-of-motion through all-of-space/time, as conserved force, could only emerge as an object at the end of a retroductive scientific account of motion, in much the way that Isaac Newton developed that idea. Efficient causation in a perceptual experience is just not sufficiently content laden to generate Newtonian force, as an object.

But taking the motion of A ball and B ball as a transitional property of a perceptual scene is really all that anyone needs to build the idea of transuent or efficient kausation out of the initial notion of a formal kause. The formal kause idea, remember, was that the observer judged an intrusion upon his or her consciousness as having a source. The observer can identify the source as her thoughts, her memories, her kneecap or the piano in the next room, as long as in so identifying the source she is connecting some x with some r. In the billiard-balls case, she is performing the formal kause analysis, as I described it, for both balls. When the transitional property, motion, is rejected as a part of either ball, it can still be analyzed as an adjectival property of both, like the light flashes. That is really all that transuent or efficient motion needs to be, for everyday experience. Searle's 'something making something else happen' definition of causation can be taken as a generalization over 'moving', 'exploding', 'growing', 'burning', 'shrivelling', 'flowing', and a variety of other change verbals, each of which, in an individual case, only describes a transitional property of a thing. The generalization is a form of objectification that doesn't need to be done for understanding of a present experience, and probably would only be done by someone who was trying to work a sophisticated, scientific notion of causation back into an ordinary perceptual experience. Certainly, everyone with some scientific education does this, and it is a reasonable thing to do. But I am pointing out that it is more than is needed to understand transition. A formal kause, and a transitional property are all that one really needs to understand practical, perceptual, everyday cases of change. An observer can separate one from the other by a blind statistical count, and analyse experience accordingly.

To summarize my response to the objection: A ball does not make B ball move. Rather, an observer analyses two balls as kausal objects, and judges an experience of motion as an adjectival, inessential property of both balls. What else the observer later decides to think about this property, is quite open. For purposes of understanding the scene, all that the observer needs to do is reject motion as a part of the object. This rejection can be accomplished by blind statistical count of x's in consciousness. Probability, and the accompanying notion of an efficient cause, are thus, very useful for understanding, but insufficient to generate a full-blown scientific notion of a cause. For that Pearl's full-blown, y-type theoretical analysis, or a more sophisticated deductive-nomological account is needed.

The Insurance Company Objection

And, of course, insurance companies do compile statistics *to* predict who will cause accidents. But in doing so, they are patently projecting agency on to actuary tables that can only questionably bear the weight. The protest of the good, nineteen-year-old driver that *he* doesn't drink and drive, doesn't speed and doesn't show off in his car is reasonable. Singular conclusions cannot intellectually legitimately be drawn from statistical generalities, no matter how politically legal it may be for insurance companies to draw them. The statistics compiling process should be viewed as a process aimed at increasing understanding, not at predicting the future. The statistics teach us that drinking and driving, speeding and macho bravado *have been* responsible for most serious accidents; not that Joe Gooddriver, age nineteen, *will* cause accidents.

Judea Pearl, however, points out that there is a systematic relationship between the generalizations created by statistical analyses, such as 'macho attributes cause accidents' and singular claims of causal event occurrence, such as 'Barry Baddriver's intoxication and excessive speed caused the accident at North and Third last night'. Pearl describes the relationship in these terms.

> Thus, the distinction between type and token claims is a matter of degree in the structural (Pearl's) account. The more episode-specific evidence we gather, the closer we come to the ideals of token claims and actual causes . . . Probable Sufficiency (PS) is close to a type-level claim because the actual scenario is not taken into account, and is in fact, excluded from consideration. Probable Necessity (PN) makes some reference to the actual scenario, albeit, a rudimentary one (i.e., that x and y are true) . . . [W]e will attempt to come closer to the notion of an actual cause by taking additional information into consideration.[12]

The actual cause, in Pearl's analysis must still be a singular event, with all of its context and specific details of occurrence recorded. Pearl characterizes a singular event cause as a 'causal beam,' which he describes as a 'structural- semantic explication of the notion of a process.'[13] In so analyzing the situation, Pearl is agreeing that insurance company actuary tables are quite removed from actual cases of causation, which always occur someplace, such as at North and Third.

Thus, Pearl's analysis of the relationship among actual causes, necessary causes and sufficient causes explains how the platonic number crunching of actuaries relates, in an indirect way, to actual causes. The quantitative analysis that generates insurance statistics has removed legitimate conclusions from the domain of object-positing all together. Statistical number-crunching of the actuarial type is y-type property attributing labor. Objects or individuals of any kind are missing from that domain, including Barry Baddriver. The insurance companies can look for individuals who embody the

[12] Pearl, *Causality*, p. 311.

[13] *Ibid.* p. 313.

'baddriver' qualities, but it is always a question of judgment whether they are accurately applying the properties to the individual. And of course, some 'gooddrivers' wind up paying too much for insurance because they are young males, while some 'baddrivers' escape with few surcharges because they are in low risk demographic groups.

Statistical analyses at the necessary and sufficient levels do isolate properties that can be correlated in a general way to general types of risks, and identify processes that are functionally connected to accidents in mathematically calculatable ways. Thus, Pearl's notion that interventions in causal DAGs are 'surgeries' and his analysis of causal functions as 'manipulations' capture the intuition that producing ability to estimate an outcome is, for some purposes of inquiry, more important than merely formally understanding a scene. But still, the judgment is missing from the caluculations, and essential to ever know an actual cause.

My responses to the insurance company objection, as well as my more general conclusions about probability and statistics are, thus, 1) that this type of reasoning is based on object-positing and formal kausation. In the basic form, statistical reasoning is the perceptual ability to perform the blind sorting process used in formal kausation to sort experiences into kauses, objects, and transitional properties. But, 2) once systematic quantificational methods, formulas, actuary tables and the like are brought into statistical reasoning, it becomes a property-attributing procedure, and leaves object-positing behind. The fact that both types of reasoning intersect in probability makes it a very powerful intellectual tool. In general, the use of both thinking methods will strengthen any inquiry.

I will now turn to an analysis of the relationship of deductive-nomological causation to my account of kausation, leaving retroductive causation for last.

Deductive-Nomological Causation

Carl Hempel considers most scientific accounts of causation to be conformable to a formula in which general scientific laws, such as the law of gravity, are combined with other, preferably observation sentences, to yield an explanandum. The explanandum rates as explanatory because it subsumes the observations, which might be test results or experimental data, under the 'covering laws'. The covering laws explain why the data is the way it is. Hempel formalizes the structure of deductive-nomological explanations this way.

L₁, L₂, ...Lᵣ Explanans sentences

C₁, C₂, ...Cᵣ
E   Explanandum sentence[14]

The L sentences in the explanans represent covering laws, the C sentences represent observations of data, and the conclusion, E, is deductively warranted by subsumption of the observations under the laws.

Corresponding to the distinction between covering laws and observation sentences in the formula, Hempel also discusses two kinds of principles at work in good scientific theories. He distinguishes between 'internal principles' and 'bridge principles' in this way.

> The former [internal principles] will characterize the basic entities and processes invoked by the theory and the laws to which they are assumed to conform. The latter [bridge principles] will indicate how the processes envisaged by the theory are related to the empirical phenomena with which we are already acquainted, and which the theory may then explain, predict, or retrodict . . . [15]

It should be immediately apparent that very little of Hempel's account is concerned with object-positing procedures, as I have described them. The empirical phenomena are just something ' . . . with which we are already acquainted . . . ' . Even as listed in his formula for deductive-nomological explanations, the C-sentences are already structured as premises that will play a role in a truth-functional deductive argument. Minimally, this means that they must be full-fledged propositions of standard form, which are formalizable in the notation of symbolic logic. When formalized, the C- sentences would be structured in a way that would represent any object as an existentially quantified variable, x, and the properties of the object would be listed as a predicate, P. The P part of the sentence would be the truth-functionally operative part. The capacity of the structure to support substitution gives it its truth-functional power, but also reduces the status of the posited object to near insignificance. It is the property predicated of the object that becomes deductively important, not the posited object, itself.

Thus, Hempel's schema describes an almost exclusively property-attributing, y-type thinking process. I have already ceded to Russell, Quine, Carnap, and like minded philosophers mastery of the intricacies of truth-functional relations in propositions structured in the

---

[14]   Carl Hempel, *Philosophy of Natural Science*, Prentice Hall Inc. Englewood Cliffs, New Jersey, 1966, p. 51.
[15]   *Ibid*. p. 72-73.

notation of symbolic logic. So, my task here is to show how deductive thinking procedures, like Hempel's, which are almost exclusively y-type procedures, can rate as causal laws when kausation is part of the object-positing process, and thus, is not to be found anywhere in these laws.

Deductive-nomological laws rate as causal laws, not because they describe kausation taking place, but because they presume that the rational structures from which these laws are deduced must, of necessity, describe the interactions of the attributed properties, and hence, must describe any possible world in which those properties interact in the described ways. Quantifiable formulae can be used to describe transitions in properties because in any possible world in which those structures were instantiated, they would exhibit those structural properties. I shall argue at length later in this paper that the connection between reality and the property attributing process is different from the connection between reality and the object-positing process, although both processes can lead to knowledge and truth.

But the situation with respect to D-N causal laws is more complex than the last paragraph would indicate for two reasons. One is that although my distinction between object-positing and property-attributing can be made by way of analysis, in practice, both processes are usually interacting. Hempel's formulae seldom occur in the purified platonic versions envisaged by him in describing his theory. So, in scientific practice, including most of the examples of scientific laws cited by Hempel to illustrate his theory, scientists help themselves liberally to both direct experimentation and the coining of new terminology for surprising observations. Science is well steeped in the object-positing process at the level of observation, in addition to availing itself of D-N techniques at its more systematic levels.

The other way in which D-N laws can rate as causal laws is that the object-positing process can be reincorporated into scientific reasoning at the highest levels of investigation, where it is used to postulate theoretical entities for science. Hempel doesn't distinguish between theoretical entities and observational ones 'with which we are already acquainted.' But I will follow the lead of other philosophers in addressing retroductive accounts of causation separately.

Hence, my temporarily hasty conclusion on Hempel's version of deductive-nomological causation is that he has smuggled kausation into his account by ignoring the fact that his principles have banned it. The difficulties that Mackie and Sanford had in trying to get time into their platonic versions of D-N Laws are a clear indication that this is what has occurred. But to further defend this criticism of Hempel, I will have to also argue at length that the formalized structures of symbolic logic do not denote uniquely, and that retroductive kausation does not fit Hempel's formula. The latter project is next, the former project will be addressed later in this book.

Retroductive Causation

Ernan McMullin has argued that theoretical scientific theories really do not fit the D-N model of causation at all. These are some of the things that McMullin says about retroductive explanation, in marking it off from D-N lawlikeness.

> What constitutes this [retroductive explanation] as explanatory is not the inclusion of these regularities into yet other regularities so much as the introduction of theoretical entities, that is, entities the warrant for whose relevance to this context (and often for whose very existence) is their effectiveness in accounting for the observed regularities.[16]

In other words, the intellectual process involved in giving theoretical, scientific explanations reverses or forestalls the tendency of property-attributing thinking processes to regress into increasingly more abstract and amorphous properties by taking an object-positing stance towards the system of properties and regularities, itself. One could, then, view retroductive explanations as something of a ploy, dragged in to prevent scientific explanations from running off into the void after a third man.

But, there are persuasive reasons for taking the reintroduction of object-positing at this level in scientific theorizing as realistically as one would take it at the perceptual level. McMullin agrees with Wesley Salmon's reasons for taking retroductive explanation as explanation involving real entities. McMullin lists those reasons as follows.

> Brownian motion can be explained retroductively by postulating the existence of microentities . . . the number of which, per mole of gas . . . can be estimated with the aid of some quantitative data concerning the motion. One can, by means of the same postulate, account for a multitude of other phenomena of quite disparate sorts, such as electrolysis and alpha decay.
> The postulated microentities come out in each case to exactly the same number per mole. The number is so large and so precisely known that it seems all together unlikely that different sorts of entities could be involved; a single kind of entity, the molecule, exerting several different kinds of causal agency, seems to be the only reasonable explanation. The

---

[16] Ernan McMullin, 'Explanation in Natural Science', in *Midwest Studies in Philosophy IX, op.cit.*, p. 206.

instrumentalist ploy fails here because it can offer no plausible reason why the theoretical construct invoked to explain Brownian motion should turn out to be conceptually identical with the entity that explains electrolysis.[17]

However, if one is a realist about the ability of the object positing process to yield knowledge, the postulation of molecules, or of any other type of theoretical entity, is no problem. The same interaction between a body of data and a conscious mind is taking place in the Salmon story as I have claimed takes place between sensory data and a mind at the perceptual level. Salmon's scientist sorts a collection of x's in her experience into those that are kausative, which she names as objects, and those that are too transitory, which she counts as properties or adjectival on the objects. The object, classified as kausative is awarded status as r, which in this case is intentionally marked by a number $6.0225.10^{23}$. In my account, molecules turn out to be as substantial as tables and chairs.

This is not, of course, to say that molecules are in any sense certain. The certainty that was attached to the D-N method is abandoned along with, or to the degree that, the quantitative method is abandoned. Once the number is naming an entity rather than quantifying over an ordinal position, the possibility of ambiguity or of other denotative errors enters the scene. Hence, phlogiston was as much a product of the scientific object-positing process as molecules are.

Retroduction, thus, cannot operate without a solid D-N basis, because the quality of the supporting D-N basis increases the likelihood of productive retroductive objects, and decreases the likelihood of unproductive ones. This situation directly parallels the perceptual situation, in which increased experience of perceptual objects increases the likelihood of productive interpretations of what is being seen.

My conclusion on retroductive kausal analysis is, therefore, that kausality reenters scientific analysis at this level, because the object-positing process comes back into use. D-N chauvinists like Hempel fail to recognize both the degree to which their theories purport to identify and individuate aspects of reality, and the degree to which their observations are independent of any phenomena whatsoever, and hence, fail to be empirical theories.

Retroduction remains the most powerful tool available to science despite the potential for judgmental error because it combines the best of both the object-positing and property-attributing capacities of mind at the most sophisticated level of thought. This is why pro-

---

[17] *Ibid.* p. 213.

ductive scientific theories have the capacity to command intellectual awe from those who appreciate their explanatory dominance.

Summary of the Semantic Account of Causation

I'll conclude this chapter with a fast summary of the major points that I have demonstrated in it.

Object-positing is a process that relates a knower's intention to name some aspect of his or her world, which I mark with an x, to the aspect of his or her world that is so marked and named, which I call r. The relationship between x and r is redundant identity. Kausation is part of the object-positing process, just described. It is the way in which some aspect of someone's world impinges on his or her consciousness, when the knower focuses on it, or pays attention to it. 'Impingement' differs from efficient causation in that it is a two way, conscious, active, intentional and judgmental relationship. The types of candidates for an r impinging on a conscious mind range from physical objects outside the knower, through states of his or her own body, dreams, sudden intellectual insights, etc.

Kausation is, thus recalcitrantly determinate in the sense that it circumscribes the ways in which reality can effect thought. It is also ineliminably intentional to the extent that the nature of the x in thought becomes the determining principle, or point of view, for the marking off of the r for attention.

Some of the circulating theories of causation fit into my schema as follows.

1. *Formal kausation*: The kause that is operative in object-positing. Its main purpose is to develop understanding.

2. *Teleological kausation*: Adds agency to the understanding gained in a formal kause, by narrowing the possible points of view to that of just the agent. This narrowing of point of view is necessary for moral and for some psychological reasoning, but too restrictive for thinking in general or science in particular.

3. *Probabilistic kausation*: This type of kause is a simple count procedure applied to x's in thought, to assist the thinker in performing the formal kause analysis, at the level of direct awareness. But, it can also be embellished with quantitative methodology that increases its capacity to analyze complex data, because it is borrowed from y-type thinking processes. But the increase in organizational capacity gained by the addition of quantitative methods, is gained at the expense of judgment and contact with reality.

4. *Deductive-Nomological kausation*: This model of causation renounces object-positing almost completely in favor of property-attributing. A high level of organizational capacity is gained

through the incorporation of syntax and quantification into scientific methodology. But, temporal order, kausation, particular objects, and sensory awareness are lost in the retreat into a universal point of view. D-N methodology gains enormous deductive power from its use of logical principles and quantificational techniques. But contact with reality is sacrificed in the ascent to Platonic heaven.

5. *Retroductive kausation*: This model of kausation reincorporates the object-positing process, this time applying it to the laws and principles of D-N model kausation, themselves, as it was applied to perceptual data at the level of simple perception. It is the most powerful tool of science because it incorporates both types of thinking process. Conception of the most abstract sort, i.e. 'molecule', thus is seen to be of a piece with the most basic sensory type of judgment, i.e. 'I'm hungry'. Both are intentional judgments about the kause of an x in thought. In this they are essentially different from quantitative analyses, which are completely general, and rely only on syntactical relations for their results.

Chapter 6

What Objects Are

By now it should be apparent that according to the account of knowledge producing processes being presented in this book, objects are the products of the object-positing process. Thus, an object is an indexically located 'this', as experienced by someone, and marked in terms of its kausal capacity and stability, with a name, which is selected through an intentional point of view. As a philosophical claim about the nature of an object, this account must be defended, both as reasonable in itself, and as more reasonable than some alternative accounts that are available in the philosophical literature.

In addition, there are a wide variety of notions that are related to the idea of an object, all of which must be explainable in terms of my account, if the account is to be deemed reasonable. Some of the related notions are linguistic, such as the ideas of names, reference, denotation, meaning, or sense, all of which are implicated with the idea of an object. Some of the ideas are ontological, and deal with questions about the existence of objects or 'being' in a more amorphous sense. Some of the notions are logical, and are concerned with the roles of objects in propositions, or in arguments.

In this chapter of this book, I will expand my account of an object, to show that this 'anthropomorphic' account of objects as impingements on direct awareness is reasonable. In the next chapter, I will show how the related linguistic, ontological and logical ideas can be understood in terms of my account of an object. Then, I will argue that this account is more reasonable than either phenomenalistic accounts like Husserl's, which it resembles, or modal accounts like Stalnaker's, to which it is the antithesis. I will often cite Searle's position, both as a supporting kindred hypothesis about objects and intentionality, and to clarify points that I believe I have more explicitly worked out than he has.

The Expanded Account of a Posited Object

My account of a posited object requires that an object be accessible to direct awareness, have a kausal influence, have an intention that selects a point of view with respect to it, and have stability as a 'this something.' I have already analyzed the role of the kausal influence in the previous chapter. Stability is the quality of an x in thought that determines that someone will judge the x an object, rather than an adjectival property or 'background', when analyzing his or her experience of it. I have also already discussed this judgment process under my discussion of kausation. So, I will add one point worth adding to my analysis of the stability of an object, then discuss the relationship between intention and point of view, in my account. I will wind up this chapter with a discussion of the forms of direct awareness that I believe can contribute data for object positing to a conscious mind.

The Role of Stability

First, my additional point on the role of stability in the determination of an object is that the requirement for stability is somewhat relative. In object-positing, a judgment is made that distinguishes objects from adjectival properties. This distinction is relatively made. What rates as an object, from one point of view, might rate as adjectival from some other point of view. The preference for stability reflects only Aristotle's preference for substance, as that which is predicated of nothing, but of which other things are predicated.[1] But for Aristotle, substance is still a somewhat relative notion. For, subject matters, and intelligible objects, like the number three, rate as substances, in addition to physical things like tables and chairs. Furthermore, substances can be 'Chinese boxed' within one another, for Aristotle, as, a syllable, within a word, within a sentence, within a paragraph. The stipulation that an object should be stable does not rule out these types of relativity in objects.

Aristotle also says of substances that, a) they are separate individual things, and that b) they, while remaining one thing, can accept contraries, while c) they have no contraries themselves.[2] These limits, while somewhat restricting the relativity of the tendencies that I was discussing in the last paragraph, can also be described as criteria for stability. They are the types of considerations that someone would have in mind when sorting x's in thought.

[1]   Aristotle, *The Categories*, 2b, 11-15, in *Basic Works of Aristotle, op.cit.* p. 9.

[2]   *Ibid.*, p. 9–11.

The Interrelationship of Intentionality
and a Point of View

To discuss the interrelationship between intentionality and point of view, I must first point out how minimal my requirements for this relationship are. I said that the relationship between an x in thought, and some aspect of reality, r, which x is individuating was one of identity, by which I mean that the x is what is used to pick out and define the r. Aristotle might put his similar observation about a substance by saying that the r represents the matter, the x represents the essence or the formal cause. I'm resisting putting things in this way, however, for two reasons. One, the word 'essence' has picked up so much philosophical baggage since Aristotle that it has become unwieldy and overstuffed. And two, even for Aristotle, the essence had to be a fully articulated definition, which I think drags too much syntactic clarity into the object-positing process.

The x needs only to be capable of being indexically isolated and intended. A stomach rumble, vague anxiety, a blip on a computer screen, an imprecise intellectual parallel, or a mouse under a bush can all be noticed by an inquisitive mind, and thus marked as a 'that' in thought. This minimal capacity for indexical marking is much less than Aristotle requires of an essence, or than John Searle requires of an intentional state. And it is really all I need to provide the directedness of attention that is necessary to provide a minimal point of view.[3]

To describe what I mean by a 'minimal point of view' I will describe how points of view grow in human experience. This account reflects the work of child development analysts, like Maria Montessori,[4] and Lev Vygotsky.[5]

The type of point of view that would be included in an indexically selected intentional state of the minimal kind just discussed would be a personal, individual, point of view. The person would not necessarily assume at the outset that the impingement that he or she was noticing as a blip, or a vague feeling, was a kaused object, distinct from the person's own thinking and sensory apparatus. An infant would start out with minimal intentional attention and an overly personally specific point of view, of this most general kind. As a child learns to distinguish points of view other than the highly

[3]   See I. Rock and A. Mack, *Inattentional Blindness*, MIT Press, Cambridge MA, 1998, for the role of attention in seeing.

[4]   Maria Montessori invented the Montessori pre-school system for educating young children.

[5]   Lev Vygotsky, *Thought and Language*, trans. & ed. Alex Kozulin, MIT Press, Cambridge MA, 1986.

me-specific, it can also formulate intentions of kaused objects that are not solipsistically ego-related. The minimal, highly personalized point of view is always available to anyone, who can formulate intentions from it at any time. But with even a young child's level of maturity, it becomes possible to formulate other, more sophisticated types of intentions, oriented towards other points of view.

The number of points of view that are available to a person will depend on his or her education and experience. The points of view of sociology, history, biology, physics, psychology or any other academic discipline are usually learned in academic settings. Ethnic, moral, social role, gender, nationalistic, and other enculturation related points of view are learned in family settings. Some points of view, such as those of a thing that eats and sleeps, feels, experiences pain, desires, and is grateful, are more biologically based, and are probably shared with animals. A point of view marked as spatially located or temporally bound would be general enough to apply to most impingements that could count as experiences, but is really quite intellectually sophisticated, requiring at least a capacity to think of space and time as abstract universal aspects of experience. New points of view are continually introduced to human thinking by science, art, popular culture and literature, and old ones sometimes fall into disuse and are lost.

An intention is formulated within the context of its point of view. So, for a child, not yet matured beyond a solipsistic point of view, the only types of objects that it is possible to posit are self-relative ones. For infants, the distinction between self and world is unclear, and the only type of thinking possible involves the undifferentiated self–world complex that is generated by their feelings and needs. So, a 'What is that?' question either has a 'me' centered answer, or it is unanswerable. The points of view of other people, and an independent external world, thus, become indispensable for understanding early in life. These hypothetical points of view expand the possible answers to a 'What is that?' question to other people and things. But still, in terms of an infant's minimal understanding of what other people and things are and it's tendencies to poorly understand distinctions between self and not-self, possible intentions will remain far fewer than an adult could formulate, and somewhat paltry in content.

There is thus, a dynamic, learning interplay between intentional contents and points of view. The greater one's range of possible points of view, the more sophisticated one's object-positing intentions can become. And the more experience one has, the more sophisticated one's object-positing **must** become to accommodate the experience, and the more one's range of points of view will expand.

A critic might say at this point, 'Fine, so experience promotes learning. That isn't new. Why do we need intentions and points of view to describe how this happens?' The answer to this question is that 'roadblocks' can be set up in learning, and thus in knowledge, at each of these points, indicating that they are points that must be traversed if even experience is to make a difference in thought. Someone who does not have access to a point of view in the context of which an intention is formulated, will not be able to posit the kind of objects that can be intended in that way. For instance, someone without the point of view of sociology in his or her repertoire, will not interpret anything that he or she sees as a non-cohesive group. And conversely, someone whose intentions rule out, or are blind to particular objects or types of objects, will be prevented from learning about the corresponding points of view. Someone who thinks of humans exclusively as egoistic individuals, or for whom a Hobbesian atomistic 'attractions and aversions' version of psychology is analytically true, will, consequently, have a difficult time trying to understand sociology.

The consequence of this analysis of the relationship between experience and objects, of course, is that objects impinge kausally on an experiencing person, who intentionally interprets this experience. Often, people are lazy and statically interpret new data in terms of old categories, or points of view. But sometimes, the fit between the new data encountered in experience and the old intentions, concepts, and repertoires of names that someone is trying to use to index the data will be sufficiently poor that the person experiences an 'understanding crisis', which stimulates his or her consciousness into a more dynamic learning mode. Of course, this need not happen. Some people have minds set like concrete, and persist in interpreting experience in immature or inappropriate ways regardless of being inundated with poorly fitting experience.

The intentional states in object-positing, thus can range in sophistication from minimal 'what?' reactions that focus attention in a non-specific and self-centered sort of way to sophisticated, propositionalized, knowledge-based intentions, such as wondering whether this is a cohesive or non-cohesive group, or whether this tumor is malignant or benign.

Comparison to Searle's Intentional States

Since Searle requires that his intentional states have a content, that may or may not be propositionalizable, I think that he is requiring a slightly higher level of sophistication of them than I require of my minimal ones. But the connection that he describes between the content of an intentional state and its conditions of satisfaction is very similar to the connection that I have described between the intention in object positing and the aspect of reality so intended or marked. Searle describes the relationship between the contents of his intentional states and their conditions of satisfaction this way:

> Thus, if I have a belief that it is raining, the content of my belief is: that it is raining. And the conditions of satisfaction are: that it is raining and not for example that the ground is wet or water is falling from the sky. Since all representation — whether done by the mind, language, pictures, or anything else, is *always* under certain aspects and not others, the conditions of satisfaction are represented under certain aspects.[6]

So, Searle and I agree that intentional states characterize the parts of reality that they mark, as marked by that intention.

Searle, however, substitutes what he calls a psychological mode for my point of view. His psychological modes give a force or direction to his intentions, and they range over beliefs, desires, perceptual directedness, emotional states, and other types of focus for directedness. Here is his list of potential psychological modes:

> ... belief, fear, hope, desire, love, hate, aversion, liking, disliking, doubting, wondering whether, joy, elation, depression, anxiety, pride, remorse, sorrow, grief, guilt, rejoicing, irritation, puzzlement, acceptance, forgiveness, hostility, affection, expectation, wishing, wanting, imagining, fantasy, shame, lust, disgust, animosity, terror, pleasure, abhorrence, aspiration, amusement, and disappointment.[7]

I think that Searle has been misled by his agent-propelled account of causation to include these psychological modes as essential parts of intentional states. For the most part, they do not add context clarification to the content of his intentional states. And, for the sake of understanding, that is what intentional states need. My points of view, rather, provide the context clarification that will inform an intentional content, or be informed by it, in the way that interaction aimed at understanding and learning requires.

Searle's psychological modes, with the exception of seeing, puzzlement and fantasy, are not descriptive of perceptual, formal-kause based intentions. Rather, they describe emotional, affective states.

[6]   *Intentionality, op. cit.* p. 13.

[7]   *Ibid.*, p. 4.

Although it is clear that affective states and cognitive states do interact in some ways, I think that it is possible to separate them for purposes of analysis, and I think that it is important to do so, in order to understand either of them.

The reason why I think that it is important to distinguish between affective and cognitive states is that they seem, from observation of certain unusual cases, to have separate sources and growth patterns in people. For instance, people with trisomy 21, or Downs' syndrome are often quite capable affectively, sometimes showing considerable social warmth and talent for acting and musical expression, even if their intellectual or cognitive capacities are very limited. The reverse situation occurs in psychopathology, where, in some cases, persons who are almost totally dysfunctional on the affective level, can suffer no deficits at all in intellectual or conceptual capacity.

So, I will disagree with Searle about the need for a psychological mode in an intentional state. I think that an intentional state does need a point of view, to give it a context, but I don't think it needs to be affectively driven. Some intentional states clearly are affectively driven, but then they are more like actions of agents, than basic cases of formal-kause understanding.

I hope that this exposition of intentions and points of view has adequately explained, for the present at least, the role of each in determining what an object is. I will now turn to an analysis of the types of direct awareness through which objects can present themselves kausally.

Types of Direct Awareness for Objects

For something to rate as an object, I have said that some type of direct awareness of it must be possible. Again, I would impose only minimal limits on what could rate as direct awareness. Data from the five sensory organs, will, of course count as types of direct awareness. But I would add a variety of other types of experiences as being sources of data for direct awareness as well.

Some of the sources of direct awareness that I would include in discussion are kinesthetic or overall-bodily sensations, affective states, the conscious experience of needs emerging from subconscious drives, dreams, memories, daydreams, creative mental play, intellectual synthesizing of a more analytical type, and religious experience. I will discuss each of these in turn, to clarify what I mean when I say that they can be directly experienced.

The Five Senses

Sensory data is, of course, the basic building block of every form of empiricism. For Locke, the five senses brought in simple ideas; little atomistic bits of color, sound, odor, texture, and taste, that the mind, then, had to assemble into objects.[8] For Hume, they were atomistic impressions in a stream of consciousness.[9] I think that I can be a bit vague about analyzing what, exactly, 'comes in' through the five senses, as long as I have made clear that it is *not* a sense-datum, of the type that Price[10] and Moore[11] discussed. I have argued that sensory awareness is unmediated. It is no more mediated in the case of spotting a gray mouse than it is in the case of becoming aware that one is hungry. I will concur with Locke that the data from each sensory source is unique to itself, and independent of the data from any other source.

An interesting question that has sometimes been raised about the alleged independence of sensory media from one another concerns the universality of certain cross-sensory metaphors in human languages. For instance, all languages call red a 'loud' color, and soft musical tones 'sweet'. I think that these metaphors reflect similarities in the ways that people synthesize sensory data, and affectively relate to it, rather than similarities in the bits of data, themselves. Since formal kause synthesizing, and affective interaction with one's environment are both universal human experiences, all languages would mark ways in which this synthesizing takes place, similarly. For now, I will assume that anyone who has ever read an empiricist text knows what rates as sensory data from the five senses, and I will pass on to my more controversial additions to the traditional list.

Kinesthetic and Bodily Awareness Sensations

Locke struggled to add 'solidity' to his list of simple ideas,[12] but, as Berkeley pointed out, Locke really underestimated the sensory importance of kinesthetic awareness.[13] People have a wide variety of

---

[8]   John Locke, *An Essay Concerning Human Understanding*, ed. Peter Nidditch, Oxford University Press, London, England, 1975, p. 55 ff. and Book II, p. 104 ff.

[9]   Hume, *Treatise, op. cit.*, Book I.

[10] H. Price, *Perception*, Greenwood Press Publishers, Westport, Conn. 1932 (1981).

[11] G.E. Moore, *Some Main Problems of Philosophy*, George Allen and Unwin, Ltd., London, 1952, pp. 30–33.

[12] *Ibid.*, p. 122–127.

[13] George Berkeley, *A Treatise Concerning the Principles of Human Knowledge*, ed. Colin Turbayne, Library of the Liberal Arts, Bobbs-Merrill Publishing, Inc., Indianapolis, Indiana, 1977, p. 27 ff.

types of sensation that relate to overall bodily conditions, such as: balance, placement in space, awareness of air circulation, heat or cold in the immediate environment, bodily position (curled up, out flat, standing, sitting, crouched or prone?) weight, being enclosed or in an open space, moving or still. No one has to look down to know whether her toes are curled or straight in her shoes.

For most people, I suppose, kinesthetic awareness is not highly developed. But the high level of development that certain people achieve in knowledge of kinesthesis points to the importance of this source of sensory knowledge. For instance, blind people can learn to judge how close to a topological drop-off they are by analyzing breeze currents against their skin. An upward draft indicates a stair well, building or cliff edge. Also, some blind people can learn to determine direction by analyzing slight temperature differences in their skin on the respective sides of their faces caused by orientation to the sun. Even in weak sunlight, the side of one's face that is facing the sun will be a degree or two warmer than the side that is away from the sun.

Gymnasts and ballerinas also must have developed capacities to analyze kinesthetic sensations. A gymnast doing a back flip on a balance beam cannot see the beam to tell if she is lined up correctly to land on it, until it would be too late to correct her position. She has to learn, instead, to feel her position in space above the beam with enough precision to know whether she will land on it or not, in time to move away from it if she is off-balance. If she hits it incorrectly, off-balance, she will be hurt by the beam. So, it is very important to her to be able to feel the correct position in space during a flip.

Likewise, ballerinas do pirouettes by learning the position in space in which their bodies are rotationally balanced. This equilibrium position is learned, by both ballerinas and gymnasts, through concentration on kinesthetic sensations, trial, error and correction.

Actually, everyone has a variety of types of kinesthetic knowledge, such as knowledge of the standard height of stair risers. A staircase with stairs that are not the standard height and depth will trip everyone that tries to walk up or down it. A door knob that is not located in the standard place on a door will be a source of continual fumbling and hand bunking.

I think that these examples should be sufficient to demonstrate the importance of kinesthetic sensations as a direct source of sensory knowledge. Berkeley's drubbing of Locke on this issue had certainly already pointed out that five senses weren't quite enough to describe the range of sensory awareness. But I think that Berkeley's reduction of objects to sensations is a mistake that arose because Locke had intermediary sense-data representations in his theory, and Berkeley left them there, reducing objects to them.

I can avoid this reduction by pointing out that the direct aware-ness of solidity requires no more intermediation than does the direct awareness of a position of balance in space. Without a mental repre-sentation to which to reduce objects, the objects, as sources of kausal influence, hold their own. My tactic, thus, is more likely to get me accused of making an object of a felt position of rotational balance than of reducing a material object to a mental event. Actually, I believe I can avoid even the former reduction, by stressing Aris-totle's 'room for some relativity' in substances, to which I already alluded at the beginning of this chapter. I will also discuss this more later. For now, I'll turn to presenting other sources of direct aware-ness.

Sub-Consciously Motivated Drives, Needs, and Anxieties

I also believe that people can have direct awareness of drives, needs and anxieties, as well as other affective states, even though they may be unaware of the psychoanalytic or biological 'sources' of those feelings. I think that I can be a minimalist about how much content the psychoanalytic 'sources' of drives and needs may have. Since I am doing cognitive philosophy and not psychoanalytic psychology, I think I can avoid discussing the subconscious basis of these feelings altogether, and deal only with their conscious effects. I will evade the psychoanalysis issue by saying that there is something about having a human brain and a human genetic structure and organization, that results in certain conscious feelings, needs and tendencies, of which people do become directly aware.

I take this claim as being no more controversial than a claim that there are certain facts about intestines and blood sugar levels that result in direct awareness of hunger, or than a claim that there are certain facts about nervous systems and tissue damage that result in direct awareness of pain. Thus, I leave the sub-conscious aspects of all of these experiences to the neurologist, the psychiatrist, and related health professionals, and concentrate only on those parts of those experiences that are capable of becoming directly accessible to conscious awareness.

So, of what kinds of affectively driven feelings are people directly aware? Following Maslow's hierarchy of needs,[14] I would say that people have direct awareness of needs for security, self-esteem,

[14] Maslow, *New Knowledge in Human Values, op. cit.*

social relationships, health, a sense of well-being, and a feeling of equilibrium, or of being in control of their world. Some people may not be sufficiently articulate to express these needs in these terms, but even so, when these, most basic human needs are not met, people become desperate. Reactions to this desperation include 'fight or flight' activities, 'acting out' their rage at their deprivation of these things in violence, self-destructive behavior, and dysfunctional psychiatric responses.

In an *Ethics of Punishment* class that I was teaching in a prison, an inmate student described the practice of 'wilding' to me in these terms;

> When I walk down the street in Queens, anybody could stick a knife in my back or blow my head off, and the cops wouldn't even come. I couldn't even get into a hospital emergency room. So, sometimes I just feel like bashing somebody over the head with a baseball bat, for no reason at all.[15]

I would say that this inmate student was directly aware of severe deprivation of security and well-being in the neighborhood in which he lived. His response, though ineffective and immature, was as biologically natural as seeking food when hungry. People who are deprived of basic needs are desperate and self-defensive people. Although they may be very unclear, as my student was, about why they are deprived or about what might effectively resolve the deprivation, the deprivation, itself, nags so insistently at the inner core of their existence and thinking processes, that any response, even an ineffective and self-destructive one, seems better to them than none. As Mohandas Gandhi pointed out, violence begets violence. Another inmate student in the same class had no trouble at all in tying his lack of concern for the well-being of other people to his own experience of sexual abuse in childhood. To him, the connection between being abused and becoming an abuser who accepts abuse as appropriate activity was immediate, and apparent.

Again, following Maslow, I would say that once the most basic needs for safety and security, food, etc. are reasonably well met, people can become directly aware of higher level needs, such as needs to be creative, to find outlets for sexual and reproductive desires, to earn the respect and esteem of their fellow citizens, to establish intimate relatedness with friends and lovers, and to engage in other self-fulfilling activities. Again, some people may be less than completely articulate in describing these needs, but their overall satisfac-

---

[15] Richard Thompson, inmate in Greene Correctional Facility, Coxackie, New York, October 1991.

tion or dissatisfaction with life will be clearly tied to how many of these needs are met, and how well they are met.

People directly experience deprivation in any of these areas as dissatisfaction in life, boredom, and frustration. Fulfillment or satisfaction are, correspondingly, directly experienced in contentment, equilibrium, and vitality. These direct experiences, even of the negative sort, are clearly not as explosive as feelings of deprivation of the more basic needs are. But, even these can become quite incendiary, as Langston Hughes rhetorically points out in *Harlem*, where he rhetorically asks, 'What happens to a dream deferred?' and rhetorically responds that it might,

> . . . dry up like a raisin in the sun?
> Or fester like a sore —
> and then run?
> Does it stink like rotten meat?
>
> Or crust and sugar over —
> like a syrupy sweet?
> Maybe it just sags like a heavy load.
>
> Or does it explode?'[16]

Whether a higher-level frustration crusts or sags or explodes probably depends on how important that particular source of satisfaction was to that particular person. I think that in this area people can do some psychological bargaining and negotiating without becoming volatile or self-destructive. But some compromises would probably exceed what the person who is being expected to make them can endure, here as well.

I don't think that I should have to argue very much for either the existence or the importance of these types of psychological needs and drives. In claiming that people have direct access to data concerning these needs and drives, I am only claiming that deprivation or dissatisfaction in any of these areas can be felt, in as direct a way as someone can feel hunger or see a mouse. Correspondingly, contentment is a directly felt experience of satisfaction of needs. To deny that this type of direct sensory awareness of affective states plays a role in human thinking, as behaviorists do, seems to me simply perverse, or self-deceiving.

A far more reasonable analysis of the, acknowledged, existence and operation of this type of psychological experience is to say that it provides a source of xs for thought. The reality r to which the x is

---

[16] Langston Hughes, '*Harlem (A Dream Deferred)*', in *The Norton Introduction to Literature*, 3rd edn., eds. Bain, Beatty, and Hunter, W.W. Norton Co. New York, N.Y., 1981, p. 600.

being indexed may, in this case, be projected outward, as psychoanalysts would say occurs in racial and sexual bigotry, or as my student appears to be doing in his conjecture that wilding is a solution to his own sense of fear of attack. Or, the x may be more accurately indexed as an aspect of one's own psychological make-up. When more accurately understood, in this way, the x can provide the basis for a more rational investigation into the source of the sense of dissatisfaction, as well as into possible solutions to it.

This is a whole area of human thinking that I believe is currently receiving far too little attention and analysis from professionals in philosophy and psychology in the western tradition. Eastern philosophy and psychology have admitted the existence of psychological projection and other forms of psychological self-deception concerning basic needs since the time of the Buddha's Enlightenment.[17] And Freud stressed these modes of self-deception and ignorance of one's own motives in his psychoanalytic analysis of human nature. But, in the twentieth century, the dominance of behaviorism and stress on third-person objective accounts of psychological processes in western philosophy and psychology led to an intellectual climate in which any reference to first-person singular experience was viewed as suspect and rated as 'unscientific'. While some philosophers, such as Sidney Shoemaker[18] and Naomi Eilan,[19] are currently arguing for the need to include first-person singular accounts in philosophies about mind and thinking, there is still suspicion and distrust of introspective psychological claims among analytical philosophers.

These considerations are one further reason why I believe that it is so important to abandon Quine's denial approach to x-type thinking processes, and begin to deal with experiences in their own terms. The attempts of cognitive scientists like the Churchlands and Stalnaker to deny that they exist, or to reduce these experiences to platonic propositions, just perpetuates and further entrenches the denial approach of behaviorism in analyses of thinking. I believe that very little academic clarity is gained by this approach, and a lot of truth and reality is lost.

---

[17] There are many available sources on the Buddha's enlightenment. One is *Many Peoples Many Faiths,* by Robert S. Ellwood, Jr., Prentice Hall, Inc. Englewood Cliffs, New Jersey, 1987, chap. 4.

[18] Sydney Shoemaker, 'Self and Substance' in *Philosophical Perspectives 11 – Mind Causation and the World,* ed. James Tomberlin, Blackwell Publishers, Boston, 1997, p. 283–303.

[19] Naomi Eilan, 'Consciousness and the Self', in *The Body and the Self,* ed. J.L. Bermudez, A. Marcel and N. Eilan, MIT Press, Cambridge, MA, 1995 p. 337–357.

To conclude this section, then, I consider direct access to sensory experience of one's own affective states, psychological needs, desires and anxieties to be one of the basic sources of xs for thought. As in any other type of direct experience, the r identified by the experience can be misunderstood, but it will be indexically related to and identified with the x. In this case, the fact that people so often invent 'objects' to which to index these experiences is an indication that I am on the right track in describing this process as an object-positing process. Whether the objects in question are only metaphors for the experiences, as in the Hughes poem, or whether they are actual objective projections, as in the projection of violence on persons to whom one wishes to do violence, the thinking process is doing the same thing with these direct experiences that it does with an experience of seeing a mouse. The objects in question are less 'substantial', in Aristotle's sense, but every bit as real. This claim really amounts to no more than a claim that a dysfunctional fear of violence is as real as hunger, which, in turn, is as real as a mouse, or a chair.

Dreams and Memories

Two more sources of direct awareness in experience to which I believe that people have access are dreams and memories. As in the case of psychological drives, I am not going to discuss from whatever subconscious or biochemical sources or motivations these experiences might emerge. I think that it is sufficient for me to say that these are experiences that people have, and thus, to which people have access for x's in thought. Many creative writers and intellectuals report having first conceived of seed ideas in dreams. And some people claim that they can use their dreaming capacity to solve problems. I don't wish to discuss or evaluate these claims beyond what I need to establish my minimal claim: that dreams and memories can yield x's to be used by the object-positing process in thought.

To argue for this minimal claim, all that I need to establish is that dreams and memories can have sensory content, of which the dreamer or rememberer can be aware. Further, this content has to parallel the types of sensory contact that I have already discussed in sensation and psychological awareness, in the last three sections. The important respects in which this parallel must occur are that dreams and memories must have content that is accessible to direct awareness, in some sense sensory or imagistic, or deeply needs-related way.

Dream reports, at any rate, clearly indicate that dreams do meet this criterion for being experiences. Dreams possessing sensory and psychological content, often of an imagistic, visual, auditory, kinesthetic or need-related sort are the most common types of dreams that people have. Taken as experiences, the image of a mouse or feeling of fear that someone experiences in a dream, can rate as much as a source of an x in thought as can a mouse sighting or a 'real' experience of fear. The difference between the real mouse sighting and the dream image of the mouse is, of course, in the kause of the experience. It is to the credit of my theory that non-psychotic people do, in fact, have little trouble distinguishing between dream mice and real mice, or between nightmares and real experiences of fear.

Likewise, memories are usually imagistic, sensory and needs-related types of experiences. Some people report doing arithmetical computations on mathematical 'forms' that are memorized, colored, imagistic 'towers' or 'spirals' that they mentally transverse as they recite the computations. In memories, in particular, it is obvious that emotional or affective states interact with the cognitive element, for highly emotionally charged memories are far more vivid, and more easily recalled than more mundane sorts of memories.

Since the sleep research of the last few decades has established both the universality and the content of dreams, I really can't envisage any objections that anyone is likely to raise against my minimal claim that dreams are a type of experience that can provide data for thought. They resemble sensory or psychological experiences in content, but differ from them in kausation. So, the object-positing process will analyze dreams in parallel ways, with the qualification that the kause will be specified as a dream rather than as an object.

Memories are mid-way between dreams and immediate real experiences, in this sense. A memory is classed by the process as once objectively kaused, but now, more dream-like. At the borders between these types of experiences, mistakes in kausal attribution may be made, just as mistakes of equivocation can be made in uses of homonyms. But in general, the contexts make the kauses apparent. And the 'objects' posited are, thus, qualified as dream or memory objects rather than as real immediate experiences.

Memory needs Kauses and not Causes

To discuss why memory needs kauses and not causes, let me review what each is. A kause is an experiential impingement on awareness, that might arise from a range of sources including one's thinking, one's bodily condition, one's sensory environment, and one's social environment. In contrast, a cause is an efficient transfer of mechanical motion or force from one place to another; Aristotle's initiating 'push' that brings about a change. Memory needs a kause rather than a cause because a) no 'push' or change takes place in anyone's body or environment when they remember something, b) even if such a change did take place, the original objects in the remembered event would have only peripheral connections with the present change, and c) memory is not as iconic as the 'information transfer' paradigm would indicate.

I think that computer analogies and information transfer paradigms are doing a lot of dirty work in current theorizing on the nature of memory. The information transfer position relies on data that indicates that memories are stored in the brain biochemically just like data is stored in a computer. The experimental evidence in favor of this view comes from brain damage and aphasia cases, in which it is apparent that 'stored' information in a brain can be partially or completely destroyed by brain damage. Also, instances of partial recall, or 'tip of the tongue' cases of dredging up memory indicate that semantic and syntactic similarity play roles in memory evocation.[20]

But I think that the advocates of this position are reading more into the computer metaphor than the data will support. The storage mechanisms of a brain and a computer may be similar in important respects, but it doesn't follow from this observation that information is 'input' to memory of a disc or silicon chip sort, or that remembering is an act of 'calling up a program', or that what is stored remains unaltered until it is 'called up'. My problem with these ways of pushing the metaphor is that a human, unlike a machine, is a dynamic system that both grows and decays with time. A human interacts with an environment that alters all of his or her states, biological, intellectual, emotional, and psychological, continually. A memory, unlike a silicon chip, is not subject to logically specific parameters of expression at the outset, is altered by other experiences that a person has over time, is emotionally and psychologically influenced, is cognitively penetrable through suggestion or new learning, and will be altered in recall by the social and point-of-view environment in which it is to be expressed.[21]

The causal-transfer view presents a picture of memory in which a propositional description of some episode passes into data-storage in a brain, then is 'recalled', unaltered at a later date. Some memories, such as memorized ditties or poems, may work this way. But a

---

[20] Lyle Bourne, Roger Dominowski, Elizabeth Loftus, and Alice F. Healy, *Cognitive Processes*, Prentice Hall, Inc., Englewood Cliffs, New Jersey, 1986, pp. 166–170.
[21] *Ibid.*, chaps. 2–6.

typical memory is neither that linguistically specific, nor that linguistically limited in scope. Most involve a range of sensory connections that are not propositional in nature. For example, a memory of a car that one once owned will involve various visual 'pictures' of the car's appearance, its smell, its engine noises, affective responses to it (was it a source of pride or embarrassment? Did happy or unhappy events take place in it? etc.). Very little of this is captured in the proposition, 'I once owned a Volkswagen.' But, even the pared-down proposition is subject to alteration and 'enhancement' or 'forgetting' based on the other qualities remembered in conjunction with it. For instance, if it had been a source of great pride and happy times, the most mechanically inferior rust bucket could be elevated to a high-quality auto in retrospect. Conversely, had a close friend died in it, the former owner might have trouble remembering its make and color or even that he owned it.

These considerations reflect what psychologists call the reconstructive aspects of memory. A memory is a mixture of 'data recall' and creative fabrication, aimed at 'leveling' or 'assimilating' what is remembered to other things that one also knows or believes.[22]

In a sense, the Volkswagen is the cause of someone's memory of it, because it was the kause of the initial sensory indexings on which the initial experiences of the car are fixed. However, many years later, the act of reconstructing either the sentence 'I once owned a Volkswagen,' or the mental sensory image of the appearance, the smell and the feel of the car, will be kaused by what is left and sifted in the brain's storage system. What will be there, at this point in time, will have been altered by intervening memories, learning, diseases suffered, and social perspectives changed. Sometimes the alteration is not great, but memory is rarely iconic or echoic.[23]

The memories that are iconic or echoic are of two types: very short term memories, such as the three-minute recall of a telephone number, and extremely traumatic memories, such as the extremely detailed slow-motion 'video-replay' memories by which victims of horrifying accidents, war episodes and violence are sometimes plagued. The short term echoic and iconic memories are interesting because the mind's capacity to do this appears to be the basis for memorization, in the sense of committing a poem or a telephone number to long term memory. But other than its contribution to the study of mnemonics, it has little to do with ordinary cases of long term remembering. The trauma cases have more to do with long

---

[22] see Atkinson, chap 8.
[23] Bourne et. al., chap. 3.

term memory, but it is hard to say *what* they have to do with long-term memory.

Law courts sometimes now acknowledge the iconic nature of traumatic memories, accepting testimony from violence and abuse victims years after the initial incidents occurred. But even these cases are somewhat problematic, because a victim of abuse is as likely to repress or deny the memory as he or she is to iconically remember it. Questions then arise about whether hypnosis-induced memories ought to be allowable in court along with regular testimony, and whether statutes of limitations ought to be dropped in these cases, because victims might suddenly 'remember' repressed incidents years later. There have been dramatic cases of both hypnosis-induced testimony that was later independently collaborated, even though the victim never consciously remembered the initial incidents, and testimony that was professed to be traumatically iconic, but was later disconfirmed despite the insistence of the victim. The Israeli embarrassment over the Ivan the Terrible/Djumanik case is one of the latter types of case.

If even these, admittedly iconic, cases of memory fail to follow the information-transfer model, what of ordinary cases? It is a platitude in police work that no two eye witnesses ever watch the same crime, and that witnesses picking culprits from line-ups are highly susceptible to suggestion.[24] It seems clearly to be the case that what is remembered is as much a function of what one initially believed was likely to happen, what one expected to happen, what one wants to remember, what fits well into one's later, revised, world view, and what one wishes to appear as to one's peers when relating the memory, as it is a function of any 'data' that might be transferred to a brain, stored and recalled. What is remembered is sifted, edited, sorted and revised much more than it is transferred.[25] So, my conclusion on memory is that we distinguish it from dreams and daydreams by the fact that a memory was once rooted in sensory experience, but is currently self-kaused. That is enough to include the initial cause, but does not suppose that iconic information transfer is taking place, in a case of memory. Research evidence indicates that this is the best that can reasonably be expected of memory.[26]

Since I consider this analysis of dreams and memories relatively uncontroversial, for any reader who has followed my analysis up to

---

[24]   *Ibid.*, pp. 115–120.

[25]   *Ibid.*

[26]   also, see Atkinson, et. al., chap. 8.

this point, I will pass on to my next source of xs in thought — creative mental play.

Creative Mental Play

The types of mental awareness that I have been speaking of as sources of xs for thought so far in this chapter, all contain some element of passive reception, in the sense that people can receive this type of sensory data even if they are relatively passive about reaching out to understand their world. That is, even a person with a very limited capacity for intentionalizing objects and a very limited repertoire of points of view would still experience sensory, kinesthetic, psycho-analytic, memory and dream experiences.

Creative mental play, however, requires curiosity and a learning approach to experience, if one is even to intentionalize in this area at all. So, it is possible that not all people engage in providing themselves with the types of objects that can be posited in this area. So, my argument for this source of xs for the object-positing process will claim only that some people do engage in creative mental play, and that those who do can, thereby, enrich their repertoires of available objects and points of view.

One type of thinking that I would classify in this category is the type of mental playing with images that artists do, when they are trying to devise ideas for projects, or merely amusing themselves. Sometimes this kind of play can be done with implements such as a camera or a pencil or in a medium, such as paint or clay, but as often as not, it is a strictly mental juggling and juxtaposing of colors, shapes, shadows, or objects to mentally 'see' what will happen.

Likewise, musicians 'jam' with tunes, melodies and tones. Some can do this with or without their instruments and bands. Great composers like Beethoven are said to have been able to compose entire symphonies 'in their heads'. I do not believe that this type of conceptual play can be reduced to a language-of-thought type score manipulation exercise, because even musicians who cannot read sheet music, like some jazz and rock musicians, claim to compose 'in their heads'. This, I submit, is a case of object positing in which the object in question is a song or a tune. The mental play with tones and notes that comes before the writing or playing of the song is a case of someone amusing him or herself by playing directly with auditory sensations, which are eventually arranged into a structure that strikes their arranger as pleasing. The produced song is an object, posited at the end of an intentional note juggling game, which might have initially been aimed at nothing other than amusing the juggler.

In addition, poets play with words, writers with scenes and episodes, dancers with choreography and movements, athletes and
craftspersons with techniques, and children with everything. In
each case, I would say creative minds are manipulating experiential
data to formulate intentions and generate objects. The thinking process might not progress much beyond the play stage, especially if the
person doing the playing does not have the requisite technical skills
to execute the artifacts envisioned. But creative artists, of course,
both improve their own techniques and produce the objects through
which they earn their livings through a continual interplay between
mental play of this sensory juggling type and work on technique
improvement.

Again, a critic might object that this is all very ho-hum. Imagination produces art; so what else is new? What is new, in the aftermath
of the twentieth century at least, is a recognition by a philosophical
theory of thinking that this occurs. Attempts, like Ryle's, to reduce
the clown's pratfalls to behavioral performances shortchange the
thinking process. When Ryle adverbializes the performance and
denies the prior mental play that planned the choreography,[27] he
sacrifices understanding of thinking for compliance with
behavioristic constraints on methodology. I submit, again, that more
is lost than gained in the bargain.

It would be better for philosophers to admit that people engage in
creative mental play of this type, and use it to generate not only
objects, in the sense or artifacts, plays, performances, songs, paint-
ings and stories, but also intentions and points of view, of less substantial sorts.

So, I will conclude my discussion of creative mental play by reas-
serting that this imaginative type of mental activity is also a source of
xs for the object positing process in thought. Just as people were
unlikely to confuse dream or memory experiences with real ones,
because the kause is different, people are also unlikely to confuse the
products of their imaginative mental play with real, dream, or memory experiences. As in the psychological needs case, projection is
possible in imaginative and creative productions. The ability of art
to enable artists or audiences to 'lose themselves' in a work of art
through projection is part of what gives art its psychological power
to engage, and work catharsis. But the type of sensory play involved
in art or craft is often lighter, and can be aimed more at amusement
than a psychological needs analysis might be, and thus, can be
detached from 'heavy' human concerns. Still, it is a source of data for

---

[27]   Gilbert Ryle, *The Concept of Mind, op.cit.* pp. 33–34.

thought that enriches human ability to intentionalize, posit objects, formulate points of view, and make judgments about the kauses of experience.

Religious or Mystical Experience

Like creative mental play, religious or mystical experience may be a type of experience that only some people have, while others do not. Again, my claims for the existence of this area in human experience will be minimal: I am claiming only that some people experience their own existence as a continuum of what Robert S. Ellwood calls an unconditioned reality.[28] That is, a reality that is unlimited by the spatial, temporal, knowledge, and power constraints of the world of ordinary experience.

William James' famous study, *The Varieties of Religious Experience*,[29] discusses a range of mystical experiences, from minimal 'feelings' that time is an illusion through full-blown visions and re-interpretations of all of experience in terms of awe inspiring contact with numinous 'others'. James characterizes numinous experience as having four marks, or essential qualities that distinguish these types of experiences from other, more mundane cases of sensory, psychological, or bodily awareness. Mystical states, according to James, are marked by their ineffability, noetic quality, transiency, and passivity.[30] They are thus distinguished from the creative mental play, dreams and memories that I have just been discussing, by their passivity and ineffability. But they share their noetic quality with sensory and psychological forms of direct awareness, which are also difficult, if not impossible to express.

As in the psychological and sensory cases, people often express their religious experience in metaphors and projections, or by round-about parables. The knowledge component often concerns what John Wisdom calls 'patterns of connections in experience',[31] or an aesthetic-like or judgmental appreciation for the way that experience coheres or can be unified. Like other sensory and psychological experiences, religious experiences are judged as kaused, and considered stable over time, although any given experience of the kausal

---

[28] Robert Ellwood, *Many Peoples, Many Faiths*, 3rd edn., Prentice Hall, Inc, Englewood Cliffs, New Jersey, 1987, p. 6.

[29] William James, *The Varieties of Religious Experience*, The New American Library of World Literature, New York, N.Y. 1958.

[30] *Ibid.*, pp. 292–293.

[31] John Wisdom, 'Gods', The Aristotelian society, re-printed in *Journeys Through Philosophy*, eds., Capaldi, Kelly and Navia, Prometheus Books, Buffalo, NY, 1982.

object is transitory. The intentions marking objects and the points of view according to which these objects are marked are often culturally or traditionally established, through doxastic practices within the various religious traditions, as described by William Alston[32]. But, in contrast with Alston, I would argue with John Hick[33] that the experiences, themselves, bear enough cross-cultural similarity to be considered more basic to human experience than the cultural expressions that they have developed within any specific religious tradition.

Even so staunch an atheist as Bertrand Russell admits the existence of mystical experience, and, with qualifications, admits its value in human thinking. In 'Mysticism and Logic', Russell cites four different marks of mystical intuition from those cited by James.[34] Russell's marks of the mystical are;

1. A conception of a reality behind the world of appearance and utterly different from it. (Like Ellwood's unconditioned reality.)

2. A belief in unity and refusal to admit division or opposition anywhere, even between good and evil.

3. A denial of the reality of time.

4. A denial of the reality of evil.[35]

Of these intuitions, Russell says of the first, intuitive denial of mundane reality, that it is an instinctive, intuitive creative force. In its apparent opposition to reason, it is the arbitrator of what is new or creative in human thinking. He says,

> Reason is a harmonizing, controlling force, rather than a creative one. Even in the most purely logical realm, it is insight that first arrives at what is new.[36]

Although Russell admits the importance of unifying insight, he denies the truth claims that are often based on this insight, especially where the unity of all existence or the denial of the reality of evil are concerned. He supports his attacks on these truth claims by a) arguing for the incoherence of the logics on which he claims they depend, i.e., Parmenedies' logic, and b) countering with his own account of logic, in terms of which he defines truth. Russell does, however,

[32] William Alston, *Perceiving God,* Cornell University Press, 1991.

[33] John Hick, 'Religious Pluralism and Salvation', in *Faith and Philosophy,* vol. 5 # 4, 1988.

[34] Bertrand Russell, 'Mysticism and Logic', in *Mysticism and Logic and other Essays,* Longmans, Green and Co., London, 1925.

[35] *Ibid.,* pp. 9–11.

[36] *Ibid.,* p. 13.

accept the intuition of timelessness, as a necessary intuition for a logical system, which, he says, can't function without eternal propositions.

Russell's summary analysis of the relationship between mystical intuitions and reason and logic is thus, that mystical intuitions may contribute valuable insights, but they have to be mitigated by a heavy dose of logic and reason, which should always dominate one's analysis of any situation.[37] So, the timelessness in the logic came from mystical insight, but once the logic has become eternal, it can repudiate its source. Very curious.

Later in this analysis, Russell presents mystical intuition as a force opposed to reason, sense, logic, science and all that is good and pure in human thinking. I think that he has misrepresented the place of religious insight. I have listed it as one more source of direct experience, along with sensory, psychological, kinesthetic, dream and memory experiences. As such, it is prone to judgmental error, but so is science, when either dealing with experience or postulating objects. Mystical insight is not so much opposed to logic and reason as it is independent of them, in the same sense that the juggling of color images in creative mental play is independent of syntax or structure. And, I would insist, the insights gained from mystical intuition's unifying impetus are the creative forces that are responsible for the postulation of most community relationships, senses of connectedness and love in human life, and peace-keeping missions in the world. Russell advocated all of those 'patterns of connections in reality', but never proposed a logical account of why he should advocate them. Nor, indeed could he. For, they are products of synthesizing mystical intuition, not of dividing and analyzing systematic logic.

When Russell abuses religion, in essays like 'Why I am not a Christian',[38] his criticisms fall most heavily on the denial of evil, which he interprets as a form of moral self-deception, and on the atrocities of the historical religious traditions, such as the Spanish Inquisition and the medieval burning of witches. I can only agree with Russell that religious as well as non-religious people sometimes indulge in moral self-deception and have used their traditions to justify atrocities. But, I don't believe that the abuses of a source of knowledge necessarily discredit the source. The abuses only demonstrate that the abusive method of employment for the information is not legitimate.

---

[37] *Ibid.*, pp. 30-32.

[38] Bertrand Russell, *Why I Am Not A Christian, and Other Essays*, Simon and Schuster, New York, 1957.

So, what of mystical insight is legitimate? This question, in my interpretation of the situation, directly parallels questions about the legitimacy of sense experience, psychological drives, memory, dreams and creative mental play. As in the other cases, I think that denying the existence or value of religious experience is pointless. It is, like the other sources of experience, a source of xs for thought, and an area of human experience on which the object-positing process will both posit objects, and develop intentions and points of view. Objects and subject matters developed here will inform and explain other areas of experience, as sensory objects may be metaphorically transferred here, to assist understanding. The status of religious or mystical objects or subject matters will be, much like the psychological ones, a matter of some difficulty to pin down, and like the psychological ones, also, known in, at times, round about ways.

But, the religious peace of a yogi or a prayerful person, or conversely, the torment of a dark night of the soul, are as real in human experience as are mouse sightings and hunger. And the self-knowledge of Mohandas Gandhi, Mother Theresa of Calcutta, or the Dali Lama indicate the level of attainment of knowledge that is possible in this area.

So, in the case of religious experience, as in the case of the other sources of direct experience that I have been discussing, my conclusion is that the denial approach should be abandoned, and the source of knowledge should be analyzed for what it is. This entails that the acknowledged masters of understanding in the field, from Moses, Ezekiel and Jesus through Buddha, Mohammed, the Dali Lama, Hindu swamis, shamans, Lao Tzu and the Zen masters, should be approached for what wisdom they have to offer, in the same way that we seek wisdom from artists, psychologists and scientists. That is, they should be neither uncritically dogmatized and slavishly followed, nor universally excluded from consideration by someone trying to understand his or her own experience. The direct experience on which religious systems are built is one of the most productive wellsprings of information and self-understanding in human nature, but perhaps also, one of the most easily misused and misunderstood. As such, I believe that attention to this source of human experience is important. Dogmatism and denial are both poor choices for methodology of approach.

Intellectual Synthesis

Among my x-type experiences, I would also include Eureka! type intellectual discoveries. Of course, it is a platitude of learning that unprepared minds never develop intellectual insights and that intellectual brilliance is 99% perspiration and only 1% inspiration. However, that 1% is still, something different from the other 99% of the work involved in discovery.

The bulk of intellectual work is of a 'compiling' nature, involving research, reading, formulating propositions or equations, writing, arguing, data gathering, deducing or inducing consequences of the gathered information, or pushing an hypothesis to its next logical step. As such, most intellectual work consists of 'small' extensions of knowledge, achieved with great labor, through pushing the border of knowledge a little further in some direction in which it was already moving, anyway. This is the perspiration side of intellectual work. For the most part, it is driven by y-type reasoning processes, and involves little object positing, as I already mentioned in my discussion of deductive nomological accounts of science.

The 1% exception occurs when someone who is doing intellectual work, looks at the equations upside down, and sees a new structure in them, dreams about a metaphor for the relationship that redescribes the entire environment, reorients the entire subject around a new axis and initiates a new formula for understanding it, or otherwise overturns the accepted approach in favor of something radically different, and new. The impetus to advocate such a radical departure from accepted practice is often reported by an inventor or innovator as a 'revelation' that hits the recipient, however well prepared, with the force and clarity of a religious conversion, and with the equivalent conviction that this was a 'bolt out of the blue', rather than a natural consequence of the last preparatory step taken.

I submit that discoveries of this type, though relatively rare, are one of the major driving forces of intellectual progress. The bulk of intellectual labor, for any age, consists of following through on the nuances and consequences of someone's flash of brilliant insight, which circumscribed the methodology and direction of the subsequent labor. Aristotle, Descartes, Copernicus, Newton, and Einstein would be credited with insights of this type in science, Russell and Whitehead would join Aristotle, the scholastics and Frege for logic awards, Fra Angelico and Picasso might be listed for art, Turing for computer science, Montessori for education, Freud and Skinner for psychology, etc. In each case, the award is given, not for greatness, which many others achieved as well, but for innovation, a radical departure from prior practice.

And since these departures from prior practice do not follow the previously prescribed methods, they will rate as x-type thinking.

They arrive in someone's consciousness as a 'new thing', a 'What is that?' Even if the process by which their recipient comes to knowledge of them is more gradual than the blinding burst from the blue type of experience, which it sometimes is, still the experience will involve positing some type of object or structure, formulating an intention with respect to it, developing a point of view that circumscribes it, and judging it kausative of some range of experiences. The objects in question will usually be subject matters or abstract objects, rather than concrete physical things, in this case. But molecules, ids, perspective, preschools, geometry involving time, and symbolic logic are none the less real for the fact that they are abstractly understood. So, I conclude that intellectual insight should join sensation, creative mental play, religious experience, dreams, memories and psychological drives as another source of x's for thought, of direct awareness, and of kaused objects. As such, they can be misunderstood or misjudged. But they also provide the basis for contact with reality; Aristotle's hedonistic devil, our sole preservation from perpetual relative metaphysical drift in platonic heaven.

At this point, someone might object that abstract objects *should* go in platonic heaven. The objector might ask, 'Isn't an id or a Riemannian Geometry a platonic form, if ever there was one?' My answer to this is that the positing process that puts time in the geometry, or an id in the personality is object positing, now a retroductive process, even at the more sophisticated levels of thought. Most of what follows from the postulation of the entity will, of course, follow concatenation rules already used for y-type processes, and will thus be platonic in nature. The difference between objects and properties may get a bit fuzzy once the objects are becoming as abstract as those of retroductive intellectual analysis are. But I think that there is good reason to insist that a molecule, perspective, or a quality daycare program are still, experiential objects, not property instantiations.

Summary; Direct Awareness of Objects

In this chapter I have explained the range of types of objects, or xs, intentionally marking rs of which I believe that people can become directly aware. As a form of empiricism, my extension of the range of objects of direct awareness considerably expands both the type of experience and the sorts of objects that will form the basis of knowledge claims. Two moves, both of which I believe are reasonable, have enabled me to formulate an empiricism this rich.

One is my insistence that direct awareness identifies objects in experience. By getting rid of intermediaries and sense data, I gain access to a wider range of types of experience. Once the sense-data are gone, the internal-external distinction, that so artificially characterizes the nature of experience, also goes. Cleaning up the territory in this way reveals the common nature of a wide range of types of experience; all that I have discussed in this chapter of this book.

The other move that contributes to the development of this rich empiricism is my characterization of object-positing as a conscious, attentive, human interaction with experience. Older empiricisms characterized a recipient of experience as a static sorting box or intake unit for pre-packaged colors, shapes, sounds and the like. In my analysis of object-positing, nothing is static and very little is pre-packaged. Only death renders human thinking truly static, although bigotry does impose premature *rigor mortis* on a *res cogitans*.

This completes my explication of objects. I will now move on to a discussion of how my notion of an object can be used to explain a variety of linguistic, logical, and existence-related ideas, of which any viable concept of an object must make sense.

Chapter 7

The Concept of an Object

Linguistic, Logical and Metaphysical Notions

Ideas Related to the Concept of an Object

In addition to being one of the key notions in a philosophical theory about thinking on its own terms, the notion of an object is also the basis for several other notions in a philosophy about thinking. The related concepts that I have in mind are of three types: 1) linguistic ideas, such as denotation, sense and meaning, 2) logical ideas, such as the role of objects as marked by variables or constants, and the identity of various terms that mark the same referent in arguments, and 3) metaphysical notions related to existence or being in general, wherein objects are taken to be either part or the whole of all that is. In this chapter, I will briefly indicate how my notion of an object can do a better job than some of the available alternatives of explaining some of these related notions.

Related Linguistic Notions

In twentieth century analytic philosophy, A.J.Ayer led a long parade of language analysis thinkers who maintained, to a greater or lesser degree, that all philosophical problems are really problems related to the use and abuse of language. If we really understood how language functions, the movement holds, most of our philosophical 'problems' would evaporate. This faith in the insubstantiality of philosophical problems relies on a variety of concurrently developed methodologies for understanding that have proven quite powerful in analyzing both the logic of language and the imperfections of many older methodologies for understanding philosophical problems.

Two of the main twentieth century methodologies that have contributed to this faith are, of course, symbolic logic and behaviorism in psychology. Symbolic logic offers the hope that all useful language can be described with the rigor with which mathematics describes engineering, and behavioral psychology offers the hope that all human behavior, linguistic behavior inclusive, can be reduced to formulae constructable out of statistical evaluations of observed events. As a methodology in psychology, behaviorism only amounted to a restriction on approaches to research or treatment, and as such, it was helpful in focusing attention on actions and avoiding speculation about unexamined thoughts. But interpreted as a metaphysical position in philosophy, especially by philosophers like Jonathan Bennett and the Churchlands, it has become a program aimed at *eliminating* all suggestions that thoughts, intentions, judgments, drives or motives exist.

My notion of an object, obviously, rains on this parade. For one thing, the intentionality and point of view that I have built into the notion of an object, make the nature of objects both opaque to logical analysis and immune to behavioristic reduction. For another, the dependence of my notion of an object on experience entails that only things that can have experience can have a concept of an object. Unlike the relationship between a box and its engineering design, the relationship between a language and its users is dynamic and continually evolving. A thing without experience cannot engage in this dynamic process. Dogs may have the requisite experience to engage in some concept formation, but computers are definitely out. Computers may be able to mimic or model the syntax of some language use, but they do not do object positing, and they have no knowledge of objects.

I think that it is a strength of my theory, that a number of linguistic concepts that became convoluted and problematic when interpreted in terms acceptable to participants in the linguistic analysis parade, are quite straightforward when interpreted in terms of my notion of an object. Let's look at a few.

Meaning

On my interpretation of the nature of an object, meanings are back 'in the head', or at any rate, back in the object-positing process. More specifically, they are in intentions and points of view of language users. Since the intentions and points of view index the x and the r to each other, meanings are ultimately indexed to aspects of experience, from the first person singular point of view of a person whose experience the intentions characterize.

Gottlob Frege and Ludwig Wittgenstein insisted that meaning was a relationship between a proposition and a thing, in which intentions played no role, to eliminate the mushiness of both the individual mental and the social-meaning worlds. For both Frege and Wittgenstein, the goal was to get personal psychology out of propositions so that logical functions could be described more precisely. Frege can still have a syntactical truth-functional relationship between propositions and things, however, without hijacking 'meaning' for this purpose. And, many issues of reference became problematic as a result of hijacking meaning and denuding it of intentionality to use it to describe logical relations. Functional Dopplegangers, twin earthians and Kripkeian travelers could never know what they meant by the expressions they used. If intentionality and meaning are reunited, Dopplegangers will pose no problem, because they will have different experiences from their earthling cousins, and 'London is ugly' will not contradict *'Londres est jolie'* because the intentional objects will differ.[1]

This is not to say that the twin earthians and their earthling counterparts would immediately understand each other on meeting, or that Kripke's bilingual thinker can be content with his two notions of London indefinitely. But both problems are resolvable if one simply observes that the dopplegangers can come to understand that their experiences differ through discussion, and the bilingual thinker can realize that his experiences of London as a child and as an adult led him to very different understandings of differing parts of one place. Searle, in his discussion of these puzzles, points out that the intentional conditions of satisfaction for *'Londres'* and 'London' or for 'water' and 'xyz' will differ, concurring with my analysis of the situation.[2]

Thus, the most basic use of the word meaning, on my analysis of the situation as on Searle's, is to mark indexically selected aspects of experience from a first person singular, intentional point of view. Other uses of the word are developed from that one. So, for instance, the dictionary meaning of a word will be a recording of what most people use that word to index in experience. And the social or community meaning of the word will be what someone has to use the word to index, if he or she wishes to communicate with his or her peers.

---

[1] see Saul Kripke, 'A Puzzle about Belief', in *Meaning and Use*, ed. A. Margalit, Reidel, Dordrecht, 1976, pp. 239–283.
[2] John Searle, *Intentionality*, *op. cit.* p. 160 ff.

Since a language such as English is, properly speaking, a social artifact, a private language is out, because it can't contribute to social discourse. But any individual speaks truthfully if at any time he or she says that the social meaning of some term fails to characterize what he or she is thinking, or means. The burden then falls upon the social dissident to find a way to share his or her intentions, point of view, and experience with the peers who misunderstand. The dissident may be able to do this by putting his or her peers in a position to share the experience, by explaining the point of view or intentions in neutral terms, or by devising and defining a new vocabulary. Or, it might be the case that the experiences and repertoires of points of view of the dissidents and their peers differ so substantially that nothing will make communication between them work on the issue under discussion.

I think that a considerable amount of social discord arises from the fact that people do, in fact, index notions in diverse ways, then argue incessantly with one another about their diverse interpretations of a situation. On my view of the situation this is a somewhat unavoidable consequence of the fact that no two people have identical experience, and no two people intentionalize all of their experience in the same ways. But the solution is not to standardize language into a condition of rigor mortis, but rather to advocate tolerance and open-minded discussion between disputants, aimed at broadening the access of all involved parties to new ways of understanding and intentionalizing about experience.

If a participant in A.J. Ayer's parade will complain that my analysis of meaning returns linguistic analysis to the bad old days when meanings were mushy and psychological, at the expense of a neat, clean, scientific analysis for which we should be looking, I respond that imposition of rigor mortis on language is neither a truthful analysis of nor a desirable condition for a language. It is not truthful, because language *is* a method of expression for human experience, not an objective, abstract structure of the material world. And it is not desirable, because the limits that it would impose on what language can do would sap it of all of its dynamic energy. If meanings are mushy and psychological, so is life, and so is human experience; and meanings are nothing if they are not tied to life and experience. Again, we can understand nothing by denying its existence or nature.

Sense

Frege's essay that distinguished between the propositional content or 'sense' of an assertion, and the psychological or bearer-dependent 'ideas' that the sense expressed, first appeared in 1918 -1919.[3] At that point in time, Frege found it necessary to argue for the independence of logic from psychology. The rhetorical force of the essay is directed at objectors who would argue that all thought must be psychologically based, and thus, even syntactical eternal truths would require something mind-like in which they could be housed, and would be required to follow psychological laws.

Over the course of the twentieth century, however, the pendulum of philosophical opinion swung 180 degrees in the reverse direction. Searle and I are now in the minority opposition against the Churchlands, Stalnaker, Dennett, Dretske, and a host of cognitive scientists who have eliminated the Fregian sense and ideas, and believe that even psychology does not exist independently of eternal propositions.

I believe that Frege was correct, and that the distinction that he was making was, or closely paralleled, my distinction between x-type and y-type reasoning processes. This book is a sustained demonstration that the y-type processes cannot exist without an x-type base, as Frege's essay 'The Thought' was a sustained argument for the logical independence of the y-type processes from the x.

Frege devised the notion of a proposition to capture his logical reflections on beliefs and logical relations. Among the most central intuitions that he sought to explain through propositions were the notions that the same belief could be expressed in a number of linguistic formulations or languages, and that truth value is preserved across valid inferences. Frege distinguished his 'Third realm' from bearer-dependent ideas this way:

> So the result seems to be; thoughts are neither things of the outer world, nor ideas.
> A third realm must be recognized. What belongs to this corresponds with ideas in that it cannot be perceived by the senses, but with things in that it needs no bearer to the content of whose consciousness to belong. Thus, the thought, for example, which we expressed in the Pythagorean Theorem is timelessly true, true independently of whether anyone takes it to be true. It needs no bearer. It is not true for the first time when it is discovered, but is like a planet which, already before anyone has seen it, has been in interaction with other planets.[4]

---

[3]   Gottlob Frege, 'The Thought: A Logical Inquiry' trans. by A.M. and Marcelle Quinton, in *Mind*, Vol. LXV, No. 259, July 1956, pp. 289-311.
[4]   *Ibid.*, p. 302.

Thus, Frege's logical program is aimed at eliminating intentionality and relativism from discussions of truth functionality in arguments, and at restricting the scope of logical discussions to extensional properties of objects. If one's inquiry is limited to analyzing logical deducibility, as Frege's was, these aims are desirable. But the recent attempts by cognitive scientists at re-importing the logically steril-ized propositions back into Frege's psychological ideas are ad hoc attempts at reducing humans to computers. The reverse move is not intellectually justified although its predecessor was. In the next chapter, I will argue against Stalnaker's reduction of all mental activ-ity to propositional denizens of Frege's third realm. For now, I will clarify what I mean by the sense of a statement.

With Frege, I agree that people entertain two types of thoughts. The experiences involved in object-positing correspond to Frege's ideas. They are bearer-dependent, intentional, context-dependent, indexical, bits of mental data. They are the element in Aristotle's for-mula for knowledge that required 'acquaintance with the thing.' These experiences give the basic meaning of a term or expression for a person. So, for instance, I can learn a good bit about pineapple fla-voring from books and discussions without ever tasting it. How-ever, until I taste it, the words, 'pineapple flavoring' are really without a sense or meaning for me. Sense is thus, directly tied to meaning in the experience of object-positing.

However, once an experience is named, which it is as part of the object-positing process, the name can take on a linguistic life of its own. Names, as I have already suggested, cannot be completely idiosyncratic, if one wishes to communicate with one's peers. A name that works, that is, one that succeeds both in indexing an expe-riential meaning and in communicating that meaning to others, can also be the existentially quantified object of a proposition. So, sense is also directly tied to the meaningfulness of terms, as used in propo-sitions. Sense is, thus, a 'bridge concept' that connects x-type think-ing to y-type thinking. A proposition is the proposition that it is *because* it has the sense of someone's first person singular experience of something. And, the person can express true thoughts in proposi-tions *because* his or her experience has the sense that is articulated in the proposition.

Let's look at some examples. A child who has tasted a pineapple, but doesn't have the word for it, still means something very specific when he says he wants more of yummy that, and points. He has the meaning side of sense, but needs the propositionalized side of sense. In contrast, someone who can never taste a pineapple because of a severe fruit allergy can say 'pineapples are a delicious fruit', and say something true, and make sense in expressing the proposition, even though the terms are, and must remain, technically meaningless for her. Our allergic person has the proposition side of the sense of 'pineapple,' but not the meaning side. To say this is to say that she has learned to manipulate a string of words in a socially acceptable way. She is thus, like a computer, in her capacity to crunch these symbols. Her lack of capacity to distinguish between the artificial flavors of a coconut popsicle and a pineapple popsicle might reveal her 'understanding' of the proposition she uttered as a fraud. Banally, 'making sense' means getting a meaning and a true proposition containing its sense together in the same place at the same time.

To conclude my discussion of sense, thus, sense is the bridge between first person singular meanings and public, 'third realm' thoughts. Sense is what is shared by the psychological Fregian idea, and the logical Fregian thought. Without the first person singular grounding, propositions are meaningless structures, and without the publicly accessible propositions, ideas are idiosyncratic experiences. Senses are thus, at the borderline between x and y-type thinking processes. They are what tie the two processes together, and make it possible for people to discuss their experience and come to understand what they hear or read.

Names or Labels and Denotation

As I have already indicated, a name is the word used by someone to index some aspect of his or her experience in object positing. Like sense, it will carry the experience with it into public discourse, if the social meanings and the propositional structures into which it is expressed are adequate to communicate the name.

But, I want to be quite broad and fuzzy about the use of the word 'name' when I use it to mark the product of object positing. Perhaps 'labels' or 'terms' would be better words to use, because they carry less philosophical baggage. Certainly, names or labels should cover proper and common nouns, but also, abstract nouns, collective nouns, names for subject matters, or perhaps, any verbals that could stand as grammatical subjects or objects of sentences. In short, anything that can be marked as a 'that' in experience, can be, in this very broad sense, named.

Thus, a color, as a platonic entity, may be a property, not a thing. But, when trying to match a blouse to a skirt, my 'Aha, there it is!' indexes the 'it' to a specific experience of a thing. The thing indexed might be named magenta, plum or electric purple, but it is not, in context, a property at all. Nor is it a shirt. Rather, it is a temporally bound, indexically selected bit of my experience marked as that-color-thing. It is one of those relatively existent subject matters that, left to its own devises, could generate quite a bit of metaphysical drift. As such, it can be 'named' in this broad sense. But naming this transitory bit will not generate either a platonic form for purpleness in object positing or a permanent thing 'magenta-thing'. Aviators do something like this when they refer to 'the blue'.

I hope that it will become apparent as I continue this discussion that the constructed 'magenta-thing' of the last paragraph is the mirror-image in the object-positing process of attempts that various philosophers have made of 'propertizing' objects in exclusively y-type theories. Of course it is possible to 'reduce' an object to a set of properties. And, to have an exclusively y-type account of anything it is necessary to do so. But, in insisting, as Russell does, that he has, thereby, explained objects, he misses half the story. The rest of the story is that an account of 'objectified' properties can also be given from the standpoint of an x-type account of reality. My 'magenta thing' does as good a job of making a thing out of what is ordinarily considered a property as his sets of properties do of making objects into y-type properties. If I wanted to be perverse, I could insist that I have, thus, explained properties and eliminated the need for y-type reasoning, at all.

Of course, the philosophical conclusion to be reached from this observation is that neither reduction is really 'eliminating.' All that either does is show how the two sides of object positing and property attributing look as mirror reflections of each other. As a sense stands between a meaning and a proposition, a name stands between an objectified property and a property-reduced object, holding metaphysical drift at bay. Since the name will be used in both the experience and the proposition, if used unequivocally in each, the experience will be tied to the propositional expression by the name, and the proposition will be tied to experience by the name.

Kripke's initial Baptisms cannot accomplish this tying job, because he has the name tying the indexing to the wrong things. He has most of an account of how names get carried through social chains and become socially useful, but none of an account about how anyone, including the initial namer, learns what the name means. Historical chains, as I argued earlier, can only give social meaning, not experience. And without experience, the name dangles from platonic space, as did my allergic taster's name for pineapple.

So, names are, primarily, the labels that someone attaches to a bit of his or her experience. If a name unequivocally carries that meaning to a proposition, there it will, secondarily, denote the set of properties in the extension of the term. Most properly, a name denotes an experience. Secondarily, it denotes the properties that are socially considered extensions of the term.

Why the priority for the experience? I believe the priority *must* be ordered in this way because of some puzzles about the meaning of names that, again, a theory like Kripke's can't solve. Suppose someone tells me that Joe, a human friend of his, is a gorilla. If the sentence means the historical chain of social expectations we are going to get a very different interpretation of the meaning of the sentence than we will get if we say that it means what someone who knows gorillas experiences. Kripke can't solve this puzzle because the historical social chain of information is, in this case, passing on a false stereotype. I think we have *every* reason to believe Jane Goodall and discount the historical bigotries, and *no* reason to prefer the social and cultural chain's stereotype and discount the person who has had the experience of studying gorillas. The reasonable analysis of the statement 'Joe is a gorilla' is that if its utterer meant 'Joe is fierce and violent' he said something that failed to express his meaning. If he meant Joe lives in trees, or is hairy and strong-armed, of course, that is another matter. The bottom line is experience counts for truthful meaning, and trumps social chains, especially when the social chain is inaccurate.

So, to conclude this section, a name denotes the experience for which it is used as an object-positing label. That is the primary denotation of a name, and any confusions that might arise when the name is used in a proposition or a social context would have to be resolved by returning to its experiential source in object-positing. If used unequivocally, it can also mark object locations in property attributing, tying them back to experience and object-positing. The name holds metaphysical drift at bay by asserting both the experiential existence and the propositional propriety of the named. Mid-sized objects, of course, will be the bulk of things named.

I believe that I have demonstrated in this section that the linguistic terms that have been so troublesome to analytic and cognitive science philosophers are pretty straight-forward when interpreted in light of my analysis of thinking processes. I will now turn to a demonstration of how some logical notions related to the concept of an object should be understood using my concept of an object.

Related Logical Notions: Propositions, Identity, and Deducibility

In addition to playing a role in the linguistic ideas that we just considered, the notion of an object is also related to some logical concepts, such as the notion of a proposition, the notion of identity, and the notion of deducibility in arguments. In this section of this chapter we will look at these ideas, to see how my concept of an object can help explain them.

Propositions

Propositions were the vehicle that Frege devised to be the mind-independent bearers of truth and deducibility in his third realm. Wittgenstein and Russell and Whitehead developed symbolic logic, using propositions as the atomic units of the system. The basic notion was that a proposition contained an assertive claim about some feature of the world. Some quality, property, or relationship was predicated on some thing in a well-formed way in any adequate proposition.

Because these assertions were devised to be isolated from the vagaries and variabilities of common language and psychological reality, their most important features were the predicated properties in the assertions. The logical analysis of the relationships between propositions that the propositions were designed to allow was to be an analysis about how relationships between the properties predicated could be described. For objects to count at all in Frege's third realm, they would be either reduced to sets of properties for which identity conditions could be clearly stated, or reduced to variables that really marked nothing but a space in the proposition at which some indeterminate thing was receiving a predication.

Of course, for purposes of doing logical analysis in platonic heaven, this move is helpful. For instance, predicate functions are necessary to articulate a concept such as the notion that there are two of something.[5] But, as I have shown in the last section, it is only an intellectual sleight of hand, that can as easily be reversed. From the perspective of the object-positing side of the thinking process, properties can be objectified as easily as objects can be reduced to sets of properties or to nothing, here.

So, a proposition is a vehicle, used by y-type, property-attributing thinking processes to describe the platonic features of human experience, or those features of human experience that can be described as relations and properties. Obviously, some features of human

---

[5] Thanks to Stewart Thau for this observation.

thinking are best or perhaps, only, describable in this way. Frege's example is the Pythagorean Theorem. This isn't the type of thing that nags at the intestines or looks yellow on the horizon. Instead, it is known by considering the relationships that obtain between three lines, when certain restraints are imposed on what one can do with them. Knowledge of the theorem can occur as a direct awareness in intellectual insight, but apart from that, it is wholly non-experiential. Thinking about the theorem appears to be simply not thinking about experience, or about anything that could in any important sense be called human at all.

Thus, the essential features of propositions are those features that relate to deducibility, and describing functional relationships among propositions. They are de dicto, as opposed to de re considerations. Quine's claim that a system of symbolic logic 'limns the essential features of reality' has to be qualified. The features limned are the logical features, only. As we saw in my discussion of direct awareness in object positing, human experience is rich with de re features that the structure of the logical system reduces to a variable, or to nothing.

In a later chapter, I will explain the relationship between x and y type thinking processes in more detail. For now, I will just observe that propositions are useful vehicles for employment in a logical system. They are the atomistic units of y-type thinking, as objects in direct awareness are the data of x-type thinking processes. Objects, in propositions, reduce to sets of properties or to nothing. Logical systems may say true things about objects, *if* the name or the sense of the original, experiential object carries over to the proposition, and is not mangled by a derivation. It will always be a question of judgment, not logic, whether this proviso has been violated in a particular case or not. The slingshot argument is a clear case in which judgment rules that this proviso has been violated.

So, my conclusion about the role of x-type, experiential objects, in propositions, is that their meaning *may* carry over into the lists of properties or space of predication in a proposition, *provided that* the name or the sense is preserved, and the meaning has been preserved through the name or the sense.

A logical system, can, of course, operate as a purely formal structure, independently of any objects at all. But then, it would be absurd to claim that it is limning the essential features of reality, in a de re sense. For reality de re must contain objects.

Identity

I have already discussed, in the causation chapter, the meaning of
the expression 'x = r', as I use it to explain sameness of meaning. To
say that the point of view of an observer and the aspect of reality
thereby marked are identical, is merely to say that the two sides of
the x = r relationship are interdefinable. In the object positing and
experiential thinking processes, that is all there is to the notion of
identity. Identity means sameness of meaning or sameness of sense,
as sense is built up out of experiential, first person singular meaning,
or indexical 'thisness'.

The mathematical or property-attributing notions of identity will,
thus, be systematically connected to this basic notion of identity,
especially when they denote 'same meaning', or 'name for the same
thing'. But, more formal syntactical notions of identity sometimes
also introduce new ideas, which are not present at the experiential
level. For instance, identity relations that identify same or similar
structural relationships, or same or similar sets in a domain, can be
both completely non-experiential and completely logically clear, as
y-type notions.

For instance, the expression $(\sim p \lor q) \equiv (p \rightarrow q)$ claims an identity
relationship between formal propositional structures that would be
a true relationship for any propositions exhibiting these structures.
Two observations about this identity relation are important to point
out. One is that this is a universal claim for any propositions that
might have the expressed structure. The claim is, thus, about the
structure, not about the content of the propositions. Two, it does not
follow from the truth of the identity expressed in the axiom of
replacement for material implication, that there actually exist *any*
propositions that bear that structure. Logicians know from experience that this structure is useful to describe a wide variety of inferences in language. But true identities can as well exist between
formal structures with impossible or fictional content, as in topology.

So, my conclusion about identity is that notions related to identity
straddle both sides of x and y type thinking processes. The core
notion, of sameness of meaning, name or sense, or same object, is an
experiential, x-type notion. Transferred to the y-type reasoning
domain, more content is added to the idea, as it comes to mark sameness of structure or form or sameness of set membership. In the case
of formalized propositions, the structural identity can replace the
meaning or sense identity altogether, to provide the freedom from
psychological vagaries that Frege and Russell sought, in order to do

logic. The benefit of the replacement is, of course, that formal structures can be systematically crunched as numbers can be added. The cost of the replacement is that sense and meaning, and with them contact with reality, are put in suspension by the transfer. Again, the slingshot argument shows how to lose reality by holding on to formal structure.

My notion of an object is helpful in making the above distinctions, because my notion distinguishes clearly between the experimental 'that thing' that is, as Aristotle would say, the thing with which someone is acquainted de re, and the structural 'something or another satisfying criterion x', that gives the formal type qualifications for the application of a de dicto concept to a case. An object can be described in either way, of course. I am insisting throughout this book, however, that the experiential x-type process is the primary, core access to an object that anyone has. The reason for the primacy of the experiential is, again, that disputes about an object must be resolved by returning to the experiential basis of the notion of that object. To seek the resolution of a dispute about the nature of an object by chasing further concepts or structures representing it would be to chase a third man.

So, on my concept of an object, identity turns out to be a multi-level idea, with a variety of meanings at its various levels. The most properly logical and formal syntactical notions belong in y-type reasoning processes, while the most properly experiential semantic notions are tied to first person singular experience. While equivocation is possible among the various meanings of 'identity', the notions can be systematically tied to each other, as well, through such notions as same name, same sense, and same meaning. So equivocation is not inevitable between x-type and y-type uses of the term 'identity'. In optimal circumstances, the logical structures in a deduction would carry the identity of an x and an r through a derivation, unequivocally. Only intentions and judgment, however, can tell when these optimal circumstances obtain.

Deducibility

'Deducibility' is a more centrally logical, and thus, more strictly y-type notion than is either 'identity' or 'proposition'. It was the rules of inference and deduction, more than anything, that Frege and Russell wanted to insist were independent of individual psychology, or of human thinking all together. Frege insisted that inferences like the Pythagorean Theorem would exist in his third realm even if no one had ever thought of them. In saying this, Frege gives a metaphysical, realistic, account of these structural relations between his thoughts. Some more recent theorists, such as Hartry Field and David Lewis, have described Frege's third realm thoughts as descriptions of 'possible worlds'. By this, Lewis and Field mean that a complete consistent list of such thoughts describe a way that the world could be.[6]

My predilections on this issue favor Lewis' and Field's analysis of the third realm, as describing only possibilities, over Frege's realistic commitment to free-floating thoughts which no one has yet thought of. However, I'm not sure that this distinction marks a real difference. I will explain what I think the denizens of platonic heaven are in some detail in a later chapter. For now, I'll just characterize deducibility as an analysis of structural relationships between various types of pure abstract structures, and explain what I mean by this statement, and what role my concept of an object plays in it.

When I call deducibility an analysis of structural relationships between various types of pure abstract structures, what I mean is that people have an ability to reason, in the abstract, about connections between properties that must occur because of the types of properties that the ones under consideration are. For instance, once I've described a recursive sequence of numbers, there are certain other properties, besides being recursive, that will follow from the fact that the sequence has that property. Likewise, once I've described a triangle, geometrical theorems about angle ratios will follow. Deducibility is a property that propositions have, by reason of their structure. Once propositions have been described as eternal, well-formed, preservers of sense in truth-functional relations, logicians can pretty much ignore the sense and meaning, and spend their time thinking about well-formedness, implication, disjunction, and other, more specifically logical properties that follow from the structure of the propositions. Their only remaining obligation to sense and meaning is to see that they remain intact across structural transpositions.

So, objects, as products of the object-positing process, play very little role in deducibility. Objects are just occupants of the places marked by the variables and constants that get moved from thither to yon in a deduction. As such, the only property that they have *vis a vis* the deduction is unchangeableness.

Someone might object at this point, 'But what about the structures, themselves, aren't they, themselves, objects?' Certainly, Frege's realistic stance towards them indicates that he saw triangles, recursive sequences, and material implications as being as real as cars, tables, and trees. And of course these, as much as my 'magenta thing' could be objectified and located in experience, either as instantiations of intellectual insight, or as instantiated in pyramids, rows of marching soldiers, and newspaper arguments. But, I think that there are reasons to avoid objectifying these structures.

For one thing, as Plato rightly pointed out, when I am discussing the geometrical properties of a triangle, I am discussing the properties of all possible triangles. 'All possible triangles' is neither a particular triangle that I am now considering nor one that I saw yesterday. To describe what I am considering accurately, it is not any triangle at all, not even a mental or platonic one. Think of Berkeley's nominalist objection that the abstract triangle cannot be right, isosceles, obtuse, or acute, and cannot be none of the above, either. Rather, what I am thinking about is some property that the concept 'triangular' must imply if it is not to become a self-contradictory concept. Thus, 'all possible triangles' marks a limit on a concept, 'triangularity', that is deducible from the nature of the concept.

For another thing, the universality of concepts such as deducibility, recursive sequence and extended spatial structure, makes them strange objects, if someone wants to make objects out of them. Suppose I know the Pythagorean Theorem. I might have this stored away in memory as a picture-diagram, as an equation, or as a paragraph. Is it all of these, one, or none of them? We might say it describes the corner of my bookshelf, whether I ever mentally transpose my diagram of it on the bookshelf or not. Or, we might say that no bookshelf that has ever existed exhibited the Pythagorean Theorem exactly. Is it everywhere or nowhere? Or is it the case that because it is everywhere it is nowhere? I refer to 'it' in the singular, but the concept 'triangularity' hardly picks out a singular individual. Words like 'Pythagorean theorem' and 'material implication' pick out clear concepts, perhaps to a far greater extent than experiential names do. But to call them objects strikes me as a bit fishy, at any rate.

Consider a possible worlds interpretation of the Fregian third realm, instead. What a geometrical structure is, as a projection of what three or four or n dimensional space can do, is a description of all possible space, as constrained by n dimensions. A logical structure is a description of what all possible logical implications could look like, with respect to their structural properties. Arithmetic is a description of all possible recursive sequences, and all possible deducible properties of recursive systems.

This analysis lets us say, with Quine, that these structures 'limn the structure of reality', at least with respect to the properties and qualities under consideration, without agreeing with Quine that nothing that fails to fit this structure can rate as real. Rather, we would say that something spatial must be geometrical, something that exhibits material implication is logical, etc. but not conversely, if something isn't structured this way, it doesn't exist.

Thus, the logical concept of deducibility, on my account, is a concept of a description of all possible arguments, with respect to certain features, such as having well-formed propositions, using material implications, De Morgan's law, modus ponens, and related rules. Objects are merely placeholders, either as variables or as constants in these transpositions; they are what is preserved unmolested by the transposition. The logical structures in the arguments are not, themselves, properly called objects because they are more accurately described as possible structures, than as actual anythings in particular.

The Metaphysical Notion of Existence or Being

Quine is famous for having claimed 'To be is to be the value of a variable'.[7] In discussing ontological relativity, he attributes ontological commitment to what someone will existentially quantify.[8] In a sense, I agree with this analysis of the situation, because existential quantification is the vehicle used by a logical system to index the meanings, senses and names of terms back to their experiential base. But I also believe that more can be said about the respective roles of both the overall structure of logical and other concept systems, and the particular experiences that people isolate as objects, in determining what humans understand by reality or existence.

The overall structure of conceptual systems, such as arithmetic, logic, or geometry, determines the outer reaches of possibility. Thus, a human concept of existence or of being is limited to what can be theoretically structured in a conceptual system. Because theoretical systems deal only with possibility, one can only infer that if something is real, then it was possible, and not conversely that anything possible is real. But productive knowledge about reality can still be gained through purely theoretical inquiries because limits on what can be real can be discovered. It is in this sense that Frege can truly

---

[7]   W.V.O. Quine, *Pursuit of Truth*, revised edn. Harvard University Press, Cambridge, MA, 1992, p. 31.

[8]   Quine discusses this issue both in *Word and Object*, and in *Ontological Relativity and Other Essays*.

claim that the Pythagorean Theorem was 'out there', like a star, waiting to be discovered an eternity before anyone discovered it. It is an objective limit on what can possibly be done with three lines in three dimensional space.

The particular experiences that people identify as objects in object-positing, in contrast, present actual existence to thought. Here one can infer that if one has experienced something it is real, but not conversely, that if one has not experienced something it is not real. Experience is always specific and limited, and each day brings both new experience and new insight to the attentive learner. Experiential existence is, thus, an expanding horizon, both for persons individually and for the human race, as a whole. To discount someone else's existence claim without a serious attempt at learning what they are identifying in experience as real is not scientific, it is simply rude and arrogant. Logical impossibilities can, of course, be ruled out. But ordinarily, even to demonstrate that someone else's existential commitment is a commitment to something logically contradictory requires more understanding of what the other person is doing in object positing than the critic has.

So, existence, like identity, will straddle the x and y-type thinking processes, equivocally meaning different things on the two sides of thinking. On the experiential side, existence means being an object in first-person singular experience. On the conceptual side, existence means either being necessarily true, as is the Pythagorean Theorem, or being possibly existent, as opposed to being contradictory, and therefore impossible. As in the case of identity, the two equivocal meanings of 'existence' can be tied to each other through the existential quantifier, so the equivocation is neither necessarily pernicious nor impossible to control. However, it is important to keep in mind that existence means something different when it is applied to x-type thinking processes than it does when it is applied to y-type thinking processes. To obfuscate the two, or to call either one the only meaning of 'existence' brings about considerable confusion in philosophical thinking.

Summary

In this chapter of this book I believe I have demonstrated how my concept of an object can give a clearer account of some common linguistic, logical and metaphysical notions, than alternative theories in the literature at present do. I will now turn from explaining my notion of an object and some of its implications to showing how my notion of an object provides a middle ground between two common notions that are abroad; Stalnaker's notion of an object as an internalized proposition, and Husserl's notion of an object as an intentional idea. I chose these two notions to situate my notion of an object between because I believe they represent opposing extreme views of what an object is; Stalnaker's view is extremely mechanical while Husserl's is extremely phenomenalistic. I plan to show that my view captures the best of both of their views, while avoiding the pitfalls of each.

Chapter 8

Stalnaker vs. Husserl

Criticisms of Some Alternative
Notions of an Object

Stalnaker and Husserl

In this chapter I will argue with two philosophers who I believe have erred in opposing directions in trying to give an account of human thinking. Robert Stalnaker is representative of a number of analytic philosophers who have tried to platonize all thinking, by rendering even Frege's mind-dependent ideas 'propositional'. Edmund Husserl, on the opposing side, has tried to render all thinking experiential, even logic. I believe that this chapter will demonstrate why a two-part analysis of thinking, that gives both x-type and y-type thinking processes their due is necessary.

Stalnaker's Mechanized, Propositionalized Objects

Robert Stalnaker, in his book, *Inquiry*, has tried to replace the Fregian ideas, altogether, with Fregian thoughts, a.k.a., propositions. The object of this replacement is to reimport the logical properties of the propositions back into the bearer-dependent mental states from which Frege had specifically differentiated them. In a Stalnaker-like interpretation of the nature of mental states, Fregian propositions are being conflated with Fregian ideas, all of which are being rendered 'mental', so that a mechanical co-relation can be proposed between these states and states in the world, or things. In Stalnaker's version of the mental-representation-is-all-propositional view of thought, he explicitly tries to give an extensional, truth-functional account of intentionality. He starts his book, *Inquiry* with the words:

> When a person suspects or supposes, realizes, regrets, infers or imagines that something is true he is taking an attitude or changing his attitude towards a proposition.[1]

Already Stalnaker has stacked the deck against a number of kinds of mental states that I would take seriously. For instance, the way that he phrases this passage implies that the only kind of imagining that is possible is imagining in strict propositional format, 'that something is true . . . '. Imagining, I would insist, is rarely so restrictively propositional in format. As an x-type thinking process, imagining is more likely to be imagistic, sensory, and judgementally ordered, if it is ordered at all. I think that Searle would agree that we can Imagine (Sally) in much the same way that we can Love (Sally) or See (Sally). In either my account or Searle's, objects are being posited and mental play is being engaged in when people imagine.

By platonizing all thinking, Stalnaker's propositional view of mental representation becomes overly restrictive in all of the ways in which we would want an account of thinking to be flexible and unhelpful in all of the ways in which we would hope that such a theory would be explanatory. Stalnaker's propositionalized ideas have to be structured, so that they can perform the function of being isomorphic with physical structures outside the mind. But the structure required to do this would deprive them of the 'cognitive penetrability' that psychologists like Pylyshyn have shown that psychological states clearly have. And, Stalnaker's propositionalized psychological states must maintain their logical structure to remain the units of a platonic deductive system that he insists they must be. But once he has slaughtered their structure to make them fit the obvious psychological limits, he is left with very little that could properly be called a proposition.

Even on the supposedly straightforward question of what a proposition is, Stalnaker provides more confusion than insight. He says;

> A proposition is a function from possible worlds into truth-values.

and explains;

> A function may be thought of intuitively as a rule for determining a value relative to any member of a specified domain of arguments. But the identity conditions for functions are purely extensional: if functions f and g are defined for the same arguments, then they are the same function.[2]

---

[1]   Robert Stalnaker, *Inquiry*, MIT Press, Cambridge Mass, 1984, p. 1.

[2]   *Ibid.*, pp. 2–3.

In this definition of a proposition even Frege's limited and possibly indirect reference to platonic entities, like the pythagorean theorem, is gone. Stalnaker specifically tries to separate his account of propositions as mental entities from Frege's and Russell's views of propositions by insisting that his propositions aren't compounded from individuals, properties, concepts, or senses.[3] And he tries to separate his account from Davidson's and Putnam's by insisting that his propositions are neither essentially linguistic nor essentially social phenomena.[4] Further, he rejects Hartry Field's account of propositional mental states for its structurally-described notion of propositions.[5]

But once Stalnaker has rejected all of these notions of the nature of a proposition, it is very difficult to say what he has left that might be at all useful in describing mental states. Obviously, Stalnaker wishes to retain the logical properties of propositions, especially truth-functionality and set-theoretic extensional equivalence. But these logical properties are a function of a proposition's structure, as Field has it, or of its compositionality, as Frege and Russell would claim. Stalnaker thinks he has retained a highly-structured, but non-linguistic piece of machinery that he can use to resolve a problem like accounting for the way that a dog thinks. He describes a dog's thinking processes in this way;

> But the problem looks quite different if one begins with the possible worlds conception of proposition. When we ascribe attitudes to the animal what we presuppose is simply that it has some mechanism for representing and distinguishing between alternative situations. It may be a very crude one, recognizing only gross differences, and containing no representation at all of possible situations radically different from the way things actually are . . . Because propositions do not mirror the structure of sentences that express them, it is possible to use sophisticated, semantically complex sentences to ascribe attitudes to creatures with very limited cognitive capacities.[6]

But insisting that Fido believes a truth-functional proposition that relates him to a possible world in this scenario, is both unhelpful and obfuscated. It presumes that the dog does y-type thinking, involving complex conceptual structures of modal logic, that he doesn't need to think about cats, and that won't help him to avoid them.

If, instead, we take a biological naturalist's view of the situation, we can give a much clearer, Searle-type analysis of what Fido

[3]   *Ibid.*, p. 3.

[4]   *Ibid.*, p. 20-21.

[5]   *Ibid.* p. 41.

[6]   *Ibid.* p. 63.

believes. We can know that Fido has sense organs without doing any modal logic at all. We can see his eyes, ears, nose, etc. Suppose, as is reasonable, that Fido has a sensory system of thinking, and does x-type object positing. His idea of the cat across the street is, then, exclusively a visual experience of a certain furry face, accompanied by an auditory expectation of a certain yowling snarl. Now suppose that Fido is dreaming of the furry face at three times normal size, and the snarl at elevated decibel levels, as a result of which, he wakes up frightened. What about the mental pictures and sounds entertained by Fido is truth-functional?

Even if I were willing to grant (which I'm not) that there is a possible world in which the cat *is* three times normal size and growls much louder, still it would be completely useless to say that Fido's mental state consists in a relationship between him and that world. Does the higher decibel level in the snarl in that world contradict the decibel level of the cat's normal snarl? Does the added visual size of the furry face in that world render the size of the furry face in this world false?

If so, why doesn't the perceptually larger furry face on the ledge above Fido in the real world contradict the perceptually smaller furry face across the yard, when Fido is at a safe distance from the cat? In short, there does seem to be a relationship between Fido's perception of the size of the cat's face and Fido's anxiety level, which cannot be captured by functions to any possible world, and there does not seem to be a relationship between the actual size of the cat's face as opposed to possible such sizes that will capture this relationship.

As the above discussion demonstrates, sensory and experiential data, the stuff of the x-type thinking processes, is simply not truth functional. Fido determines by awakening, and determining the kause of the experience to have been a dream, that he is safe. His judgment that he is safe is a judgment on experience, done in object-positing, not an inference of any kind, much less of possible worlds functions.

We know that animals perceive because they have sensory organs and react behaviorally to sensory stimuli. We do not know that animals can do modal logic, and it seems to me, we have every reason to suppose that they don't. The fact that they do not use language is, in itself, prima facie evidence that they do not entertain propositions. But, whatever one's beliefs about a dog's logical capacities may be, it is still apparent that the perspective judgments in the above scenario are not inferences between modal propositions. And if these judgments are not modal inferences for the dog, I submit that they are not modal inferences when we perform them, either.

Kosslyn and Pomerantz have studied the relative merits of propositional and imagistic accounts of mental representation to determine if the propositional accounts can give an adequate appraisal of what occurs when people process visual data. Their findings, especially with respect to visual scanning experiments, were heavily in favor of treating sensory imagery in its own terms, rather than trying to reduce it to propositional encoding, as Stalnaker has done. Kosslyn and Pomerantz compare propositional and imagistic accounts of scanning experiments and conclude;

> The imagery account seems somewhat plausible, while the propositional account seems entirely ad hoc. A propositional account based on discrete units and links is inherently ill-suited for representation of metric, analog information.[7]

Since Searle admits both propositional and non-propositional data, he is in a position to be flexible about the types of judgments and inferences that can be used to process this information. Even biological transformations that are not in any sense logical inferences can be admitted to Searle's analysis of how mental judgments are made. Such concessions to biological naturalism might seem offensive to platonic purists, but human mental processes are not, as a matter of fact, platonically pure.

My conclusion on Stalnaker's attempt at conflating propositions with Fregian ideas so that all thinking can be described as truth-functional and platonic, is thus, that more is lost than is gained by the conflation. Certainly, people, at least, do perform propositional functions. But imagistic and intentional object-positing type thinking is not performed in this way. And these x-type thinking processes are at least half of the thinking that people do. Nothing is gained by denying either the nature or the structure of these thinking processes, or by trying to conflate them with something that they are not.

Husserl's Experientialized Logic

A century ago Edmund Husserl tried to intentionalize and phenomenalize logic, making, in my estimation, the reverse mistake of Stalnaker's. Husserl tried to reduce concepts like number, set, inference, totality, relation and unity to concrete presentations that could be somehow made accessible to direct awareness. Husserl

---

[7]   Stephen M. Kosslyn and James R. Pomerantz, 'Imagery, Propositions, and the Form of Internal Representations.', in *Readings in Philosophy of Psychology*, vol. 2, ed. Ned Block, Harvard University Press, Cambridge, Mass, 1981, p. 166.

wanted to make awareness of these concepts as direct as I have described awareness of a mouse, or of hunger as being.

In my account, however, the relational terms are data for y-type thinking processes. Concepts like set and inference represent syntactical structures that interrelate as concepts within conceptual schemas. They are structural features of thinking and reality that are exhaustively defined by their structural properties, which are statable in de dicto terms. The meanings of the terms might be apprehended in flashes of intellectual insight, but apart from relatively rare experiences of this kind, the entire domain is non-experiential.

Husserl, in contrast, renders denizens of Frege's third realm 'phenomenal' in order to explain them as aspects of experience. He distinguishes between what he calls 'assertoric seeing' and what he calls 'apodeictic seeing' to claim that the two are differing ways of experiencing reality.

> . . . We may state on Phenomenological grounds that the so to speak 'assertoric' seeing of an individual, for instance the awareness of a thing or of some individual state of things, is in its rational character essentially distinguished from an 'apodeictic' seeing, from the in-seeing of an essence or of an essential relationship; but also likewise from the modification of this in-seeing which may take place from a mixing of the two, namely, in the case of an application of an insight to something assertorically seen, and generally, in the knowledge of the necessity of a posited particular being so-and-so.[8]

Husserl thinks that he has a distinction between two types of 'seeing' here that can be used for explaining mathematics and logic. But Frege seriously abuses Husserl's presentational view of third-realm concepts in his review of Husserl's 'Philosophy of Arithmetic,' as follows;

> Psychological Logicians lack all understanding of sameness, just as they lack all understanding of definitions. This relation cannot help but remain puzzling to them for if words always designated presentations, one could never say 'A is the same as B'. For, to be able to do that, one would already have to distinguish A from B, and then these would simply be different presentations.[9]

Frege's criticism is true of Husserl's passage because the distinction between the two types of seeing in this passage does not represent a difference in kind of thinking for Husserl, but only in level of

---

[8]   Edmund Husserl, *Ideas*, trans. W.R. Boyce Gibson, Collier Macmillan Publishing, London, 1975, p. 353.

[9]   Gottlob Frege, 'Review of Husserl's "Philosophy of Arithmetic"', reprinted in *Husserl, Expositions and Appraisals*, eds. Frederick Elliston and Peter McCormick, University of Notre Dame Press, Notre Dame, Indiana, 1977, p. 318.

abstraction. Husserl insists on the need to interpret logic and perception in the same way. He claims that Phenomenology unites the most dogmatic formal logic to the most ephemeral perceptual experiences in this way:

> In particular, it [Phenomenology] enables us to understand that the a priori truths of logic concern essential connections between the possibility of the intuited filling out of the posited meaning (whereby the corresponding positive content attains synthetic intuition) and of the pure synthetic form of the posited meaning (the pure logical form) and that that possibility is at the same time the condition of possible validity.[10]

In words closer to the ones that I have been using in this book, Husserl is claiming in this passage that formal logic is a part of the object-positing process, namely, that part of the object positing process that makes relations, structures and propositions both applicable to experience and extractable from experience, via abstraction. In contrast, my account of logic acknowledges the freedom of logic from experience. Propositions are a combination of syntax and semantics, and thus, contain both logical and experiential elements. The syntactical elements are not experiential, at all.

Frege also abuses Husserl's notion of the process of abstraction in his review of 'Philosophy of Arithmetic'. On the topic of extracting logical and mathematical ideas from direct presentations in experience, Frege first quotes Husserl, then chastizes him as follows. Husserl says:

> If we take this abstraction seriously, then of course the collective connection, rather than remaining behind as a conceptual extract, also disappears with the particular content. The solution lies at hand. To abstract from something merely means: not paying any particular attention to it. (Husserl, p. 84)

Frege responds:

> The core of this exposition clearly lies in the word 'particular'. Inattention is a very strong lye which must not be applied in too concentrated a form, so as not to dissolve everything; but neither ought it to be used in too diluted a form, so that it might produce sufficient change. Everything, then, depends on the proper degree of dilution, which is difficult to hit. I, at least, did not succeed in doing so.[11]

As one can see from both of the *Ideas* passages, as well as the 'Philosophy of Arithmetic' passage, Husserl has placed apprehension of necessary connectedness, relations between unities, and other self-evident types of relations in his category of apodeictic seeing,

---

[10]   Husserl, *Ideas, op. cit.* pp. 376–377.

[11]   Frege, in *Husserl, Expositions and Appraisals, op. cit.*, pp. 319–320.

which is for him simply a change in stance or observational attitude from ordinary perceptual cases of seeing. Husserl has, thus, listed apperception of self-evident truths as another type of phenomenal experience paralleling my experiences gained through the five senses, kinesthetic awareness, psychological self-awareness, etc. Husserl believes that we 'see' the necessity of the implication ('Jill is next to Mary' implies 'Mary is next to Jill') in the same direct way that I have claimed that we see a mouse.

I agree with Frege that Husserl's analysis of logic provides an unhelpful way of understanding either how we come to know relations, or what relations are. For one thing, relations like the 'next to' relationship are completely general; they are not metaphysically tied to the existence of Mary and Jill, or, indeed, to the existence of any specific objects at all. In Frege's sense, it might be possible for this relationship to be the relationship it is even if there were no objects to be so related, or knowers to know that they were so related.

For another thing, the 'next to' relation is not learned by looking at a situation and 'abstracting' something from it, as Husserl implies that it is. The epistemological source of understanding a relationship like being 'next to' is pure thought about the meanings of terms or contents of concepts, not experience. As Frege correctly observed, the role of definitions is not given its due in a presentational account of math and logic.

For a third thing, the necessity of the relationship, its very self-evidence, is a property of it that experience does not and cannot give. The self-evidence of the implication is a logical function of the de dicto, definitional meaning of 'next to', independently of whether any things ever were next to each other in experience or not.

Consequently, the metaphysical, epistemological and logical independence of any relationship from any experience seems to require that judgments about concepts be located in some independent 'mental space', as Frege located them in his third realm. I have located them in y-type thinking processes. I think that my move segregates them nicely from experiences in genesis and nature, without isolating them all together in a Fregian third realm. As I mentioned previously, in opposition to Frege, I find disembodied thoughts that no one has and no one ever will think, a bit fishy, at best.

Thus, my conclusion on Husserl's attempt at experientializing logic is that this task, like Stalnaker's attempt at logicizing experience, fails. In my estimation, neither project is worth attempting. Logic and experience are not the same in nature. Logic is a y-type thinking process, which together with other concept, definition, and relationship-oriented thinking processes, can only be understood in its own syntactic and de dicto terms. Perception, in contrast, is intentional, particular, de re, semantical, and closely tied to experience.

My analysis of the interaction of x and y type thinking processes insures that Husserl's concern for the applicability of logical structures to empirical data will be preserved. But the conceptual autonomy of x and y-type thinking processes also allays Frege's concern that logic should not be conflated with experience or psychology.

Summary: Objects

This concludes my exposition of my account of an object. In the last few chapters I have expanded the concept of an object as an experiential posit, showing what it is not by contrasting it with other similar ideas, and explaining what it is in some detail. I have also demonstrated some of the consequences of this notion of an object for theories of language and theories of logic. Finally, I have shown how my analysis of an object stakes out the normative middle ground between two opposing types of mistakes, the logicizing of experience and the experientializing of logic.

I will now turn to a more general discussion of the relationship between the x and y type thinking processes. This, more general discussion will demonstrate both why the y-type thinking processes cannot be viewed as wholly independent of the experiential domain, as Quine thought they could, and how the x-type thinking processes fill the gaps in the y, that Quine and Plato chased after a third man trying to fill.

Chapter 9

Relation Between X-type and Y-type Thinking Processes

The Difference between the Processes and the Difference it makes

Throughout this book I have been claiming that x and y type thinking processes are fundamentally different; they have differing roles, structures, and goals, and they deal with data arising from differing sources. Both are needed for human thinking to take place, and most cases of human thinking are a mixture of both. But, they can be distinguished from each other for purposes of analysis, and it is necessary so to distinguish them to understand how each works independently, before one can understand how they work in combination. The following boxes summarize some of the main differences between x and y type thinking processes.

The X			
Structures	Data Sources	Products	Goals
intentional causation (world-to mind)	semantic identification (de re)	semantics	giving meaning to terms and names
object positing (mind-to world)	Direct experience (de re)	objects and subject matters	understanding experience

The Y			
Structures	Data Sources	Products	Goals
propositions	sentences, language use (de dicto)	syntax	standardizing thoughts
Logical operators and inferences	Abstract concepts, and definitions (de dicto)	Logical schemata and systems	sorting and interrelating thoughts

As I have described these thinking processes, they interact with one another. For instance, Pylyshyn's liquid dynamics students are importing highly systematized, y-type knowledge of liquid movement into their object-positing activity when they correctly ascertain fluid constancy levels in a perceptual scene. And, conversely, good physics must be an analysis *of* motion in experience, not of some de dicto clear definition of motion, that is, nevertheless, irrelevant to reference to de re experience.

But the domains of the x and the y-type thinking processes are also, in a sense, autonomous of each other and neither is reducible to the other. The autonomy of each domain is apparent from the fact that each contains certain data that belongs exclusively within its own area. For instance, unarticulatable experience, such as mystical insight, is exclusively x-type data, whereas impossible mathematical constructions, such as those of topology, are specifically y-type constructions.

In a mechanical sense, the connection between the x and y-type thinking processes might occur, as Quine described it, through the existential quantifier of symbolic logic. A conceptual system can admit the existence of objects by accepting either constants or variables that range over the names or senses of those objects in someone's x-type thinking processes. Conversely, objects or subject matters become systematized into theories by being classed into terms, sets, or sequences which are amenable to satisfying variables or constants in a given theoretical structure. Or, it might occur more simply, as sentences of ordinary language denoting things named or counted.

However, if we broaden our perspective from the mechanical connection between the x and the y, and ask what the entire thinking and knowledge structure that I have been constructing looks like, the final product will look quite different from Quine's system in some important respects. My main objections to Quine's (and, consequently, most modern analytic philosophers') view of the overall structure of knowledge and reality, are the following.

Experience Matters

Experience and Logic are not the same in nature. They differ in structure, content, sources, goals and products. Quine has achieved his apparent smooth transition from one end of his intellectual structure to the other by slaughtering the experiential domain and reducing its content to an insignificant shadow of the logical domain. I have already shown why I believe this is the case in earlier chapters of this book. But, without experience, logic has no grounding. And objects, causation and existence are all experienced phenomena. So, a logic system is sterile without an experiential basis.

Reality and Existence Matter

Reality can only impinge on knowledge at the x-thinking processes end of a knowledge system, through first person singular experience. Quine thinks that reality can alter the system through either the experiential or the logical ends of his Web of Beliefs. But, his analysis of how this occurs in the most theoretical parts of a knowledge structure chases a third man. I will argue for this position in the next chapter. There is a sense in which logical structures limn the outlines of reality, as Quine would put it. But that sense is only that logic outlines the range of possible existents. To know what exists in actuality is to have experience of it.

The Y-Domain is not Neat, Clear and Simple

Even the Y-end of the knowledge structure is not as neat and unequivocal as Quine and other analytic philosophers present it as being. Questions that have been raised about Intuitionist interpretations of mathematics, logics developed for quantum physics, and other alternate interpretations of logic, indicate that more, rather than less of the syntactic domain should be considered experientially based, and variable. I will argue for the variability of the logical domain after I argue for the claim that Quine's system chases a Third Man, in the next chapter.

My philosophical conclusion from my arguments against the above points will be that human thinking is a human product, which is essentially grounded in human experience. Platonic heaven may well exist, and humans may have some intellectual access to it. But the conceptual certitude of the platonic entities only partially affects the naturalistic thinking that humans do. The consequences, thus, of adopting my more naturalistic view of human thinking will be:

1. A re-estimation of the respective roles of logic and experience in contributing to human knowledge: Experience will re-emerge from its long eclipse by logic in twentieth century thought.

2. Radically platonic theories of knowledge, such as the current view that computers know the data that they store, or rate as persons because they can do calculus, will be discredited.[1]

3. The cognitive science commitment to syntactical structures as the only legitimate 'mental language' will have to be substantially modified to allow for kausal and imagistic experiential thinking processes.

4. Long abused sources of knowledge, such as first person singular experience, will re-emerge into the light of intellectual discourse. Behaviorism will remain a useful methodology for psychological research and treatment, but will cease to exert its current strangle hold on what can be said about thinking or about psychological states.

5. Some modesty will be imposed on the knowledge claims of human intellectuals. Rather than making universal, all-encompassing claims for what he has derived from his human logic, an intellectual will be restricted to more hedged knowledge claims, such as, a) m can be deduced from logic n with respect to point o, or b) science has compiled m from experience of n with respect to point o. The difference between my hedged knowledge claims and Quine's egotistical claim to have 'limned the ultimate structure of all reality' is a difference in how close we respectively consider human knowledge to be to omniscience. In Quine's view, omniscience is a ten on a scale on which human knowledge has reached a 9.5. In my view, omniscience is infinity on a scale on which human knowledge has achieved maybe 2.5. Of course, a disagreement about the size and range of a scale measuring all possible knowledge is outside the range of thinking or knowledge, altogether, and hence not resolvable by any intellectual process. But I think that the arguments in this book undermine the underlying premises of the arguments that claimed that some grand convergence of knowledge on a master theory of the world as the Unity of Science is immanent and inevitable. Science has a range of topics in experience for which it is an eminently successful method of inquiry. And Logic has another range of topics within which it rules supreme as methodology of analysis. But neither describes all of

---

[1]   Mary Anne Warren advocated the point of view that a robot that can do calculus could theoretically be self aware and attain personhood in 'On the Moral and Legal Status of Abortion' in *Morality in Practice*, sixth edn., ed, James Sterba, Wadsworth/Thompson Learning, Stamford CT, 2001, p. 135 .

reality, and restrictions of methodology in philosophy to either approach, or to both conjoined, are arbitrary restrictions on the task of philosophical inquiry. My point here is not to belittle the enormous achievements of science and logic, but only to advocate more humility before the complexity of reality, and more openness to experience, of both the first and second person types, than my analytical philosophical colleagues typically exhibit. Both x and y type thinking processes must be understood to understand even a simple sentence, such as 'The cat is on the mat'.

One argument that has arisen recently that points out a strong conflict, or paradox of reason, that results from ignoring the difference between the x and the y and the difference it makes is the conflict that Stephen Stich and some of his colleagues have called the 'Rationality Wars' controversy.[2] I will now turn to an analysis of this controversy to show the problems that arise when the experiential grounding of causation and statistics and the platonic grounding of logic are ignored. In this next section I will also include some brief comments on a feminist view of stressing the y-type reasoning processes at the expense of the x.

Rationality Wars, Statistics, Logic, and Platonic Transcendence[3]

The theory of mental structures and processes that I have outlined in this book can help to clarify some of the issues about rationality and what it is or isn't that have been raised among researchers in social statistics, artificial intelligence and feminist epistemology. Statistics researchers Holland, Holyoak, Nisbett and Thagard argue in *Induction*, that most of the processes that people actually use to do inductive, or causal, reasoning are not syntactical in structure, and are not reducible to a syntactical structure. They argue that the actual reasoning that people use is not irrational despite its failure to reflect accepted standards for good reasoning. Feminist epistemologist Elizabeth Minnich argues in *Transforming Knowledge*, that the preference for linear and quantifiable thinking processes that is the hallmark of the western epistemological tradition is inherently classist, racist and gender biased, as well as being a misrepresentation of the

---

[2] See Richard Samuels, Stephen Stich, and Michael Bishop, 'Ending the Rationaliry Wars: How to Make Disputes about Human Rationality Disappear', in *Common Sense, Reasoning and Rationality*, Vancouver Studies in Cognitive Science, Vol. 11, ed. Renee Elio, Oxford University Press, NY, 2002.

[3] For much of the discussion of rationality wars in this section, I thank Stephen Stich for e-mailing me his article, cited in the last footnote, before its publication, and I thank dancing buddies John Skinner and Scott West for discussions of the issues.

actual character of human knowledge. I will outline the arguments against syntactical hegemony espoused in each of these works, and follow the controversy that Holland et. al. were addressing a bit to show how my framework for thinking can accommodate the broader views of knowledge presented by these authors.

Induction

Holland, Holyoak, Nisbett and Thagard say that their conception of induction requires that inductive processes be viewed as pragmatic problem solving devices. They understand inductive processes as operating dynamically in both what I have called a world-to-mind direction and in a mind-to-world direction. Specifically, these authors say:

> ... [Our] central assumptions are that induction is (a) directed by problem solving activity, and (b) based on feedback regarding the success or failure of predictions generated by the system. The currently active goals of the system, coupled with an activated subset of the system's current store of knowledge, provide input to inferential mechanisms that generate plans and predictions about the behavior of the environment. The predictions are fed back to other inferential mechanisms along with receptor input. We use the words 'receptor input' in a broad sense to include not only perceptual representations of the environment, but also information about the internal states of the system (for example, detection of needs or, even, contradictory inferences.) A comparison of predictions and receptor input will yield information about predictive successes and failures, which will in turn, trigger specific types of inductive changes in the knowledge store.[4]

Obviously, these authors see the mental condition of a system, whether human or machine, as a dynamic interrelationship in which the system is processing information about itself and its environment (x's for thought) in terms of statistical predictions based on prior conceptualization, which is largely inductively learned, and not innate in syntax, as Chomsky would have it. Further, the system is modifying its reasoning rules and conceptual structures to accommodate the feedback that it is receiving from the environment (r's, which become x's once conceptualized.)

Holland et al. describe the mental restructuring of concepts that takes place in inductive reasoning this way.

> Rather than simply applying operators to a fixed problem representation, the representation itself may be transformed by re-categorizing

---

[4]   John Holland, Keith Holyoak, Richard Nisbett and Paul Thagard, *Induction, Processes of Inference, Learning and Discovery*, MIT Press, Cambridge, MA 1989, p. 9.

problem components and by retrieving associations and analogies. Such restructuring implies that search takes place not only in the space of potential 'next states' along a temporal dimension, but also through the space of alternative categorizations of the entities involved in the problem.[5]

Both the role and the variability of what I have called point of view in creating and sustaining thinking processes is stressed in this passage.

Indeed, the entire system of thinking rules constitutes a modifiable 'mental model', much like a Kantian schema, which is arranged into a hierarchy of rules, according to Holland et. al. Other rules, as well as feedback from the environment can be used to modify the hierarchy, should this seem necessary to the system's goals at any time. Rules, as well as categories, are both created and modified using data or feedback from the environment. The formation of rules and corresponding categories follows a structure that the authors call a quasi-morphism, which is a refined and technical version of the mental process of r's converting into x's that I discussed in my analysis of kausation. In the Holland et. al. version of induction, a transition function interacts with categorizations of data to produce a mental model of the environment. Progressive repetitions of the interaction of the model's predictions with the environment, bring about progressive modifications in the model.[6]

Holland et al. have constructed computer models that computationally implement an inductive system like the one that I described as operating in kausation, and while they admit that they must use syntactical computer structures to construct the system, they point out that the y-type syntactical elements in their system are dynamically modified as needed by the current transformation of data interpretation taking place in a quasi-morphism. Their system is bottom up, and would agree with Quine's ontological relativity thesis that no rule is unrevisable, given sufficiently incommensurate experience.

Hence, according to these authors, even computer operations, to be adaptive and useful, must include input from an environment. I have argued elsewhere in this book that mere data input to a computer cannot be equivalent to human experience, and so can not develop a full x-type reasoning process. But these authors are pointing out the inadequacies of purely syntactical reasoning processes to run even an adaptive and learning computer. In the Three Prisoner's Paradox we will see why input to a computer from the environment,

[5] *Ibid.*, p. 11–12.

[6] *Induction*, pp. 34–35.

whether it is statistical or logical, can only simulate, and not dupli-
cate what humans get from experience.

The Three Prisoners' Paradox Statistics, Logic or Practical Reason?

Massimo Piatelli-Palmarini, Ruma Falk, and other cognitive scientists have recently been discussing a problem that is sometimes
called the Monty Hall problem, for the three doors in the guessing
game show, and is sometimes called the three prisoners' paradox,
for a description of the problem in terms of three prisoners. The
problem invites a reader to determine whether the probability of
success for a possibly pardoned prisoner or a game show contestant
improves or changes when the prisoner or contestant gains new
information. I'll give Ruma Falk's three prisoners version of the
problem here for discussion.

> Tom, Dick and Harry are awaiting execution while imprisoned in sepa-
> rate cells in some remote country. The Monarch arbitrarily decides to
> pardon one of the three. The decision who is the lucky one has been
> determined by a fair draw. He will be freed, but his name is not immedi-
> ately announced and the warden is forbidden to inform any of the pris-
> oners of his fate. Dick argues that he already knows that at least one of
> Tom and Harry must be executed, thus convincing the compassionate
> warden that by naming one of them he will not be violating his instruc-
> tions. The Warden names Harry. Thereupon Dick cheers up, reasoning:
> 'Before, my chances of a pardon were only 1/3; now only Tom and
> myself are candidates for a pardon, and since we are both equally likely
> to receive it, my chance of being freed has increased to 1/2.
>
> Suppose, however, that the Warden had named Tom. By the same rea-
> soning, this piece of information would be equally encouraging to Dick.
> It looks like, whoever the warden names, Dick's chances are affected
> favorably. In fact, just imagining the interchange with the warden
> would have the same effect . . . Can all this be true? More than that, the
> warden need not actually exist. Just a thought experiment on Dick's part
> involving a *hypothetical warden* would raise Dick's probability of sur-
> vival. What is true for Dick, however, is valid for Tom and Harry as well,
> so that each prisoner's probability of going free is raised to 1/2, thereby
> violating the requirement for the sum of probabilities of all elementary
> events in a discrete sample space.[7]

Falk, and many other analysts of this problem see it as a problem
arising from the fact that most people are too unskilled in probability
mathematics to realize that the *correct* answer to the problem is the
answer given by the application of Bayes's Law to the problem,

---

[7]   Ruma Falk, 'A Closer look at the Probabilities of the notorious three prisoners',
       Cognition, Vol. 43, pp. 198, 1992.

which will result in Dick still having only a 1/3 chance of being the spared prisoner after he's received new information, while Tom's chances of being the spared one have risen to 2/3, absorbing all of the former 2/3 probability of either Tom or Harry being spared.

Piatelli-Palmarini agrees with Falk that it is simply poor, pre-probability theory reasoning on the part of intellectually untrained people that results in the 'mistaken' thinking pattern by which Dick believes that his chances of survival have risen to 1/2. Both authors trace such mistaken thinking patterns to the enlightenment blindness about inductive reasoning that infected such otherwise brilliant minds as Hume and LaPlace. Piatelli-Palmarini concludes that the problem is not a real paradox, like the truth paradoxes of set theory, but is simply correctable erroneous reasoning due to ignorance.[8]

I think that the problem is a real paradox of rationality, pitting x-type reasoning processes against y-type reasoning processes, in a situation in which the two methods of approach will yield different results as the 'correct' answer. First, I will present the alternate analyses of the problem, and then I will discuss why I see the problem as a true paradox of rationality.

The Logical Purist's Solution

First, let's look at the problem from the perspective of a logical purist, who thinks that reasoning must follow the laws of symbolic logic to rate as rational. Noam Chomsky, for example, believes that all thinking involves innate syntactical structures that embody language and accurately reflect the world. Jay Rosenberg believes that there is a structural isomorphism between the structure of symbolic logic and the structure of reality. For either author the True/False sortal system is adequate to describe any first-order real world situation, and use of symbolic logic to comprehend reality **is** rationality. These authors will agree with Bertrand Russell that semantics is reducible to syntax in a logic system. How will symbolic logic approach the three prisoners' problem?

The three prisoners' problem becomes a derivation of statements from other statements, all of which can be true or false. What Dick learns from the warden is that one component of a possibly true disjunctive statement is false.

Dick will be pardoned, or Tom will be pardoned or Harry will be pardoned. 1. [(D v T) v H]

[8]   Massimo Piatelli-Palmarini, *Inevitable Illusions*, John Wiley and Sons, Inc, NY 1994, pp. 159–169

The Warden: 'It's not Harry' 2. ~ H

From 1 & 2, Dick can conclude 3. (D v T)

The applicable rule is disjunction elimination, and the key word in the rule is **elimination**. 'Harry will be pardoned' is proven **false**. H ceases to be an issue under consideration, altogether. H has no residual value to transfer anyplace, and if it did, there would certainly be no reason to transfer the residual value to Tom rather than to Dick.

Having eliminated Harry as the potential pardonee, there are only two possible pardonees remaining as candidates for the pardon: Dick and Tom. Since either ~ D or ~ T will equally leave the statement (D v T) true, but at least one of them must be true to make the statement true, (D v T) is a 50/50 toss-up, from line three of the argument until ~ D or ~ T turns out to be true. Only the execution of one of the prisoners will change the 50/50 odds of (D v T) in line 3. This reasoning is a consequence of how disjunction rules work in logic. The logical purist's line of reasoning is good logic, not poor statistics.

The Statistician's Version

Using Bayes's law, the statistician, in contrast, assigns 1/3 chance of pardon, initially to each prisoner. This means that Dick has 1/3 chance of survival at the outset, while Harry and Tom together have 2/3 chance. The elimination of Harry from the pool of potential pardonees does not redistribute either the total probability, or Harry's unusable portion thereof equally among the remaining candidates. Rather, the elimination of Harry from the pool gives his entire share of the probability of a pardon to Tom. So, Tom benefits from Harry's exclusion, but Dick does not.

Computer models running large numbers of trials for this type of situation show that Tom wins the pardon 2/3 of the time, (or the game show contestant wins by switching doors 2/3 of the time), so the statisticians can demonstrate, on large runs, at any rate, that the Bayes's solution to the problem produces a higher probability of success.

The Evolutionary Psychologist's Solution

Evolutionary psychologists add another spin to the issue, by insisting that the mind is modular, and that independent units of evolutionarily developed thinking mechanisms perform different thinking tasks.[9] So, logical reasoning mechanisms, statistical reasoning mechanisms, and various locally effective but mathematically wrong mechanisms, might all be just different ways to approach a

---

[9]   see Samuels, Stich and Bishop, *op. cit.*

problem, and one should not be surprised to find that different results are reached depending on which method of approach is used to address an issue. The evolutionary psychologists acknowledge that methodologies must be domain-specific, and argue that there still is a right and a wrong way to use any given heuristic, once the environment has been properly taken into account.

So, which approach is more rational, the logical purists, the statisticians or the evolutionary psychologists? The logicians say (D v T) is a toss up, while the statisticians say T is a rational winner. The evolutionary psychologists say both the reasoning modules and the environment have to be taken into account to determine what the rational thing to do is.

Issues to Sort out

Epistemological or Metaphysical Parameters?

One issue that is clearly relevant to the discussion is the question of the relation of the above problem to parameters delimiting someone's knowledge or to parameters delimiting possibilities for reality. Logicians are typically interested only in possibilities delimiting all possible realities, especially with respect to whether a claim is true or false, and not at all in what someone knows or doesn't know. So, new information has modal metaphysical, not existential epistemic import. The statisticians and evolutionary psychologists, in contrast, are taking point of view seriously as a parameter, and considering new information a shift in that parameter. This gives the statisticians and evolutionary psychologists more than a two-sortal T/F grid with which to work, and puts their work partially on the object-positing side of mental operations. This is especially clear in the case of the evolutionary psychologists, who specify that the entire rubric can not be understood without reference to the environment. The logician's analysis, in contrast, is exclusively a y type reasoning process. The fact that different conclusions are reached depending on which type of reasoning process one uses indicates that neither process can be used in a hegemonic way, ignoring the fact that other thinking tools are available. As Putnam and Hume had previously pointed out, reality does not come equipped with a manual of instructions directing users about what they should count, or how they should count it. So, although mathematics may be platonically pure, the use of mathematical principles is not.

One attempt at a solution to this dilemma is presented in 'Domain specific reasoning: social contracts, cheating and perspective change', by Gerd Gigerenzer and Klaus Hug.[10] Gigerenzer and Hug argue that the types of inductive reasoning that operate in a bottom-up way use principles that reach different results from those that a logical purist would reach using only the principles of symbolic logic. In particular, Gigerenzer and Hug point out that conditional inference rules from symbolic logic are regularly violated by people who see themselves as making judgments based on what the authors call a 'cheating detection algorithm'.

Rather than concluding that the test subjects using the cheating detection algorithm were poor logicians, or good statisticians, Gigerenzer and Hug conclude from their research that domain specific reasoning is more appropriate in many contexts, and that the subject matter content, which has long been ruled irrelevant by logical purists, as well as by statistical purists, is and should be the determining consideration in choosing principles to use for reasoning about a situation. Their general conclusion about the conflict between statistical and logical rules in problems like the prisoner's problem is the following.

> The general point is that there is no simple and unique division line between structure and content, or between information relevant and irrelevant to rational reasoning. What counts as the relevant structure for reasoning about a domain therefore seems to need a domain-specific theory. Thus we need to define what the relevant structural properties are – modal operators, prior probabilities, likelihoods, perspectives, cheating detection, and the like – rather than to leave this job to one out of many possible logics, usually selected by convention.[11]

Thus, these authors would agree with my analysis of the rational situation presented in this book, according to which different types of reasoning processes emerge from x-type and y-type thinking approaches, perspectives and point of view determine what may be thought within a context, and objects and kausation are both source and product of the x-type reasoning process. The platonic purity of the y-type reasoning processes cannot be superimposed on any content domain in an uncritically isomorphic way without doing violence to the inherent character of the domain. Unless the objects and kauses of experience are having an impact on the structures being used to understand them, they are badly misunderstood.

The final conclusion reached by Gigerenzer and Hug is that both statisticians and logicians are being unreasonable in insisting on the correctness of the principles of their disciplines in resolving prob-

[10]   Gerd Gigerenzer and Klaus Hug, 'Domain Specific Reasoning: Social Contracts, cheating and perspective change', in *Cognition,* vol. 43, 1992, pp. 127–171.
[11]   *Ibid.,* p. 168.

lems like the prisoner's problem or the Monty Hall problem. Their final observation is:

> The dissociation of research on deductive and probabalistic reasoning is as obsolete as the parallels between the two programs are striking. We expect that the two fields will converge in the next few years, as a consequence of the growing role of pragmatic principles, such as perspectives, cost-benefit analyses, and cheating-detection, in both fields.[12]

While I agree that the dissociation of research between deductive and inductive reasoning processes is obsolete, I am not as sure as Gigerenzer and Hug that the programs can simply be melded, or will inevitably converge. Rather I think that the inherent differences between the two programs need to be both recognized and respected. I am more inclined to think that the relationship between the x-type and y-type reasoning processes, the Aristotelian hedonistic devil and Platonic heaven, will turn out to be more like that between the Chinese yin and yang: opposites in necessary balance, not 'wrong' contradictories of 'right solutions', whoever may have offered the result.

Statistical or Logical Social Policy?

Another issue that is often discussed in connection with the prisoners' dilemma, and that is offered as justification for the 'rightness' of the statistician's solution to the problem, is the fact that the logician's version of the problem, however intuitively plausible it may be if the choice is presented in isolation, as the prisoner's or Monty Hall choice appears in the problem, can be shown to be mathematically incorrect by multiplying cases. If Monty has 100 doors to open, or there are 1000 prisoners of whom only one will be spared, the probability of succeeding by switching the choice becomes more apparent, as Marilyn Vos Savant and Leonard Gilman both point out.[13] But the issue is really more tricky than the mathematical 'solution' suggests. Consider a somewhat parallel dilemma in utilitarian ethics that has always plagued ethical theorists.

One clear situation in which statistical risks are distributed to a large population is in social policy decisions such as determining how much cost-for-safety in a car is worth compared to the risk of law suits over unsafe automobiles. An injury-proof car could be constructed, but would be very expensive for auto-makers to build and for consumers to buy. So auto-makers calculate probable costs from

---

[12]   *Ibid.*, p. 169.

[13]   This problem is discussed by Gilman in 'The Car and the Goats', in *The American Mathematical Monthly*, vol. 99 n. 1, Jan 1992, pp. 3–7.

lawsuits for unsafe cars, and probable costs of preventing those deaths, and spend the lesser amount on safety for cars. The inevitable result is horrible deaths or injuries for some individuals from lack of safety in cars. The justification is that the cost of preventing those deaths exceeds the cost of paying lawsuits on them, and the auto-makers figure that they will come out financially ahead by allowing those deaths. Many decisions about social policy, by businesses or by governments follow this pattern.

Points of view become essential in analyzing this problem. For, from the point of view of the victims of the unsafe cars, nothing justifies the negligence of the auto-makers in deliberately producing unsafe vehicles. They are in a position of becoming individual victims of a bad statistical draw. In a parallel way, in the prisoners' dilemma, whether Dick's chances of being pardoned are 1/2 or 1/3 will make little difference to Dick if he in fact does not receive the pardon. These victims of circumstance will suffer such devastating individual consequences of their poor draw that, to them, the notion that their fate was 'justified' by large numbers of cases will seem perverted reasoning in the extreme. Their personal status as dispensable minorities will to them appear to cast them as sacrificial victims to someone else's benefits. This type of argument has long been raised against the type of utilitarian ethical reasoning that cost–-benefit and risk–benefit analyses represent. Hence, Kant adopts a Platonic, logical, universal categorical imperative in ethics renouncing any value for experiential or x-type information in deciding on ethical policies.

In the context of the prisoners' dilemma, this ethical discussion reveals a truth that I discussed in Chapter 5 in connection with statistical reasoning. Individual conclusions cannot be legitimately drawn from statistical analyses, and what individual results do turn up are quite capricious and only peripherally related to the large numbers that supposedly 'justify' them. All of this is far too sloppy for logical purists, of course, and one might say that it is so for good reasons. Logicians, whether of the ethical or simply analytical type, squirm at the notion that individuals become capriciously derivable or dispensable because a large number analysis deems them so. So, while the statistician's proof of the plausibility of the mathematics presented by many runs of the prisoners' dilemma may be good math, there are still questions to be raised about how this piece of reasoning would rate as logic or ethics. Again, the x-type subject matter content is far from irrelevant to the judgment of appropriateness of the y-type reasoning principles used to analyze it.

Feminist Objections to Platonism about Rationality

Feminists have also objected that there is a gender and class bias built into the western epistemological tradition's preference for abstract forms and mathematical structures in reasoning. In a society in which women were denied access to education, and confined to work involving repetitive, daily, tasks, the exultation of abstract reasoning became a circular justification for consigning women to daily, repetitive, and menial work. For, women were said to do menial chores because they were incapable of doing abstract reasoning, and of acquiring education, and to be unworthy of education and power because they did menial chores and were uneducated.[14] Minnich calls the resulting hierarchy of levels of mental value an 'hierarchically invidious monism', according to which, only one type of person rates as really human; the man who does abstract reasoning. Women and slaves were cast as 'embodied', 'mired in matter', stuck in concrete reality, and therefore, subhuman in comparison to the transcendent Platonic man who overcame his situated particularity and dwelt in the realm of the forms.

The resulting legacy of social injustices is, in itself, a reason to rethink the conception of rationality predicated on Platonism, even if the internal incoherence of Platonism were not sufficient to motivate rethinking it.

Summary

In this chapter I have argued for the difference between the x and the y type reasoning processes, and the difference it makes. The paradoxes, confusions and controversies that I have mentioned in this chapter all clearly need more attention and more work than they have been receiving in the philosophical and intellectual world. I hope that this brief indication of some of the tangles that come from confusing the difference between these thinking processes and misunderstanding their relationship to each other will motivate more attention to the x and the y and the relationship between them.

In the next chapter I will fulfill my long overdue promissory note to analyze why exclusively y-type reasoning processes in symbolic logic systems are no better off with respect to Plato's third man paradox than Plato was.

---

[14] Minnich, Elizabeth, *Transforming Knowledge*, Temple University Press, Philadelphia, PA, 1990, p. 87 f.f.

Chapter 10

The Third Man

Plato's Third Man; a Regress of 'Being'

In the *Parmenides*, Plato presents Parmenides and Socrates in a discussion of the difficulty with the idea of the Forms that came to be called the third man problem. Parmenides asks Socrates,

> How do you feel about this? I imagine your ground for believing in a single form in each case is this. When it seems to you that a number of things are large, there seems, I suppose, to be a certain single character which is the same when you look at them all; hence you think that largeness is a single thing.

> True, Socrates replied.

> But now, take largeness itself and the other things which are large. Suppose you look at all these in the same way in your mind's eye, will not yet another unity make its appearance — a largeness by virtue of which they all appear large?

> So it would seem.

> If so, a second form of largeness will present itself, over and above largeness itself and the things that share in it, and again, covering all these, yet another, which will make them all large. So, each of your forms will no longer be one, but an indefinite number.[1]

This problem arises, in my estimation, because Plato's theory of predication makes 'being' or 'existence' a property of a concept. This comes about in the theory of Forms because concepts are what is real for Plato, while occupants of experience like tables, chairs and people are imitations of the real. Later in the *Parmenides*, and also in the *Sophist*, Plato struggles with 'the being of not-being'. There Plato questions how it can be true to say of something that it does not exist. It follows from the theory of the Forms that one is asserting the existence of some entity whose nature is non-being; obviously a problem.

---

[1] Plato, *The Parmenides*, in *The Collected Dialogues of Plato*, eds. Edith Hamilton and Huntington Cairns, Princeton University Press, Princeton, New Jersey, 1961, Par. 131 e -132 b, p. 926.

The solution to the dilemma is to see that Plato has the realm of reality and the realm of possibility reversed. The conceptual realm is a playground for possibilities, not a demarcation of the real. Reality is experience, first person singular contact with trees, people, and other intentional objects. The problem of the 'being' of concepts, then evaporates.

For, distinctions made with respect to existence within the y domain do not, then, circularly, become analyses of the status of a y-entity with respect to itself. Rather, existence questions refer, externally, to the referent of some y concept as it picks out an experience in the x domain. A statement of the non-existence of a unicorn is not, circularly, an assertion of the non-existence of an analytically existent Form. Rather it is a comment on a concept that describes a possibility, asserting that this particular, internally lucid concept, nevertheless, fails to have a concrete x-type correlate to which it could refer.

The regress problem for Plato also arises even for the postulation of a number or a unit, if these are to be circularly defined as denizens of a Fregian third realm. Parmenides also points out to Socrates, that even 'the one', postulated as a platonic form for unity, is problematic.

> Therefore, any 'one that is' is a whole, and also has parts.
>
> Again, take each of these parts of the one being — its unity and its being. Unity can never be lacking to the part 'being' nor being to the part 'unity'. Thus, each of the two parts, in its turn, will possess both unity and being; any part proves to consist of at least two parts, and so on forever, by the same reasoning. Whatever part we arrive at always possesses these two parts, for a 'one' always has being, and a being always has unity. Hence, any part always proves to be two and can never be one.
>
> In this way, then, what is 'one being' must be unlimited in multitude.[2]

In my analysis, the statement that 'the one has being' is not, circularly, a statement that a concept 'one' has as a part another concept, 'being', and that each of these concepts requires the property 'being' in order to be said to be. Rather, 'one has being' means that the concept 'one' is applicable to experience, say in counting one pen. Plato is, of course, right to place numbers in general, including 'one' in the realm of the Forms. But the need to see a recursive counting system as playing with possibilities, rather than citing realities, becomes especially apparent if one considers that numbers like zero and the square root of two are justified, not by things they mark, but by roles

---

[2]   Plato, *The Parmenides*, 142,d,e, in *Plato, The Collected Dialogues*, eds. Edith Hamilton and Huntington Cairns, Bollingen Foundation, Princeton University Press, Princeton, New Jersey, 1973, p. 936.

that they can play in a recursive system of concepts. In this way, I can, but Plato can't, say that '0' is a valuable number because of the role that it plays in a recursive system, without asserting the existence of 'nothing.'

By claiming that reality is the intentional experience that a human has of trees, tables, and other people, I keep questions of existence in their proper place. The realm of concepts is autonomous of the realm of the real, in the sense that impossible and non-existent entities can be conceived, as well as possible worlds which are radically different from the actual world. And in a qualified sense, these possible worlds can be said to be; that is, as possibilities. But questions about the existence of these conceptual will-of-the-wisps are always about their relationship to experience. Questions about their relationships to further, more abstract, ideation can, of course, be asked, but they are not questions about existence, in the straightforward sense that Plato supposed they were.

Likewise, I believe that more modern platonists have caught themselves in logical labyrinths by trying to define concepts as existents, or to define the entire conceptual realm as reality. I will now briefly summarize a discussion by Alexander Rosenberg of Mackie's and Shoemakers' respective accounts of causal laws as conditional propositions, both of which exhibit the third man regress that any platonic account of those laws will generate.

The Third Man in a Counterfactual-Conditional Account of Causation; a Regress of Powers and Properties

Most recent attempts at reducing kausation to a platonic entity have featured some variation of an analysis of causes that claims that causes are counterfactual conditional statements. These analyses claim that causes are propositions with a counterfactual conditional syntax; hence, they fit in a system of symbolic logic and are reducible to the laws of physics and mathematics.

In an article entitled 'Mackie and Shoemaker on Dispositions and Properties', Alexander Rosenberg points out the circularity that is endemic in this type of account.

> If properties are clusters of causal powers, and if causal powers are properties, then causal powers are, themselves, clusters of causal powers. In spite of the circularity of the relations among properties and causal powers, it may be hoped that causal powers could be graded along a dimension of more and more generality and fundamentality. After all, properties will be those entities denoted by the predicates of causal laws, and if causal laws reflect an axiomatic hierarchy, then we may well be

able to read off not only the causal powers that there are from the laws, but also, how they cluster to generate the properties that they constitute. Thus, there will be a descent of causal powers until we reach the properties mentioned in the ultimate, unexplained, laws of physics. If Shoemaker is correct, these properties will have to be dispositional, because all properties are. On the other hand, they cannot themselves be composed of further causal powers, more fundamental than they are, for they are the properties related to the most fundamental laws of physics.[3]

In this article, Rosenberg is arguing that Mackie's interpretation of the nature of a causal property does a better job than Shoemaker's of rendering the circularity cited in this passage less vicious. But, from my point of view, any attempt at patching up a platonic, property-oriented analysis of causation is equivalent to sticking a band-aid on massive, internal hemorrhaging. No platonic analysis of the nature of a 'causal power' is going to succeed in escaping the eternal regress of explanations described above by Rosenberg.

No platonic account of a causal power can exit this regress because, like Plato, these philosophers have construed all existence as concepts; causation is a counterfactual conditional proposition, causal powers are properties, the relationship between the two is the entailment relationship of symbolic logic, and all of the above are ultimately reducible to the equations of physics. But, as I pointed out in the Causation Chapter, these folks have missed 1) the intentionality of kausation, 2) the logical opacity of causal contexts, and 3) the objects named in kausal object-positing, which have evaporated all together from counterfactual conditional accounts.

As Rosenberg describes the progress of the regress of explanations, explanations and properties become more 'fundamental' as they approach the mathematical purity of laws of physics. But he points out that, even once there, a stopping point has not been reached. The reason for this is our by now familiar third man. When concepts are used to explain concepts, further concepts must always be generated to explain the explanatoriness of the last concept. An exit from the circle must move *out* of the realm of concepts, altogether; into experience. The laws of physics are not more 'fundamental' than other concepts, they are merely more abstract and mathematical.

Rosenberg observes that Mackie believes that the way out of the circle is to claim that every dispositional property '. . . has an occurrent categorical base in manifest, non-dispositional properties',[4]

---

[3]   Alexander Rosenberg, 'Mackie and Shoemaker on Dispositions and Properties', in *Midwest Studies in Philosophy IX 1984, Causation and Causal Theories, op. cit.*, p. 85.

[4]   *Ibid.*, p. 90.

which are identified in a Kripkean way; 'The identity criteria for a kind give the essences of its members, . . . they express necessary truths about the kind and its members.'[5]

Both Kripke and Mackie seem to think that this move gets them into de re reference to experience and out of the realm of concepts, but as I argued against Kripke in an earlier chapter, more radical surgery is needed. Kripke is still playing with possible worlds, in a way that is pre-semantic. Rosenberg points out that even Mackie saw the problems that I have claimed arise with respect to Kripke's failure to achieve reference and identification of essences and kinds. Rosenberg quotes Mackie as saying:

> These de re modalities are, in a very broad sense, de dicto after all. Though these necessities apply to individual things and natural kinds . . . that they do so is primarily a feature of the way we think and speak, of how we handle identity in association with counter-factual possibility . . . [6]

Mackie, thus, sees the problems that his account of the 'occurrent categorical base' for causal properties will have, but fails to see that he has really not done much better than a dispositional properties theorist in exiting the regress. Rosenberg seems to agree with me on this point, but he also seems to despair of doing better.

Again, concepts have modal properties, experience and reality do not. Kausation is an aspect of experience, and any syntactic model of kausation will lose its essential features: intentionality and object-positing, substituting y-type features for the eliminated x-type ones. But, it is exactly the x-type thinking process that is needed to index kausation. Mackie, Shoemaker, and Kripke are all chasing a third man in seeking real kausation in possible worlds.

So, in a platonic account of causation, as in a platonic account of existence, the third man strikes again. But the problem is more endemic in platonic world views than these two examples would indicate. I will now turn to a brief summary of some arguments[7] for the claim that any logical/mathematical conceptual system that purports to account for the structural properties of all reality is, likewise, a victim of the third man. Quine will be my hostile witness for the prosecution, but the problem is not restricted to Quine's particular version of a logical system. Quine is just my best witness, because he is most clear and honest about the beliefs to which his logical system commits him.

---

[5]   *Ibid.*, p. 87.

[6]   *Ibid.*, p. 89.

[7]   from my Master's thesis, Syracuse University, 1979.

The Third Man in a Logical System: a Regress of Metatheories

Willard V.O. Quine believes that he has shown, in works like *Word and Object* and *Philosophy of Logic,* how science, mathematics and formal logic constitute a comprehensive intellectual structure for 'limning the true and ultimate structure of reality.'[8] He believes that his structure is like a self-rebuilding ship, that is organically organized, and tied to reality at both ends: the empirical end represents observation and experience, while the logical end represents broadly logical, platonic truths. At the empirical end, the existential quantifier and satisfaction relations ensure that only objects which will fit the structure of the system may enter, and conversely, the object-positing capacity of the structural system ensures that all needed objects will be posited.

In this book I have been agreeing with the mechanics of the Quinean view of how object-positing and theoretical structures interrelate through the existential quantifier. My disagreement with Quine, in the beginning of the book, over his commitment to behaviorism and his rejection of most x-type data, pointed out, however, that his anemic view of object-positing is too sickly to perform the mechanics he proposes.

At the logical end of Quine's system, however, I believe he has himself entangled in the same third man problem that we have already seen in Plato and in counterfactual conditional accounts of causation. Quine believes that a 'proxy function' can enable him to anchor broadly logical truths on to reality at the most abstract end of his system, by tying structures in one theory onto structures in another, 'background theory'. He believes that proxy functions and background theories can be used to explain one theory in terms of another, while avoiding an infinite regress of theories, or reduction of all theories to numbers, as in Pythagoreanism.

Since Quine's third man problem affects entire structures of logical/mathematical systems, the conclusion that will be drawn from this argument will be that all y-type thinking processes are similarly affected by regress problems. Hence, y-type thinking processes do not 'limn the true and ultimate structure of reality,' or establish a world of 'being' to oppose to our shadow world of 'becoming'. Rather, Frege's third realm, Plato's heaven, and Quine's system of symbolic logic describe possible worlds. Reality is only to be met with in experience.

---

[8]   W.V.O. Quine, *Word and Object,* MIT Press, Cambridge, Mass., 1960, p. 231.

'Reality-Anchoring' Structures in Quine's System and Why They are Needed

To begin analyzing Quine's third man problem, I have to explain the structures that he believes can stave off this problem for him in his system. For each theoretical structure that Quine discusses, and for each place in a theoretical structure that is marked by a constant or a variable, Quine offers an account of a relationship that exists either between that structural item and reality or between that structural item and some other theoretical structure.

When the theoretical structure under consideration is a symbolized canonical paraphrasing of a sentence, the relationships in terms of which it is to be understood are:

1. Reference: Which ties the paraphrased item to reality, and

2. Translation: Which ties the paraphrased item to other theories.

When the theoretical structure under consideration is an open sentence in canonical notation, the relationships in terms of which the structure is to be understood are:

1. Satisfaction: Which ties the open sentence to reality, and

2. Validity: Which ensures the consistency of an open sentence with the rest of its home theory.

When the object-positing structures of theories are considered most generally, the relationships in terms of which they are to be understood are:

1. Translation through a Proxy Function: Which connects the object-positing structure in an object language or theory to an object-positing structure in a background language, and

2. Modeling: Which relates an object-positing structure in one theory to those of another theory, which need not be a background theory.

Quine cites the parallel nature of these relationships in this passage.

> Regress in ontology is reminiscent of the now familiar regress in the semantics of truth and kindred notions – satisfaction, naming. We know from Tarski's work how the semantics, in this sense, of a theory regularly demands an in some way more inclusive theory. This similarity should perhaps not surprise us, since both ontology and satisfaction are matters of reference. In their elusiveness, at any rate – in their emptiness now and again except relative to a broader background – both truth and ontology may in a sudden rather clear and even tolerant sense be said to belong to transcendental metaphysics.[9]

---

[9]   W.V.O. Quine, 'Ontological Relativity', in *Ontological Relativity and Other Essays*, Columbia University Press, New York, 1969, pp. 67–68.

The emptiness that Quine attributes to these structures results, however, not from the fact that they belong to 'transcendental metaphysics', but rather from the fact that they are circular and regressive as he has described them. He, like Plato, Mackie, and Shoemaker, is looking for reality in the wrong place; in further, more abstract ideation rather than in experience.

First, let's look at how Quine believes that reference, satisfaction, and translation through a proxy function can tie his theoretical structures to reality, while translation into other theories, validity and modeling ensure smooth intertheoretic transitions.

Semantic Ascent through Primary 'Reality Anchors'; Reference, Satisfaction, and Translation through a Proxy Function

Quine's accounts of reference, satisfaction, and translation through a proxy function all are presented against the background of his famous theses about the inscrutability of reference and the relativity of ontology.

The referential indeterminacy thesis claims that reference is an idiosyncratic, non-translatable, passing trait of an individual's personal ontology. To evade what Quine considers the vacancy of a notion of truth that would result from the indeterminacy of reference, he proposes that reference and satisfaction can, through semantic ascent, become more concrete by becoming tied into the logical truths of a theory.

The ontological relativity thesis claims that reference to objects made by a theory is meaningless without the specification of a background theory in which the ontological commitments of the object theory are explained. The reasons for this skepticism about ontology are the indeterminacy of reference for terms, within a term's own theory and the circularity of explanations that might be offered concerning the ontological commitments of the theory inter-theoretically. To evade these problems, ontological commitments must be specified in a meta-theory, or background theory, which ties the ontology of the object theory into reality through a proxy function.

Indeterminacy Thesis

In Quine's comments about the indeterminacy of reference, he would seem to be granting me the importance of a first person singular point of view. But he grants the point only to deny its value; he thinks that truth amounts to nothing if it amounts to this, and so he looks for truth, not in the first person singular, but through 'semantic ascent' into a theoretical structure that has been sterilized of the worthless first person singular. So, from reference we must move immediately to satisfaction through semantic ascent.

Semantic Ascent

Quine describes semantic ascent in this way.

> We choose a standard grammar in which the simple sentences are got by predication and all further sentences are generated from these by negation, conjunction, and existential quantification. Predication, in this grammar, consists always in adjoining predicates to variables and not to names. So, all the simple sentences are *open* sentences, like 'x walks' and 'x is greater than y'; they have free variables. Consequently, they are neither true nor false; they are only satisfied by certain things or pairs of things or triples, etc. The open sentence 'x walks' is satisfied by each walker and nothing else.[10]

The open sentences, because they are neither true nor false but only satisfied by things or sets or sequences of things, are supposedly able to avoid the indeterminacy of reference. But Quine concedes that this ascent to logical form is a bit circular, himself.

> Already at the bottom of the tree, thus, Logic's pursuit of truth conditions encounters a complication. The relevant logical trait of negation is not just that negation makes true closed sentences out of false ones and vice versa. We must add that the negation of an open sentence with one variable is satisfied by just the things that that sentence was not satisfied by; also that the negation of an open sentence with two variables is satisfied by just the pairs that the sentence was not satisfied by; and so on.[11]

Despite this acknowledged circularity, however, Quine thinks that semantic ascent to open sentences has freed him from commitment to chancy reference, replacing it with secure predicate satisfaction. But the concession in the above passage seems to undermine the switch from denoted objects to satisfied predicates. For, if the things that the variables originally stood for must be the same ones negated in the open sentence, the machinery already has an opportunity for reality to slip away.

Satisfaction and Open Sentences

The situation becomes even worse if we consider how Quine describes the understanding of a satisfaction relationship. This, he says, is contingent only on the understanding of the predicates involved.

---

[10] W.V.O. Quine, *Philosophy of Logic*, Prentice Hall, Inc, Englewood Cliffs, New Jersey, 1970, p. 36.
[11] *Ibid.* p. 36.

The sentence consisting of 'conquered' flanked by the alphabetically i^{th} and j^{th} variables is satisfied by a sequence if and only if the ith thing in the sequence conquered the jth . . . This is what it means to say of any predication in the object language that it is satisfied by a given sequence of things. One is told this only insofar . . . as one already understands the predicates themselves.[12]

Quine thinks that he has here semantically ascended to predicates from reference to objects. But how could understanding the predicate 'conquered' assist one in knowing the meaning or truth value of a sentence without a corresponding understanding of the objects that are the referents of the quantified variables and so occur in the sequences? How would an understanding of the word 'conquered' assist one in knowing the truth value of 'Caesar conquered Gaul' without a corresponding understanding of the subjects to which 'Caesar' and 'Gaul' refer? Without such an understanding, I can't even distinguish between the two sequences <Caesar, Gaul> and <Pancho Villa, New Orleans>, much less tell which of the sequences is true and which is false.

The Truth Predicate

Quine thinks that he can evade the dilemma cited in the last paragraph through the use of a 'truth predicate.' A truth predicate asserts the existence of a Z which is a relationship between a set of ordered pairs (a sequence) and an open sentence.

Quine claims that a truth predicate, as a formal structure, can perform a type of semantic ascent that gets one focused on formal structures rather than objects. He believes, also, that the truth predicate can perform this role within the context of his one, unitary, interrelated system, while still dealing with truth paradoxes. He admits when discussing truth paradoxes,

The truth predicate is clearly the trouble spot. The inevitable conclusion is that the truth predicate, for all its transparency, and seeming triviality, is incoherent unless constricted.[13]

Any kind of truth predicate is notoriously subject to the paradoxes of truth cited by Tarski. Like the paradox of the Cretan Liar and the paradoxical truth values of a statement like 'This sentence is false,' a truth predicate must be defined *externally* to a language, in a metalanguage, in order to be able to define truth for any given language. Hence, the semantic ascent here envisioned by Quine must go *out-*

---

[12]   *Ibid.*, p. 40.

[13]   W.V.O. Quine, *Pursuit of Truth*, revised ed., Harvard University Press, Cambridge, MA, 1996, p. 83.

side the language for which it is defining truth, or it is an impractical and pointless formalization of an inevitably paradoxical statement.

Quine, however, believes that his truth predicate operates *within* his unitary system, and succeeds in bringing him from less formal simple sentences, through semantic ascent to the most abstract logical levels in his system. He thinks he can accomplish this by declaring satisfaction inductive, rather than direct, and then attaching the truth predicate to the abstract, inductive notion of satisfaction. He claims that this maneuver frees him from the exigencies of my contrast between <Caesar, Gaul> and <Pancho Villa, New Orleans> because Caesar, Gaul, Pancho Villa and New Orleans have all become abstract objects, during the induction. He explains how he thinks the inductive slide to abstract objects from Caesar, etc. solves the problem here;

> The two-place predicate 'satisfies' remains well defined in its inductive way, but a grasp of the predicate and how to use it carries no assurance of the existence of a corresponding abstract object, a corresponding set of ordered pairs. And failing such a pair set ...[the formal definition] fails to translate 'x satisfies y'. Though the satisfaction predicate is well explained even within the formal language by the recursion, it does not get reduced to the prior notation of that language. Satisfaction, and truth along with it, retain the status that truth already enjoyed under the disquotation account; clear intelligibility without full eliminability.[14]

So, the fact that the inductive definition of the sequences as abstract objects removes the reference from the real objects to abstract sequences, enables us to tie the abstract sequences to logical truths, and thus, connect the truth predicate, through logical truths to satisfaction.

Quine defines a logical truth as:

> ... one whose truth or falsity is assured by its logical structure. A sentence is logically true if only truths come of it by substitution of sentences for its simple component sentences.[15]

And he believes that the only difference between these logically true sentences and their lowly simple open counterparts is a difference between whether all sequences satisfy them, or only some or none do. He believes that a truth predicate is one of these high-level logical truths.

---

[14] *Ibid.* p. 87-88.

[15] Quine, *Philosophy of Logic,* p. 55.

Logical Truths

To maintain this position, against an argument for a claim like mine, that x and y type thinking processes are different in kind, Quine presents the following explanation.

> A logical truth, staying true as it does under all lexical substitutions, admittedly depends upon none of those features of the world that are reflected in lexical distinctions; but may it not depend on other features of the world, features that our language reflects in its grammatical constructions rather than in its lexicon? It would be pointless to protest that grammar varies from language to language, for so does lexicon. Perhaps the logical truths owe their truth to certain traits of reality which are reflected in one way by the grammar of our language, in another way by the grammar of another language, and in a third way by the combined grammar and lexicon of a third language.[16]

By this suggestion, Quine conflates truths that are a result of tautological constructions such as $(p \rightarrow p)$ to truths of empirical observation. The most empirically observational statement can lose the taint of relativity by ascending, through a truth predicate, to a more certain, 'logically true' part of its own theory, at which truth becomes universal and obvious.

Thus reference ascends to satisfaction, which becomes 'blessed' as defined in terms of the most obvious logical truths of a theory. As reality anchors, reference ties a sequence to a satisfaction relation. The satisfaction relation and the truth predicate tie simple open sentences to logical truths, all of which are intimately bound up in the most obvious general features of a theory.

Ontological Relativity Thesis

Whether a theory is then bound to reality will be a question of how the theory can be tied in to other theories, no less obvious than itself. Reference and satisfaction, through truth predicates hooking sequences on to logical truths, provide inter-theoretic reality anchors. Once those matters have been explained in terms of each other, the proxy function provides an intra-theoretic reality anchor, by explaining the ontological commitments of an object language or theory in terms of a background language or theory. Hence, ascent to a background language or theory is just one more kind of semantic ascent, in terms of which we are to explain our reference. Quine's goals for a background theory are that it should be able to;

    a)   explain the terms and ontological commitments of its object theory,

---

[16]   *Ibid.*, p. 95.

b) while reducing bloated or excessive ontologies to more economical ones,

c) without justifying the reduction of all theories to pythagoreanism, or a claim that all objects are numbers.

In order to accomplish these goals, he establishes specific criteria for a proxy function, which will be used for inter-theoretic translation.

The Proxy Function

Quine claims that all proxy functions must provide a direct one-to-one pairing of objects in the object language to objects in the background language. The purpose for this demand is to ensure that the translation is a translation of the object language, and that it preserves all important references there. Quine thinks that three levels of stringency might be imposed on a proxy function, depending on the purpose of the translation.

1. Monotheoretic Definitions: This type of translation is somewhat simple and arbitrary, because the relativity problem is somewhat trivial in this case. As long as a one-to-one paring can be established, the translation is adequate.

2. Ontological Reduction: Quine's criteria for an adequate proxy function are stricter when one ontology is to be reduced to another, via proxy function. In this case, the proxy function must be able to give an account of how the old things, in the object theory, are being reduced to the new things, in the back-ground theory.[17]

3. Non-Denumerable Set Reduction: Quine would impose very strict criteria for this type of reduction. He argues against the Lowenheim-Skolem Theorem that this simply can't be done, because no one-to-one proxy function can be established that will reduce a non-denumerable domain to a denumerable one.

Quine believes that the buck stops at level three. Semantic ascent has dragged us from reference, to satisfaction, to truth predicates, to logical truths, to proxy functions, and on to background theories. But the complexity of the circle has concealed from him the fact that he is still chasing a third man.

The Proxy Function's Dysfunction

Level one, of Quine's criteria for the proxy function, above, is relatively uncontroversial; each item in one theory is simply re-specified in terms of the background theory. Since nothing is lost or gained in

---

[17] Quine discusses this issue in 'Ontological Reduction and the World of Numbers', in *The Journal of Philosophy*, Vol. LXI, No. 7, March 26, 1964, p. 214.

the transaction, no problems arise. But when we turn to what Quine says about levels two and three, it turns out that his reality anchor won't hold.

Level two is designed to allow ontological reduction. When one theory has a bloated or excessive ontology, Quine says that the bloat can be reduced out through the proxy function. He gives an example of how this would be done in the case of an economic theory that made no capital on the numerical distinctness of persons.

> Suppose its universe comprises persons, but its predicates are incapable of distinguishing between persons whose incomes are equal. The inter-personal relation of equality of income enjoys, within the theory, the substitutivity property of the identity relation itself.[18]
>
> The proxy function would assign to each person his income. It is not one-to-one; distinct persons give way to identical incomes. The reason that such a reduction is acceptable is that it merges the identities of only such individuals as never had been distinguishable by the predicates of the original theory. Nothing in the old theory is contravened by the new identities.[19]

However, the background theory plays an important role in this type of reduction according to Quine, because;

> It is only relative to a background theory in which more can be said of personal identity than equality of income that we are able even to appreciate the above account of the fragment of economic theory, hinging, as the account does, on a contrast between persons and incomes.[20]

At this point in Quine's discussion, the role of the background theory becomes regressive. We have reduced theory A, in which there are persons, but no differentiating predicates to apply to persons of equal income, to theory B, in which there are no such persons. But, to understand either A or B or the reduction that has taken place between them, we must appeal to background theory C, in which no reduction takes place at all. Quine argues, as follows, that this regression does not represent a failure on the part of the reduction.

> If the new objects happen to be among the old so that V is a sub-class of U, then the old theory with the universe U can itself sometimes qualify as the background theory in which to describe its own ontological reduction. But we can do no better than that. We cannot declare our new ontological economies without recourse to the uneconomical old ontology.
>
> This sounds perhaps, like a predicament; as if no ontological economy is justifiable unless it is a false economy and the repudiated objects exist

---

[18]   Quine, 'Ontological Relativity', op. cit., p. 55.

[19]   *Ibid.*, p. 56.

[20]   *Ibid.*, p. 55.

after all. But actually, this is wrong. There is no more cause for worry here, than there is in reductio ad absurdum, where we assume a false-hood that we are out to disprove. If what we want to show is that the universe U is excessive, and that only part exists or need exist, then we are quite within our rights to assume all of U for the space of the argument. We show thereby, that if all of U were needed, than not all of U would be needed.[21]

So, we are to understand that the economic theory that I have called A is going to serve as a background theory for its own reduction, and that persons will be eliminated from it, as in a reductio ad absurdum argument. At the end of the argument, only theory B will remain, and it will not contain any persons.

But Quine has controverted one of his own goals for background theories in this description of a reductio ad absurdum elimination of a bloated ontology: avoiding pythagoreanism. For, if a function, Fxa, can be established between persons and incomes, why not between numbers and anything that they can count? Why not establish functions like non-identity, being within a range, or being symmetrically related to a theory? In these terms, any class of objects, whether denumerable or not, could be reduced to any one object, or any universe of objects could be reduced to any other universe of objects. And a clear account of how we had done it could be given: the function. So, if this kind of substitutability, and reduction through reductio ad absurdum works at all, it works too well. The reduction proves that all ontologies are reducible to numbers.

If we persist in trying to nail Quine down on the role of the background theory, we see that he is defending two versions of how a background theory can work in an ontological reduction. Either:

1) The background theory can be party to its own reduction, in which case there should initially be only two theories under consideration, and only one of them should be left after the reduction,

or:

2) the background theory can be party to a reduction of one subordinate theory to another, where there are three theories in consideration at first, and two remain after the reduction.

Quine says that the case of reducing the persons out of the economic theory, via reductio ad absurdum, is a case of the first type. However, he is almost certainly mistaken about this. If he has proven the non-existence of persons in the above passages at all, he has surely done so only against the background of some further language or system that recognizes the existence of persons. In fact,

[21] *Ibid.*, p. 55.

he seems to concede in the following passage that no reduction of the first type ever could take place.

> ... there is no absolute sense in speaking of the objects of a theory. It very creditably brands this pythagoreanism itself as meaningless. For there is no absolute sense in saying that all of the objects of a theory are numbers, or that they are sets, or bodies or something else; this makes no sense except relative to some background theory. The relevant predicates — 'number', 'set', 'body', or whatever — would be distinguished from one another in the background theory by the roles they play in the laws of that theory.[22]

It seems to me that if this argument against pythagoreanism works at all, it also bans a reductio argument of the type that Quine said the economic theory's reduction was, above. For, in that case, wouldn't it be true that either the reduction is meaningless because persons and incomes are distinguished in the background theory, or if the reduction gains an economy over persons, there, it could also gain economies over everything but numbers to establish pythagoreanism? So, if there is a possibility of a reduction of the first type, a genuine reductio ad absurdum reduction, it proves pythagoreanism if it proves anything.

However, a type two reduction, in which three theories are initially under consideration, and two remain at the end of the reduction, is clearly chasing a third man. For the background theory is devised to explain the object theory, and must, itself, be explained in terms of some further, yet more amorphous, background theory. No actual reduction can ever take place, because each background theory must have a more extensive ontology than its object theory. The need for a fuller ontology in the background theory is evident from the fact that either pythagoreanism is wiping away all non-numerical ontologies, or reductio ad absurdum reductions aren't happening.

Hence, my analysis of Quine's account of ontological reduction shows that he has two choices; a) pythagoreanism, or b) a regress of perpetually more amorphous background theories postulated to explain ontological commitment.

Quine still believes, however, that the buck stops with his third level of stringency on proxy functions; the level that would be needed to reduce a non-denumerable universe to a denumerable one. There, Quine simply claims that this can't be done because no one-to-one proxy function could be stated that would retain the distinctness of the objects in the non-denumerable universe through its denumerable substitutes. Also, such a reduction would require a

---

[22]   'Ontological Relativity', op. cit., p. 60.

background theory that was stronger than the theory to be reduced. He argues that the Lowenheim-Skolem theorem does not succeed on the grounds that it can cite no proxy function.

> The theorem is that all but a denumerable part of an ontology can be dropped and not be missed . . . . I see in the proof even of the strong Lowenheim-Skolem theorem no reason to suppose that a proxy function can be formulated anywhere that will map an indenumerable ontology, say the real numbers, into a denumerable one.
> On the face of it, of course, such a proxy function is out of the question. It would have to be one-to-one, as we saw, to provide distinct images of distinct real numbers; and a one-to-one mapping of an indenumerable domain into a denumerable one is a contradiction.[23]

Again, as in the reductio ad absurdum case, I don't see why ad hoc limits imposed on the system to prevent just one possibility should be accepted. Why is the absence of a one-to-one mapping fatal in this case, when it was perfectly all right to reduce persons to incomes? If a function can equate a class of separate persons to a single income, why can't a function similarly be devised that, say, equates all real numbers greater than x but less than y to a mean of x and y? If, on the one hand, we are not assuming that we have thereby disproved the existence of the unused reals, which continue to subsist in a background theory, this should not be a problem. If, on the other hand, Quine is insisting that these functions prove the non-existence of anything, via reductio ad absurdum, I would say that he is in at least as much trouble over repudiated people as he is over repudiated real numbers.

My observation on the proxy function, is thus, that it can't do what Quine wants it to do as a reality anchor. If the function allows actual reductio elimination of ontological items, it permits pythagoreanism, and the elimination of the non-denumerable reals, as well. If Quine's limits on the function prevent those reductions, then they prevent any ontological economy, and we are faced with a regress of more and more amorphous background theories at the tail end of our semantic ascent.

The Background Theory

At the outset of this journey through semantic ascent, Quine promised that we were headed toward a unitary, mathematically structured system of logical truths that outlines the true and ultimate nature of all reality. We were led to believe that our quest for reference and knowledge of what is would find a resting place in the pla-

---

[23] *Ibid.* pp. 60 - 61.

tonic heaven of logical truth. Once there, we would find an ultimate, true, and completely explanatory science. However, we have arrived, and when we knocked on the door, it was not science that answered, but the third man. What we find is another door, to another theory; one more extensive and amorphous than the last. The 'ultimate' background theory will only give us more of the same.

Indeed, general systematic considerations with which Quine readily concurs guarantee that this must be so. Quine discusses this issue when he describes his protosyntax for mathematical logic:

> Logic, like protosyntax, itself, is protosyntactically incompletable.
>   It follows, in particular, that the notion of a theorem which was developed in earlier chapters and defined protosyntactically in #58 does not accord the status of theorem to all those logical formulae which are true statements — or else, worse, that it accords the status of theorem to some falsehoods. And, as the foregoing argument shows, any alternative notion of theorem which we might devise will suffer a similar fate, so long as we insist on protosyntactical definability. Nor is the demand of protosyntactical definability easily waived; it seems already to be more liberal than the normal practical demand on constructivity — the demand that for each theorem there exist an at least fortuitously discoverable method of confirming its theoremhood.[24]

This passage looks like an open admission that any background theory for a syntactical system, i.e., any metatheory, protosyntax or metalogic, to which one could turn in semantic ascent will be more extensive and more amorphous than its object theory. The result of the ascent will always be missing truths, and provable falsehoods, brought about by the necessary incompleteness of the system. An ultimate, true structure of reality does not appear to be here to find.

In his conclusion of his discussion of incompleteness in protosyntax and in logic, Quine seems to concede this point.

> Thus, even if we go so far as to waive the demand of protosyntactical definability in order to come by a notion of logical theorem which will cover all logical truths and exclude all falsehoods, the outlook remains dark; we should have to renounce syntactical definability, as well. Indeed, a notion of theorem capable of exhausting those logical formulae which are true and excluding those which are false will be definable only in a medium so rich and complex as not to admit of a model anywhere in the reaches of the theory of logic which is under investigation.[25]

Quine sent us to this background theory looking for a reality anchor, but we have not found one. Indeed, I feel like the neophyte factory

---

[24] W.V.O. Quine, *Mathematical Logic*, revised edition, Harvard University Press, Cambridge, Mass. 1981, p. 316.
[25] *Ibid.* p. 318.

worker who gets sent to fourteen departments in search of a sky-hook; I've been had.

The Third Man in any Exclusively Y-type System

Of course, the conclusion to be reached from our fruitless search for reality in Quine's system is that y-type thinking processes cannot produce what Quine is demanding of them. The factors that give us contact with reality: experience, kausation, objects and intentionality, are not there. This claim does not deny the value of syntactically structured thinking processes. They provide all the structure and system that we have in thinking. But, it does point out that the basis for any thinking system that claims to be about the nature of reality has to be found in experience, not in systems and structures. Systems and structures can help organize x-type data, but they can also provide groundless but interesting mind games. Quine has presented us with a groundless but interesting mind game in his ascent through more and more amorphous background theories and proxy functions.

This is not a problem, as long as we remember that what we are doing is playing mind games. Y-type thinking processes are useful tools for manipulating possible worlds. But if we want them to apply to the real world, we have to make the effort of connecting them to it, through experience. Good science does this. It is neither good science nor good thinking to mistake the tool for the reality that it may, or may not, be used to describe. And, the third man is the inevitable result of confusing Frege's third realm with reality.

To conclude this chapter, I have shown here that attempts to reduce x-type thinking processes to y-type ones cannot yield an account of truth, any more than they can yield an account of reality. I will now turn to the task of establishing that the y-type realm is not as neat and unitary as many philosophers presume that it is, in any case.

Chapter 11

Is Platonic Heaven All That Pure?

The Y-Domain does not Cohere as a Monolithic, Unitary Structure, as Platonists Presume

In this section of this book, I will suggest ways in which the conclusion of the last chapter ought to be understood. In my critique of Quine, I have already pointed out that there is no overarching, unitary, completely logical/mathematical 'complete science' to be found through semantic ascent to logical forms from propositions. In this section I will indicate that not only is there no such monolithic logico-mathematical structure to which to ascend in this way, but also, what y-type thinking processes there are in the y-thinking realm are a diverse and possibly empirically effected polyglot of thinking methods and procedures, that may have little relationship to each other apart from the fact that they are all autonomous modal systems of concepts. To show the diversity of the realm, I will pick at the monolithic view of Plato's heaven from several different points of view. I will show:

A. The influence of experience on logic,

B. The possibility of alternatives to classic logic,

C. The non-equivalence of math and logic, and

D. How incompleteness and inconsistency considerations limit what can be claimed for a y-type system.

These considerations will not amount to an argument for abandoning classical logic, or even for resisting discussions of similarities and analogies among differing parts of the y-realm. But, they will recommend some humility about claims to be made for the extent and clarity of the y-domain. And they will indicate that the final arbiter of truth, or even of any definition of truth, is experience, and our success in analyzing it. Blessings from platonic heaven are not even necessary, much less sufficient for truth.

The Influence of Experience on Logic

To argue that experience has an influence on logic, I am going to pick at some of the platonic dogmas about both experience and logic that are around in the philosophical literature. First, I will argue that the psychological autonomy that Frege seeks for logic does not require metaphysical autonomy for platonic entities. It requires only a far more limited degree of autonomy that asserts only the independence of human will or decision making for the realm. Second, I will argue that platonists suffer from an overly restrictive notion of experience when they equate all learning from experience with sense perception. Third, I will argue that truth is empirical, and logic is a tool for understanding experience. As such it is, to a limited degree, capable of being honed for its task. But, should it prove wholly inadequate to a task, the correct response would be to find another tool, not to junk the task.

Psychological Autonomy does not Require Metaphysical Autonomy

I've already granted to Frege and Russell the autonomy of the third realm. But, I think that it is important to be explicit about what that means. Frege clearly meant *metaphysical* autonomy: that even if no human beings or creatures with thinking apparatus anything like ours had ever existed, still, (p ⊃ p) would be true. For Frege, the tautology was an eternal sentence that was part of cosmic reason, whether anyone ever said it in any language or not. His reason for insisting on this view of the matter was to free the tautology from human psychology; humans simply have nothing to do with its stucture or nature, although we can understand it.

I don't think that it is necessary to assert the existence of disembodied thoughts in order to achieve the autonomy of psychology that Frege rightly seeks in this case. There are lots of things about our own natures that humans neither create nor control, but merely discover if we are sufficiently attentive. For instance, humans do not choose their own sexes, heights, nutritional needs, genetic propensities to disease, eye colors, or needs for oxygen. Nor are any of these matters negotiable. Unlike personality, affective make-up, and character, these dimensions of human life are merely brute facts about the way a person is. Each of them has inevitable consequences that serve as limits on what the person can do; for instance, men are inevitably deprived of the capacity to bear a child.

Perhaps the y-thinking processes are facts about systematic thinking that parallel these types of facts about humans. They are non-psychological in the sense that they are independent of anything that humans will or control. Like bone structure, they set limits on what humans can think or do. As we cannot fly, because our bones are too heavy, so we cannot think that p does not entail p. But just as this does not imply that heavy bones are free-floating facts about the universe that would exist even if there were no animals for them to reside in, it also does not imply that (p ⊃ p) is a free-floating thought, that would exist even if there were no creatures that think. Rather, it is merely a recalcitrant fact about human thought, as opposed to negotiable ones like ego contents and desires.

Perhaps it would be true to say that necessarily any creature that did thinking would have to think that p entails p. But this statement is not really more esoteric than saying that any creature that weighed over 100 pounds and had a strong skeletal structure would be too dense to fly. What the tautological implication statement claims is that, in a Kantian sense, there are ways in which things must be understood, if they are to be understood. As Kant pointed out, that statement does not necessarily imply that noumena, independently of any thinking, must be the way that thought represents phenomena to be. The necessity applies only to our understanding, not to the natures of the things, themselves.

In light of what I have said about the direct perception of things like bones, Kant's observation can not here be interpreted as referring to unknowable noumena. The noumena/ phenomena distinction must be drawn in a different way in a direct realism than in Kant's system. But I can say that there are limits on what people are free to think about either bones or implications. And the limits come from recalcitrant parameters in nature in both cases. And just as people can learn more about bones, through study and careful attention to the properties they have, they can also learn more about thinking processes through study and attention. These processes are, thus, both recalcitrantly independent of psychology and accessible to knowledge; logical knowledge in this case.

The Platonists Share an Excessively Restricted Idea of Experience

Frege would, further, point out that we do not learn that p implies p from experience, agreeing with Plato that 'lovers of sights and sounds' are doomed to a lifetime of ignorance. But, I believe that both Plato and Frege are using overly restricted notions of experience in this judgment. As I have pointed out in my discussion of x-type thinking processes, sights and sounds are not the only types of experience to which people have access. People have experiences like hunger and meditative calm. Implication may be the type of fact that can be encountered in y-type thinking the way that a need for food can be learned by turning one's attention to one's stomach grumbles. I will discuss this point further when I discuss intuitionist interpretations of math, later in this chapter.

Logic is a Tool for Understanding Experience, Not Truth Itself

P implies p is true, but as Hume pointed out, it is a rather contentless truth. It only becomes significant when it is interpreted in terms of some content. This observation implies, first, as Kant rightly pointed out, that you had to do something with it that produced something synthetic out of its pristine but useless analyticity before it could be truly said to represent a bit of knowledge. Second, the observation indicates that $(p \supset p)$ is a thinking process that has to be, in some sense 'filled in' with experiential content. Of course, this can be done in a fanciful way, as a mind game, and these games are fun for humans to play. The Mad Hatter's Tea Party, in *Alice in Wonderland*, for instance, is fun with logic. But the fact that truth does not reside in the structures used by Lewis Carroll to construct the conversations at the party should be pretty apparent. When the content that is plugged into the structures is nonsense, the arguments yield nonsense, regardless of their formal validity. It is extra-logical considerations that determine whether an argument is sound or not; i.e., experience. As computer technicians are fond of saying; 'Garbage in, garbage out'.

Third, Hume's observation of the contentlessness of logic also indicates that truth can not reside in logical structures. These structures can preserve truth across inferences. But how does a logician decide that truth *has been* preserved across inferences? Obviously, she starts with a notion of something that is true. This must be something that she learned from experience, because she is bringing it with her to the beginning of her logical investigation. Then, she judges whether *its* truth has been preserved by seeing if *it* is still there at the end of the argument. How would she know if *it* was still there? The logic of the situation certainly isn't going to tell her. Rather, intentional kausation will be her reality check, at the end as well as at the beginning of her logical investigation.

A corollary that directly follows from the contentlessness of logical structure is also the fact that logic is a thinking tool. It is a very powerful thinking tool, but humans are its users, not its slaves. Should this tool prove inadequate to deal with some subject matter or type of experience that we want or need to understand, we have options. We can attempt to hone the tool to our needs, as Putnam's suggestions for quantum logics recommend. Or, we can find other methods for thinking about whatever it is that doesn't fit the tool. As we 'got around' our excessive bone weight by inventing airplanes in which to fly, we may also be able to find ways to circumvent the restrictions imposed on our thinking power by logic, if the restrictions prove prohibitive to our understanding, in some respect.

These considerations do not add up to a claim that logic is empirical. But they do indicate that logic is not as immune to considerations related to experience as many logicians would like to claim. At any rate, to the degree that it is so completely immune, it is also merely intellectual entertainment. It only becomes a valuable tool when used. And, by then, its pristine purity is also tainted with experiential content.

Possible Alternative Logics

David Bostock has suggested that we should take very seriously both the idea that there might be alternative interpretations of logic from the classical one and also the idea that logic should be viewed as, in some sense, empirical. He argues that the fact that most logicians cannot now conceive of alternatives is no more persuasive than Kant's commitment to Euclidean geometry was in light of the subsequent development of the Riemannian and Lobachevskian alternatives. Bostock points out:

> Nowadays we have all become convinced that the claims of Euclidean geometry are indeed empirical claims because we do now understand how things might be otherwise. Understanding has been generated first by showing that there are 'alternative geometries', and second by showing how one could choose between these alternatives on empirical grounds.[1]

Bostock undertakes the first of these tasks in this article. He discusses the alterations in classical logic that are brought about by the

---

[1] David Bostock, 'Logic and Empiricism', *Mind*, vol. XCIC No. 396, October 1990, p. 573

intuitionist's elimination of the law of excluded middle, and by a logic designed for quantum theory, such as Putnam's. Bostock points out that the reasons for proposing the alternatives are in a sense empirical; they make certain phenomena easier to explain than they were according to the classical conceptions of logic. For instance, elimination of the principle of distribution in Putnam's quantum logic gets rid of the particle location problem that physicists have been finding unresolvable in quantum physics. The problem is eliminated by the alternate understanding of logic, because the entire situation is described differently in the new logic, and so the problem does not arise.

Bostock points out that when the structure of a logic is altered from the classical one, the formal definition of truth that applied to the old one must also be altered. He envisions a formal theory of truth, not one based on experience, but argues that empirical considerations would have a bearing on rejecting the classical conceptions of truth and logical structures, to replace them by, say, a quantum system.

> . . . one might obtain a smoother total theory of the world by simply dropping the classical conception of truth and substituting in its place a different conception, more closely tied to verifiability. The different conception of truth will naturally bring with it a different logic.[2]

Bostock argues that claims to have disproven this possibility are question begging because they use the classical conception of truth to criticize a non-classical logical system. He points out that in this respect, he sees no reason why one should use classical logic as the tool of choice for evaluating either the classical logic itself or any of its proposed alternatives.

In his conclusion, however, Bostock criticizes the Quinean view that all of logic is empirically penetrable by pointing out that whether one chose classical, quantum or intuitionist logic might be based on how well that system explained the world as a whole. But determining the structure of the system itself, and of what concept of truth it entailed would still be a priori matters. In the terms of the theory that I have been presenting, Bostock's conclusion is that x-type reasoning processes would constitute the data that we would want one of our y-type logics to explain. We would accept or reject one of the alternatives on the basis of how well it explained that data. But, contra Quine, we would not figure out the structure of those logics using our x-type data. Rather, we would, granting Frege the auton-

---

omy of the y realm, consider only systematic matters when deciding what followed as a consequence of a particular logic.

So, I believe that Bostock would welcome a theory like mine, in which it is possible to grant the autonomy of the y-type thinking processes without granting a monolithic stranglehold on all thinking to classical logic, whether classical logic is viewed as x-type or y-type in origin. Raising the suggestion that there could be possible alternatives to classical logic is, again, not to argue against classical logic, but merely to indicate that it should not be understood as the monolithic arbiter of all thought that many contemporary philosophers consider it.

Intuitionist Interpretations of Mathematical Knowledge: Math ≠ Logic

In the same volume of *Mind* as the Bostock article, Michael Detlefsen analyses the intuitionist view of mathematics to argue that mathematical knowledge is something different from, and not reducible to, logical knowledge, Peano notwithstanding. A major tenet of what I have been calling the monolithic view of logic, of course, has been the belief that Peano had succeeded in showing that the logic of mathematics and the logic of language were really the same thing. Russell and Frege, for instance, both believe that all eternal sentences are on a par as logical items, and that no logically relevant distinction can be made between a mathematical statement and an eternal sentence or proposition, formulated in symbolic logic, in this regard. Thus, one structure, that of classical logic, describes the entire third realm. Detlefsen points out that the mathematical intuitionists, such as Brouwer and Poincaré, never bought the Frege-Russell view that one structure, the structure of logic, described the entire realm of mathematical truths. But Detlefsen argues against the common understanding of *why* the intuitionists are dissidents on this topic. He says that common opinion holds that the intuitionists take issue with the law of excluded middle. But he points out that the concerns expressed by Brouwer and Poincaré relate more to the subject matter of mathematics itself, and to how it is known, than they do to any law of logic.

After rhetorically asking if there is any appreciable difference between the mathematical knowledge of someone who has the intuitive understanding of a mathematical subject area and of someone who knows axioms that apply in the area and can manipulate logical steps to form a proof, Detlefsen emphatically replies for Poincaré that there is an enormous difference, as follows.

Even perfect logical mastery of a body of axioms would not, in his view, represent genuine mathematical mastery of the mathematics thus axiomatized . . .

On Poincaré's view, then, genuine mathematical reasoning does not proceed in 'logic-sized' steps, but rather in bigger steps – steps requiring genuine insight into the given mathematical subject being inferentially developed. This sets it at odds with logical reasoning, which, *by its very topic-neutral character*, neither requires nor even admits use of such insight in making inferences. In thus forswearing all appeal to information that derives from the particularities of the specific subject matter under investigation, logical reasoning also forswears the easy loping stride of one familiar with the twists and turns of a given local terrain, and opts instead for the halting step of one who is blind to the special features of all localities, and who must therefore take only such steps as would be safe in *any*. In Poincaré's view, the security thereby attained cannot make up for the blindness which it reflects. Logical astuteness may keep one from falling into a pit, but having a cane with which to feel one's way is a poor substitute for being able to see.[3]

Now, Detlefsen's way of putting the status of mathematical knowledge provides a very interesting challenge to both the classical account of a monolithic logic system in platonic heaven, and to my alternative.

This view of mathematics is a challenge to the Frege-Russell view because it proposes that mathematics can not be understood as a branch of logic, and thus, a continuous part of the third realm. Frege's easy equation of the Pythagorean theorem to all other eternal truths simply won't work, from the Detlefsen-Poincaré point of view. On this view, geometry is geometry and logic is logic and algebra is algebra, and if they have anything in common it is more by coincidence than by design that they do.

As an analysis of mathematical knowledge, this differentiation of subject matters makes good sense to me. I am not a particularly mathematically gifted person, and in studying math in school I discovered that I had widely divergent talents for varying topics. Geometry was a breeze. I could sit back, close my eyes, and 'see' the structures and relationships being discussed in a problem. I knew what I was out to prove from the start of the proof, and could sail through it without a hitch. After a quick check at the end, I was sure I was right. Algebra, in contrast, was a nightmare. Despite being forced to do a large number of quadratic equations under conditions of great duress, at the end of the classes I still could not tell anyone what on earth a quadratic was or why it existed. When I had scram-

---

[3]   Michael Detlefsen, 'Brouwerian Intuitionism,' *Mind*, vol. XCIX, No. 396, October 1990, p. 503.

bled one badly, the teacher asked, 'Don't you see that it *can't* go that way?', to which my frustrated reply was that I saw absolutely nothing when I looked at quadratics. If I could memorize the steps, I had a chance of blundering through it without egregious errors. But being right was always more a question of good luck than of good management. I think that Poincaré would be correct to label me a geometry knower and a quadratic agnostic stumbler, even when I got a quadratic right, through luck and memorization of steps. Likewise, set theory was a breeze, while accounting was a nightmare, for me.

But, this view of mathematics might also locate math in a different place from that in which I have located it in my account of the x-type and y-type thinking processes. Specifically, math is presented by Detlefsen as a type of mental experience. So, if he and Poincaré are correct, I should move it from the y-type thinking process area into the x-type thinking process area, and place it in parallel with psychological experience, memory, dreams and the like. Mathematical insight would then rate along with intellectual insight as a kind of intentional and kausal thinking that generates objects. This seems reasonable in light of Detlefsen's comments on Poincaré's view.

However, I also share some of Frege's reluctance to make this move, because the certainty and conceptual interrelatedness of mathematics seems to require that it have the autonomy of psychology that Frege wants for his third realm. I think that the best conclusion I can reach on this question is a suggestion that maybe mathematics is, like intellectual insight in general, 1% inspiration and 99% perspiration. The inspiration comes from specifically mathematical intellectual insight, but without it one can't even get off the ground, as I never did with quadratics. However, once the inspiration gets one going, the rest of the work is y-type.

After making this very interesting observation about intuitionism in mathematics, Detlefsen proceeds to argue that current versions of intuitionist logic, featuring many values or elimination of the law of excluded middle, do not faithfully reflect the intuitionist's insight that a logical reproduction of a proof does not represent a mathematical understanding of it. In other words, eliminating the law of excluded middle does not prevent generating proofs that would fail to be mathematical by intuitionist standards. He concludes by inviting further inquiry into the topic, which he believes has been unfairly slighted by the intuitionist's opponents.

Detlefsen's interesting discussion contributes two important suggestions to my discussion of the monolithic view of logic. One, perhaps mathematics is not part of the platonic realm at all, but rather is an empirical science based primarily on mental experience of widely divergent but very specific types. Two, whatever mathematics is, it is unlikely that it is completely reducible to logic. Peano's axioms may adequately simulate the generation of a number system. But they do not completely reproduce mathematical knowledge. The axioms describe mathematics in logical terms, which are not its own terms, and are not 100% accurate substitutes. Searle points out both the limits and the benefits of simulation when he observes that simulated fires don't burn anything down. The fact that one can learn from a simulation does not entail that it is a duplication of the original.

Again, these considerations are suggestions that the y-type thinking realm is not the completely logical, unitary and systematic heaven that Plato envisioned. Perhaps even math and logic are not as systematically related to each other as Frege and Russell believe they are.

Hintikka's Independence Friendly Logic, Again

Jakko Hintikka's Independence Friendly logic also provides an Intuitionistic alternative to the Frege-Russell version of first order logic. As I pointed out in chapter nine, Hintikka claims that the descriptive and interrogative functions of language, corresponding to my x-type and y-type reasoning processes, respectively, differ in function. In particular, Hintikka argues that the Frege-Russell method of imbedding quantifiers imposes a hierarchical structure on the relationship of dependency of one quantifier on another that misrepresents the actual relationship of dependency that quantifiers have on one another. The key to getting the relationship of quantifiers to one another right, according to Hintikka, is to understand that thinkers do not have a God's eye view of reality, and are always operating with partial information. He points out that from his game-theoretic perspective on logic:

> The first question any game theorist worth his or her utility matrix will ask about semantical games is: Are they games with perfect information or not? Looked at from our anachronistic game-theoretical perspective, Frege in effect answered: Logic is a game with perfect information. In spite of its prima facie plausibility this answer is nevertheless, *sub specie logicae* not only arbitrary and restrictive, but wrong, in that it cuts off from the purview of logical methods a large class of actual uses of our logical concepts.[4]

[4]   Jakko Hintikka,*The Principles of Mathematics Revisited,* Cambridge University Press, Cambridge, UK, 1998, p. 50.

Hintikka agrees with Detlefsen that intuitionists were more concerned with mathematical knowledge and how it is acquired than with particular issues such as the law of excluded middle. But, if one focuses on knowledge of mathematical or logical truths, rather than on what facts are represented by the truths, more distinctions can be made with respect to the scope of quantifiers. The nesting or hierarchal analysis of the scope of quantifiers is not the only one possible. Hintikka distinguishes between priority scope, as the relationship of quantifiers and variables that indicates which operation should be performed first, and binding scope which indicates which variables serve the function of pronouns for which quantifiers. Conflating the two meanings of scope has made both logic and linguistics a 'royal mess', Hintikka explains:

> Frege's mistake can thus be seen as a result of conflating the two uses of parentheses. The most natural way of using them for the purpose of indicating logical priority is to require that the scopes of quantifiers are nested. But to do so precludes a merely partial overlapping of quantifier scopes, even though such a violation of the nesting requirement is a perfectly natural thing from the vantage point of binding scope.[5]

Hintikka's alternative logic, by focusing on what we know and how we know it, thus, analyses y-type reasoning processes as tools for performing tasks. And Hintikka points out that the tasks humans wish to perform using logic cover a wider range of topics than the traditionalists thought they did, and the topics they cover do not interrelate as neatly as Platonists will claim they do.

But Hintikka still claims to be a realist about mathematical and logical entities and functions. Just as I do not think that including concerns about knowledge of entities and functions in thinking derails realism, Hintikka insists that he can still be a 'closet realist'.[6] He explains as follows.

> Thus one can even think of the task of mathematical research as involving an attempt to bring as many of these strange 'arbitrary functions' to the fold of intellectually mastered and , in a sense 'known' mathematical objects. This task presupposes, ontologically speaking, the existence, rather than the inexistence of all and sundry arbitrary functions. In general, it makes sense to speak of mathematical objects as being known or not known, and of our coming to know new mathematical objects only if one assumes that they actually exist even when they are not known. [7]

---

[5] *Ibid.*, p. 55.

[6] *The Principles of Mathematics Revisited,* p. 253.

[7] *Ibid.*, p. 252.

So, Intuitionists and proponents of some alternative logics, such as Bostock, Detlefsen and Hintikka insist, with me, that the y-type reasoning processes have their own form of reality, that is independent of human will and imagination, but understood through the postulation of entities in x-type experience. While there is a sense in which platonic heaven is out there to be known, it must be tied to entities in experience, as well.

Incompleteness and Inconsistency

I have already discussed the issues of incompleteness and inconsistency in logical theories in connection with my criticism of Quine in chapter ten. To briefly summarize; a logical theory that is complete, that is, that can express all the truths expressible according to its rules and formulas, is also, necessarily, capable of generating contradictions. To eliminate contradictions, thus producing consistency, one must limit the rules and formulas to prevent the generation of paradoxes. All of this has been apparent since Gödel's proof. Generally, what the incompatibility of consistency and completeness indicate is that truth cannot be defined internally in any one system. Rather, whatever formulas or rules are used to define truth for the theory must be banned from admission to the theory, thus making it incomplete.

In my discussion of Quine on this topic, I pointed out that he is chasing a third man by pursuing truth from theory to theory, and that he never arrives at the ultimate background theory that he misleads us into believing is there. But, whether in Quine's system or any other, the incompatibility of consistency and completeness indicate that no monolithic Platonic realm can be constructed.

Penrose on Gödel and Incompleteness and Inconsistency

Roger Penrose, in *Shadows of the Mind*, gives a general argument for the position that mathematical thought is non-computational based on Gödel's theorem. Penrose analyses the argument on this issue that actually arose between Turing and Gödel to point out that mathematicians could not operate with unknowable or unknown algorithms, of the type that Turing claimed could have been developed in the human race through Darwinian evolutionary processes. Penrose discusses the possibility of an *F* (a theorem-proving machine) that could do what the Artificial Intelligence proponents suppose a mind can do with respect to computational reasoning. That is, develop algorithms in a blind, bottom-up sort of way, that could ultimately generate a y-type reasoning realm that encompassed all the reasoning that humans perform. Daniel Dennett explicitly endorses the Turing side of the Gödel/Turing discussion in the following claim.

> Darwin shows us that a bottom-up theory of creation is, indeed not only imaginable but empirically demonstrable. Absolute ignorance is fully qualified to take the place of Absolute Wisdom in all the achievements of creative skill – *all* of them.[8]

Penrose points out that while the Turing/Dennett view of how mathematical reasoning developed is conceivable, there are several key problems with it. For instance, individual mathematicians might use different procedures to reach the same mathematical truths. But he points out that if this were true, it would make the development of mathematics more puzzling, not more intellectually clear, for,

> Two algorithms need not be at all similar with regard to their internal operations, and yet they can be identical with respect to their eventual effects. However, in a certain sense, this actually makes it more puzzling how our putative unfathomable algorithm(s) for ascertaining mathematical truth might have arisen, for now we need many such algorithms, all quite distinct from one another in their detailed constructions, yet all essentially equivalent as regards their outputs.[9]

In addition to the unlikelihood that there could be such a wide variety of algorithmic methods that would, nevertheless, converge on a far more restricted number of specific algorithms, Penrose also points out that these algorithms would be poor candidates for inheritable qualities.

> The inbuilt potential mathematical algorithms (i.e. whatever inherited aspects to our mathematical thinking – presumed algorithmic – that there might be) would somehow lie coded within the DNA, as particular features of its sequences of nucleotides, and they would have arisen as a result of the same procedures whereby improvements gradually or intermittently arise in response to selective pressures.[10]

But the type of algorithm that is needed to explain mathematical ability, according to Penrose, has to be capable of some really remarkable things. For one thing, it has to be capable of conceiving of a Zermelo-Fraenkel formal system, and of a Gödelization of that for-

---

[8]   Daniel Dennett, *in Darwin's Wake, Where am I?* Presidential Address to the Eastern Division of the American Philosophical Association, in *the Proceedings and Addresses of the APA*, vol. 75, no. 2, November 2001, p.14

[9]   Roger Penrose, *Shadows of the Mind*, Oxford University Press, Oxfod, UK, 1994, pp. 146–147.

[10]   *Ibid.*, p. 145.

mal system, and many reiterizations of the Gödelization of that system. In addition, the algorithm would have to be capable of conceiving of the details of all possible mathematical discoveries, even ones that have not yet been thought of by mathematicians. And, this inheritable algorithm would have to have had all of this capacity since the time of our ancient ancestors. Penrose argues that the likelihood that such an algorithm could ever have been encoded in DNA nucleotides is extremely low.

> This putative, unknowable or incomprehensible algorithm would have to have, coded within itself, a power to do all this, yet we are being asked to believe that it arose solely by a natural selection geared to the circumstances in which our remote ancestors struggled for survival. A particular ability to do obscure mathematics can have had no direct selective advantage for its possessor, and I would argue that there would be no reason for it to have arisen.[11]

> The situation is quite different once we allow understanding to be a non-algorithmic quality. Then it need not be something that is so complicated that it is unknowable or incomprehensible. Indeed, it could be much closer to 'what mathematicians think they are doing'.[12]

Penrose asserts that the notion that a robot or Turing machine could ever achieve mathematical ability that parallels human knowledge leads to inevitable contradictions because the computational principles on which such a machine operates are not capable of understanding mathematical truths. His explanation of why this must be so is that humans use non-computational means to arrive at mathematical truths. The reason for this is:

> If one is to decide the truth of A_1 sentences for certain, in principle, then rather than depending just on random or unknowable procedures, one must have some genuine *understanding* of the *meanings* of what is actually involved in such assertions. Trial and error procedures, though they may provide some guidance towards what is needed, do not in themselves give definitive criteria of truth.[13]

So, again, agreeing with Bostock, Detlefsen, and Hintikka, Penrose is claiming that knowledge of mathematical reasoning requires a specifically human capacity. In Penrose's case, as in Hintikka's, the specifically human capacity required is the ability to do reasoning that is not computational. All of these authors agree with me that understanding and meanings are not inherent in formal computational structures.

---

[11] *Shadows of the Mind,* p. 149.

[12] *Ibid.,* pp. 149–150.

[13] *Ibid.,* p. 197.

My solution to the problem is to see the y-type thinking processes as a diverse variety of thinking tools, with interesting relationships to each other. The interrelationships among y-type reasoning processes have their own form of reality, which is the reality of possible relations among possibilities. But, truth is not in them at all; rather it is in experience. A formal definition of truth can be devised, provided its inventor remembers that it is just a formal way to analyse relations among y-structures, or to hook the y-realm up to the x. Then, there will be no need to demand consistency among diverse y-type thinking methods, or to worry about the fact that the structure is not complete. As Penrose says of the Gödel proof:

> The Gödel argument shows – for good or for bad – that there is no way of encapsulating, in a computationally checkable way, all the methods of mathematical reasoning that are humanly acceptable.[14]

For reductivists, this is clearly bad news. They cannot banish experience from the range of things discussed and counted as intellectually legitimate. My Aristotelian devil x must be given her due.

Penrose, who proclaims himself a Platonist, is arguing against material reductivism, of the evolutionary naturalist sort, and not against Platonism in the argument I've been giving on the last few pages. My primary adversaries in this book have been philosophers who are both evolutionary naturalists and Platonists, such as Quine and Dennett, who believe that platonic and materialistic reductivism are mutually supportive of one another, and unite in the computer metaphor. Penrose has shown, in the arguments cited on the last few pages, that the equation of these two forms of reductivism doesn't work as its proponents presume.

But the stress of my argument has been against the Platonism of the Quinean position, rather than against the material reductivism of it, which might seem to put me at odds with Penrose. So, here I must ask what it is about Platonism that Penrose seems to think he needs. It might be that he thinks of the mathematical objects as eternal or as spiritual in some traditionally Platonic sense. But it might also be that he simply agrees with Frege's motivation to keep math autonomous, and free of the exigencies of psychology. The latter consideration seems to be operative in the passage I quoted on page 213, in which Penrose stresses the importance of the 'convergence of outputs' and the insignificance of methods of accomplishing the mathematical outputs. He may think of the convergence of outputs as requiring a realistic realm to house the loci of convergence.

------

[14] *Ibid.*, p. 192.

It was also considerations related to the convergence of mathematical ideas that led me to side, in Chapter Four, with Hintikka's 'closet realism' about the y-type thinking processes, against Lakoff and Johnson's claim that all of thought is embodied metaphors. There is a realistic sense in which math and logic do limn the structure of reality, and so, the y-realm is as important as the x. My anti-Platonism comes in as my claim that the y-thinking processes are not *more* important than the x, contra Quine. And here, I think that Penrose, as a theoretical physicist, might well agree with me. Empirically informed, pragmatic 'closet realism' about the y-thinking structures acknowledges their importance and autonomy, but does not try to use them to abolish or denigrate the value of experience.

Summary

In this chapter of this book, I have advanced a number of considerations that are designed to erode the notion that there is a complete, logically structured platonic heaven. They do not amount to a decisive argument either for or against anything. But I think that they do indicate that there is more blind faith than good reasoning in the commitment of contemporary Platonists to a unitary, monolithic third realm.

My explanation of the y-type thinking processes and how they relate to the x-type ones is now completed. I will wrap up this book with an overview summarizing what knowledge, reality and human thinking look like when viewed as human products of x and y-type thinking processes.

Chapter 12

Overview and
Conclusion

To conclude, I will briefly summarize what the picture of knowledge and reality that I have been presenting looks like overall. I will begin with a short summary of what knowledge looks like, as acquired through the x and y thinking processes, then discuss the relationship of the x to the y, in knowledge. I will wrap up with a discussion of what reality will look like overall under this analysis of knowledge and reality.

Knowledge

Knowledge in my analysis, as in Hume's and Aristotle's accounts, will consist of two types of known products. From the x-type thinking processes, people acquire knowledge by acquaintance, de re knowledge of sensory, intellectual, or other experiential data. This type of data can be imagistic, auditory, conceptual, kinesthetic, or in other ways immediately experienced. It gives people direct, immediate contact with reality. But it is always intentional, in several senses. One, if someone isn't paying attention to it, they will miss it. Two, via the naming process, people can project their own, antecedent expectations on it, if they have any, and three, their ability to understand what they are experiencing is limited by what they do or do not know about it. Further, this type of data is always kausal. The kause may be a mouse, a stomach rumble, a dream, a burst of intellectual insight or a tidal wave. In each case, the experiential bit of data is having a direct, intentional impact on someone on the world-to-mind side of the x-type thinking process, and the person is responding with attention and a name on the mind-to-world side of the process.

What a person gets as a result of this contact with the world is a polyglot collection of experiences. A person may, at times, attempt to attach all of his or her many experiences to a single, unitary, concept of what the world is, overall, but, some people may not ever try to conceptually unify their disparate experiences. Quite possibly, people who are not particularly philosophical don't try to synthesize all of their experience into a unitary world view. Objects are anything that a person intentionally indexes and names in his or her experience.

From the y-type thinking processes, people get concepts, or relationships between ideas; de dicto knowledge of what their concepts can or must entail. The concepts may be learned from other people, books, or other y-type reasoning processes, through logical thinking, reading, conversations, or other forms of intellectual or social discourse. Y-type reasoning processes give people the ability to generalize their experience and draw inferences from it, as well as the ability to invent logically consistent possible worlds for themselves. Thus, y-type thinking processes enable people to speculate about what could be and invent what they would like to see, even if the possibilities imagined have never been experienced in reality.

What people get from y-type reasoning processes are scenarios about what the world *could be like*, but little or no information about *what it is like*. There are no objects in the y realm, only structures and relationships. These can be used to sort, organize, categorize, or structure experiences. But in the absence of experiences that will fill them in they are only elegant fantasies. People are inclined to generate cosmologies and grand all-encompassing schemes about experience out of their y-type reasoning processes. But the measure of the value of these schemes will always be how adequate they are to explain experience. In the history of philosophy, all too often philosophers have slaughtered the experiential data to force them to fit an abstract scheme, rather than adjusting the scheme to make it fit the data.

Propositions encoding knowledge reside in the 'middle' of the relationship between x and y type thinking processes. Ideally, they encode an x-type experience in a y-type syntactical format. It could be that someone could learn a proposition without any experience to which to index it. This person will subsequently learn to understand the proposition only if he or she develops a context, or point of view, in which it fits, either by further learning or further experience. Until the context is developed, the proposition, though repeatable, will remain vacant words for the person. Objects enter propositions through the mechanics of the existential quantifier, or constants. The 'same object' is maintained through syntactic transformations if at the end of an inference the same person can still use the context to index his or her initially named experience.

Thus, the overall picture of knowledge that I am presenting does not have a 'higher' and 'lower' or 'internal' and 'external' division. I believe that these ways of dividing up the various types of knowledge misrepresent its character. Rather, knowledge should be thought of as shading from inarticulately experiential at one end to fantastically structural at the other extreme end, with most practical, scientific, or communicable discourse in the middle, as a balance of syntactical and semantical elements. The picture should be seen as dynamic, and evolving, both individually, for each knower, and collectively for the whole human race. It has no monolithic, unitary structure or organization, but rather can be variously structured and interpreted depending on human needs or perspectives at a given time. Thus, overall, the collected sum of all human knowledge is both kausal and intentional, as well as structured in various appropriately logical and structural ways. This means that no unitary cosmology exhaustively describing all of human knowledge can ever be constructed. But, that is what we would expect from our examination of the limitations on the y-type reasoning processes.

The Relationship of The X and Y Type Thinking Processes to Each Other

In a technical and mechanical sense, the x and y type reasoning processes work together to form propositions. But the propositions are always in a sense hypothetical. Both new structural thinking from the y-end and new experiences from the x-end continually press for development of new concepts, revised structures, increased understanding and revised interpretations of whatever propositions the knowers, collectively or individually hold. And the interaction of the two processes must be seen as dynamic and evolving.

Truth must be understood pragmatically. The hypotheses that do the best job of explaining our experience to us are the true ones. If truth is to be understood ideally, rather than pragmatically, as some ultimate, transcendental, universal, adequate account of all reality, both human and non-human, as known by some omniscient being, then it is a y-type idea, projecting a possibility whose actuality humans cannot attain. I have no objection to philosophers postulating such a possibility as an article of religious faith. But, for human knowledge, it is quite pointless.

The only response that any human could appropriately muster to a comparison of what he or she knows, or of what all humans collectively know, to omniscience would be silent awe at our ignorance.

Reality

Reality is experience. Individually, it is what each person experiences, in a first person singular lived life. Collectively, it is what all people experience or have experienced. Some people have access to a greater variety of types of experience than others, and some seem to have special talents or sensitivities for certain areas of experience for which others seem to be 'blind' or precluded from access. Perhaps atheists are people who fail to have religious experiences, while religious mystics are masters in this area, as composers hear symphonies 'in their heads' while tone-deaf people can't keep a beat, and as mathematicians 'see' how quadratics must go, while I see nothing but a jumble of meaningless numbers and letters there.

I think that we humans have good reason to admit that other humans have experiences that we, individually don't, and so to credit 'reality' to the recorded and communicated points of view of others, at least as far as we have the capacity to understand them. I think that we have very little reason to attribute reality to Kantian 'noumena', viewed as reality existing independently of and beyond the knowledgeable reach of any human point of view ever conceived. But again, if someone wants to hypothesize such a possibility as a y-type religious or scientific act of faith, I suppose I have no particular objection. I would simply respond that I have little or no understanding of why they think they need this hypothesis, contentless and devoid of experiential reality as it must remain.

Bibliography

Almog, Joseph, 'Semantical Anthropology', in *Midwest Studies in Philosophy IX*, see French.

Alston, William, *Philosophy of Language*, Prentice Hall, Inc., Englewood Cliffs, NJ, 1964.

— *A Realist Conception of Truth*, Cornell University Press, Ithaca NY, 1996.

— *Perceiving God*, Cornell University Press, Ithaca NY, 1991.

Anderson, Peter Bøgh, Emmeche, Claus, Finnemann, Niels Ole, and Christiansen, Peder Voetmann, eds., *Downward Causation*, Aarhus University Press, Aarhus, N., 2000.

Anscombe, Elizabeth, *Intention*, Cornell University Press, Ithaca, NY 1957.

Aristotle, *The Basic Works of Aristotle*, ed. Richard McKeon, Random House, New York , 1941.

Atkinson, Rita L., Atkinson, Richard C., Smith, Edward E., and Bem, Daryl J., *Introduction to Psychology*, 10th edn., Harcourt, Brace, Jovanovich Publishers, NY, 1990.

Barwise, Jon, and Perry, John, *Situations and Attitudes*, Bradford Books, MIT Press, Cambridge, MA, 1983.

Beakley, Brian, and Ludlow, Peter, eds., *The Philosophy of Mind*, MIT Press, Cambridge, MA, 1994.

Benacerraf, Paul, 'What Numbers Could Not Be', *Philosophical Review*, vol. LXXIV, no. 1, January, 1965.

Bennett, Jonathan, *Locke, Berkeley, Hume, Central Themes*, Clarendon Press, Oxford, 1971.

Berkeley, George, *A Treatise Concerning the Principles of Human Knowledge*, ed. Colin M. Turbayne, Bobbs Merrill Co., Indianapolis, IN, 1977.

Bermúdez, José Luis, Marcel, Anthony and Eilan, Naomi, eds., *The Body and the Self*, MIT Press, Cambridge, MA, 1998.

Bever, Thomas G., Carroll, John M., and Miller, Lance A., eds., *Talking Minds*, MIT Press, Cambridge MA, 1984.

Block, Ned, *Imagery*, Bradford Books, MIT Press, Cambridge, MA, 1981.
    ed., *Readings in the Philosophy of Psychology*, vols.1 and 2, Harvard UniversityPress, Cambridge, MA, 1980.

Bostock, David, 'Logic and Empiricism', in *Mind,* vol. XCIC, no. 396, October, 1990.

Bourne, Lyle E., Dominowski, Roger L., Loftus, Elizabeth F., and Healy, Alice F. *Cognitive Processes*, 2nd edn., Prentice Hall, Inc., Englewood Cliffs, NJ, 1986.

Bownds, M. Deric, *The Biology of Mind,* Fitzgerald Science Press, Bethesda, MD, 1999.

Boyer, Carl B., *A History of Mathematics*, 2nd edn., revised by Merzbach, Uta, John Wiley and Sons Publishing, NY, 1991.

Burnet, J., *Early Greek Philosophy*, Black, London, 1920.

Caplan, David, ed. *Biological Studies of Mental Processes*, MIT Press, Cambridge, 1980.

Carnap, Rudolph, 'Meaning and Necessity', in *Meaning and Truth, The Essential Readings in Modern Semantics*, see Garfield and Kiteley.

Castaneda, Hector-Neri, 'Causes, Causity, and Energy', in *Midwest Studies in Philosophy IX*, see French.

— 'Thinking and the Structure of the World', in Critica, vol. 6, September, 1972.

Chalmers, David J., *The Conscious Mind,* Oxford University Press, Oxford, UK, 1996.

Chisholm, Roderick M., ed., *Realism and the Background of Phenomenology,* Ridgeview Publishing Co, Atascadero, CA, 1960.

Chomsky, Noam, *Reflections on Language,* Pantheon Books, Random House, NY, 1975.

— *Language and Thought,* Moyer Bell Publishing, The Frick Collection, Wakefield, RI, 1993.

— *Some Concepts and Consequences of the Theory of Government and Binding*, MIT Press, Cambridge, MA, 1982.

— *New Horizons in the Study of Language and Mind,* Cambridge University Press, Cambridge, UK, 2000.

Church, Alonzo, 'Ontological Commitment', *The Journal of Philosophy*, Vol. LV, no. 23, November, 1958.

Churchland, Paul, *Matter and Consciousness*, Bradford Books, MIT Press, 1985.

Clark, Andy, *Being There,* MIT Press, Cambridge, MA, 1998.

'Visual Awareness and Visuomotor Action', *Journal of Consciousness Studies*, vol. 6, No. 11–12, 1999.

Cooney, Brian, *The Place of Mind*, Wadsworth Thompson Learning, Belmont, CA, 2000.

Cummins, Robert, *The Nature of Psychological Explanation*, Bradford Books, MIT Press, Cambridge, MA, 1983.

Davidson, Donald, *Words and Objections, Essays on the Works of W.V. Quine,* D. Reidel Publishing Co., Holland, 1969.

— 'Truth and Meaning' in Meaning and Truth, the Essential Readings in Modern Semantics, see Garfield and Kiteley.

— 'The Method of Truth in Metaphysics', in Philosophy of Language, The Big Questions, see Nye.

— 'On the Very Idea of a Conceptual Scheme', in Philosophy of Language, The Big Questions, see Nye.

Dennett, Daniel, *Content and Consciousness*, Routledge and Kegan Paul, London UK 1969.

— *Brainstorms*, Bradford Books, MIT Press, Cambridge MA, 1978.

— 'In Darwin's Wake, Where am I?', Presidential Address to the Eastern Division of the American Philosophical Association, New York, NY, December, 2000.

Descartes, René, *The Meditations*, in *Descartes' Philosophical Writings*, trans. and ed. Anscombe, E., and Geach, P.T., Bobbs Merrill Co., Indianapolis, IN, 1971.

— *Rules for the Direction of the Mind*, in *Descartes' Philosophical Writings*, trans. and ed., Anscombe, E., and Geach, P.T., Bobbs Merrill Co., Indianapolis, IN, 1971.

Detlefsen, Michael, 'Brouwerian Intuitionism', in *Mind*, vol. XCIX, no. 396, October, 1990.

Donnellan, Keith S., 'Reference and Definite Descriptions', in *Readings in the Philosophy of Language*, see Rosenberg and Travis.

Dretske, Fred I. *Knowledge And The Flow of Information*, Bradford Books, MIT Press, Cambridge, Mass. 1981.

— and Enc, Berent, 'Causal Theories of Knowledge', in *Midwest Studies in Philosophy, IX*, see French.

— *Naturalizing the Mind*, Bradford Books, MIT Press, Cambridge, MA,1995.

Dreyfus, Hubert L., *Husserl, Intentionality and Cognitive Science*, Bradford Books, MIT Press, Cambridge, MA, 1982.

Dummett, Michael, 'The Significance of Quine's Indeterminacy Thesis', in *Synthese*, vol. 27, July–August 1974.

Ellwood, Robert S., *Many Peoples Many Faiths*, 3rd edn., Prentice Hall, Inc., Englewood Cliffs, NJ, 1987.

Falk, Ruma, 'A Closer Look at the Probabilities of the Notorious Three Prisoners', in *Cognition*, vol. 43, 1992.

Field, Hartry, 'Tarski's Theory of Truth', in *Meaning and Truth, the Essential Readings in Modern Semantics,* see Garfield and Kiteley.

Flanagan, Owen, *The Science of the Mind*, Bradford Books, MIT Press, Cambridge MA, 1984.

Fodor, Jerry, *Representations*, MIT Press, Cambridge, MA, 1981.

— *The Language of Thought*, Harvard University Press, Cambridge, MA, 1975.

— *The Modularity of Mind*, MIT Press, Cambridge, MA, 1983.

— *Psychosemantics*, MIT Press, Cambridge, MA,1987.

— *The Mind Doesn't Work That Way, The Scope and Limits of Computational Psychology*, MIT Press, Cambridge, MA, 2000.

Føllesdal, Dagfinn, 'Quantification into Causal Contexts', in *Reference and Modality*, see Linsky.

Freeman, Anthony, *The Emergence of Consciousness*, Imprint Academic, Exeter, UK, 2001.

Freeman, Walter, J. 'Consciousness, Intentionality and Causality', in *Journal of Consciousness Studies*, Vol. 6, no. 11–12, 1999, pp. 143–172.

Frege, Gottlob, 'The Thought', in *Mind*, vol. LXV. no. 259, July 1956, pp. 289–311.

— 'Review of Husserl's "Philosophy of Arithmetic"', reprinted in *Husserl, Expositions and Appraisals*, eds. Frederick Elliston and Peter McCormick, University of Notre Dame Press, Notre Dame, IN, 1977.

— 'On Sense and Nominatum', in *Meaning and Truth, the Essential Readings in Modern Semantics,* see Garfield and Kiteley.

French, Peter A., Uehling, Theodore E., and Wettstein, Howard K., eds., *Contemporary Perspectives in the Philosophy of Language*, Minnesota University Press, Minneapolis, MN, 1977.

— *Midwest Studies in Philosophy, Volume XIV, Contemporary Perspectives in the Philosophy of Language II*, University of Notre Dame Press, Notre Dame IN, 1989.

— *Midwest Studies in Philosophy IX, 1984, Causation and Causal Theories*, University of Minnesota Press, Minneapolis, MN, 1984.

Freud, Sigmund, *Character and Culture*, Collier Books, Macmillan Publishing Co., NY 1962.

— *General Psychological Theory*, Collier Books, Macmillan, Publishing Co. NY 1962.

Gallagher, Shaun, and Shear, Jonathan, *Models of the Self*, Imprint Academic, Exeter, UK, 1999.

Gallie, R.D., 'Substitutionalism and Substitutional Quantification', in *Analysis*, vol. 35, January 1975.

Garfield, Jay L. and Kiteley, Murray, eds., *Meaning and Truth, the Essential Readings in Modern Semantics*, Paragon House, NY, 1991.

Garfield, Jay L., ed., *Foundations of Cognitive Science, the Essential Readings*, Paragon House, NY 1990.

Gazzaniga, Michael S., "Consciousness and the cerebral hemispheres" in *The Cognitive Neurosciences*, MIT Press, Cambridge, MA, 1995.

Gigerenzer, Gerd, and Hug, Klaus, 'Domain Specific Reasoning: Social Contracts, cheating and perspective change.' In *Cognition*, vol. 43, 1992.

Gilman, Leonard, 'The Car and the Goats', *American Mathematical Monthly*, vol. 99 no. 1, Jan 1992.

Goodman, Nelson, *The Languages of Art*, Hackett Publishing Co., Indianapolis, IN, 1976.

— *Of Mind and Other Matters*, Harvard University Press, Cambridge, MA, 1984.

— *Ways of Worldmaking*, Hackett Publishing Co., Indianapolis, IN, 1978.

Grice, H.P., 'Meaning', in *Philosophy of Language, The Big Questions*, see Nye.

Gunderson, K., *Language, Mind and Knowledge*, Minnesota Studies in the Philosophy of Science, vol. 7, University of Minnesota Press, Minneapolis, MN, 1975.

Haack, Susan, *Evidence and Inquiry*, Blackwell Publishers, Malden, MA, 1995.

— *Philosophy of Logics*, Cambridge University Press, Cambridge, UK, 1978.

Hasker, William, *The Emergent Self*, Cornell University Press, Ithaca, NY, 1999.

Hartmann, George W., *Gestalt Psychology*, Greenwood Press, Westport, CT, 1974.

Haugeland, John, ed. *Mind Design*, Bradford Books, MIT Press, Cambridge, MA, 1981.

Hempel, Carl, *Philosophy of Natural Science*, Prentice Hall, Englewood Cliffs, NJ, 1966.

Hintikka, Jakko, *The Principles of Mathematics Revisited*, Cambridge University Press, Cambridge, UK, 1998.

Hobbes, Thomas, *Leviathan, Parts 1 and 2*, ed., Schneider, Herbert W., Bobbs Merrill Co., Indianapolis, IN, 1958.

Holland, John, Holyoak, Keith, Nisbett, Richard, and Thagard, Paul, *Induction, Processes of Inference, Learning, and Discovery*, MIT Press, Cambridge, MA, 1989.

Hughes, Langston, 'Harlem, (a Dream Deferred)', in *The Norton Introduction to Literature*, 3rd edn., eds. Bain, Beatty, and Hunter, W., Norton Co., New York 1981.

Hume, David, *A Treatise of Human Nature*, ed. Bigge, L.A. Selby, Oxford University Press, UK, 1978.

Humphrey, Nicholas, *How to Solve the Mind–Body Problem*, Imprint Academic, Exeter, UK, 2000.

Husserl, Edmund, *Ideas*, trans., Gibson, W. R. Boyce, Collier Books, NY, 1975.

Jackson, Frank, *Perception*, Cambridge University Press, UK, 1977.

James, William, *The Will to Believe*, Dover Publications, Inc. NY, 1956.

— *Pragmatism*, New American Library, Ontario, Canada, 1974.

— *The Varieties of Religious Experience*, the New American Library of World Literature, NY, 1958.

Jones, W.T., *A History of Western Philosophy*, 2nd edn., Harcourt, Brace, Jovanovich, NY, 1975.

Kant, Immanuel, *The Critique of Pure Reason*, trans. Norman Kemp Smith, St. Martin's Press, NY, 1929.

Kaplan, David, 'Quantifying in', in *Reference and Modality*, see Linsky.

— 'Dthat', in *Meaning and Truth, the Essential Readings in Modern Semantics*, see Garfield and Kiteley.

— 'On the Logic of Demonstratives', in *Meaning and Truth, the Essential Readings in Modern Semantics*, see Garfield and Kiteley.

Kim, Jaegwon, *Mind in a Physical World*, MIT Press, Cambridge, MA, 1998.

— *Philosophy of Mind*, Westview Press, Harper Collins Publishers, Boulder, CO, 1996.

Kosslyn, Stephen M., and Pomerantz, James R., 'Imagery, Propositions, and the Form of Internal Representations', in *Readings in Philosophy of Psychology*, see Block.

Kripke, Saul, *Naming and Necessity*, Harvard University Press, Cambridge, MA, 1980.

— 'A Puzzle About Belief', in *Meaning and Use*, A. Margalit, Reidel, Dordrecht, Holland, 1976.

— 'Semantical Considerations on Modal Logic', in *Reference and Modality*, see Linsky.

— 'Speaker's Reference and Semantic Reference', in *Meaning and Truth, the Essential Readings in Modern Semantics*, see Garfield and Kiteley.

Lakoff, George, *Women, Fire and Dangerous Things*, University of Chicago Press, Chicago IL, 1987.

— and Johnson, Mark, *Philosophy in the Flesh, The Embodied Mind and its Challenge to Western Thought*, Basic Books, Perseus Book Group, New York, NY, 1999.

Lewis, David, 'Possible Worlds', in *Meaning and Truth, the Essential Readings in Modern Semantics*, see Garfield and Kiteley.

Linsky, Leonard, ed., *Reference and Modality*, Oxford University Press, Oxford, UK, 1971.

Locke, John, *An Essay Concerning Human Understanding*, ed. Nidditch, Peter H., Oxford University Press, UK, 1975.

Lycan, William G., *Consciousness*, Bradford Books, MIT Press, Cambridge, MA, 1987.

— 'Robots and Minds', in *Twenty Questions, an Introduction to Philosophy*, eds. Bowie, Michaels and Solomon, Harcourt Brace Jovanovich, Publishers, NY, 1988.

Mackie, J.L., *The Cement of the Universe*, Oxford University Press, UK, 1974.

Mangan, Bruce, 'The Fringe: a Case Study in Explanatory Phenomenology' in *The View from Within*, Varela and Shear, eds. *op. cit.*

Marcus, Ruth, 'Extentionality', in *Reference and Modality*, see Linsky.

Maslow, Abraham H., *New Knowledge in Human Values*, Henry Regnery Co., Chicago, 1959.

McKim, Vaughn R., and Turner, Stephen P., eds., *Causality in Crisis? Statistical Methods and the Search for Causal Knowledge in the Social Sciences*, University of Notre Dame Press, Notre Dame, IN, 1997.

McMullin, Ernan, 'Two Ideals of Explanation in Natural Science', in *Midwest Studies in Philosophy IX,* see French.

Metzinger, Thomas, ed. *Conscious Experience*, Imprint Academic, Exeter, UK 1995.

Miller, George A. and Johnson–Laird, Philip N., *Language and Perception*, Belnap/ Harvard University Press, Cambridge MA, 1976.

Millikan, Ruth, 'Biosemantics', in *Philosophy of Language, The Big Questions,* see Nye.

— *White Queen Psychology and Other Essays for Alice,* MIT Press, Cambridge, MA, 1995.

Minnich, Elizabeth , *Transforming Knowledge*, Temple University Press, Philadelphia, PA, 1990.

Moore, G.E., *Philosophical Studies*, Harcourt, Brace, Jovanovich, NY1922.

Núñez, Rafael, and Freeman, Walter J., eds., *Reclaiming Cognition*, Imprint Academic, Exeter, UK, 1999.

Nye, Andrea, ed., *Philosophy of Language, The Big Questions*, Blackwell Publishers, Malden, MA, 1998.

Parsons, Charles, 'Ontology and Mathematics', *Philosophical Review*, April 1976.

Pearl, Judea, *Causality, Models, Reasoning and Inference*, Cambridge University Press, Cambridge, UK, 2000.

Penrose, Roger, *Shadows of the Mind*, Oxford University Press, Oxford, UK, 1994.

— *The Emperor's New Mind*, Oxford University Press, Oxford, UK 1989.

— ed., *The Large, The Small and the Human Mind,* Cambridge University Press, Cambridge, UK, 1997.

Perkins, Moreland, *Sensing the World*, Hackett Publishing Co., Indianapolis, IN, 1983.

Piatelli–Palmarini, *Inevitable Illusions*, John Wiley and Sons, NY, 1994.

Plantinga, Alvin, 'Actualism and Possible Worlds', in *Meaning and Truth, the Essential Readings in Modern Semantics*, see Garfield and Kiteley.
  The Nature of Necessity, Clarendon Press, Oxford, UK, 1974.
Plato, *The Collected Dialogues of Plato*, trans. and eds., Hamilton, Edith, and Cairns, Huntington, Princeton University Press, Princeton, NJ, 1961.
Price, H.H., *Thinking and Experience*, Harvard University Press, Cambridge, MA, 1962.
  Perception, Greenwood Press, Westport, CT, 1950.
Putnam, Hilary, 'Realism and Reason', Presidential Address to the American Philosophical Association, Eastern Division, in Boston, Mass, 1976, printed in *Proceedings and Addresses of the American Philosophical Association*, 1977.
— 'The Meaning of 'Meaning', in *Philosophical Papers II, Mind, Language, and Reality*, Cambridge University Press, Cambridge, UK, 1975.
— *Representation and Reality*, Bradford Books, MIT Press, Cambridge, MA, 1989.
— 'After Empiricism', in *Post–Analytic Philosophy*, eds. Rajchman, John and West, Cornell, Columbia University Press. NY, 1985.
— *Pragmatism*, Blackwell Publishers, Oxford, UK, 1995.
Pylyshyn, Zenon, *Computation and Cognition*, Bradford Books, MIT Press, Cambridge, MA, 1986 .
Quine, Willard V.O., *Ontological Relativity and Other Essays*, John Dewey Lectures in Philosophy, Columbia University Press, NY, 1969.
— *Mathematical Logic*, revised edn. Harvard University Press, Cambridge, MA, 1981.
— *The Roots of Reference*, Open Court Publishing Co., LaSalle, IL, 1974.
— *The Ways of Paradox and Other Essays*, Random House, NY, 1966.
— *Philosophy of Logic*, Prentice Hall, Inc. Englewood Cliffs, NJ, 1970.
— *Word and Object*, MIT Press, Cambridge, MA, 1960.
— 'Ontological Reduction and the World of Numbers', *The Journal of Philosophy*, vol. LXI, no. 7, March 26, 1964.
— *Pursuit of Truth*, revised edn., Harvard University Press, Cambridge, MA, 1992.
Reid, Thomas *Inquiry and Essays*, ed. Keith Lehrer and Ronald Beanblossom, Bobbs Merrill Co., Indianapolis, IN 1975.
Reisberg, Daniel, *Cognition, Exploring the Science of the Mind*, W.W. Norton and Co., New York, 1997.
Resnick, Michael D., *Frege and the Philosophy of Mathematics*, Cornell University Press, Ithaca, NY, 1980.
Ricoeur, Paul, *The Rule of Metaphor*, trans., Czerny, McLaughlin and Costello, University of Toronto Press, Toronto, Ontario, Canada 1975.
Rock, Irving, *The Logic of Perception*, Bradford Books, MIT Press, Cambridge, MA 1983.
  and Mack, A., *Inattentional Blindness*, MIT Press, Cambridge MA, 1998.
Rosenberg, Alexander, 'Mackie and Shoemaker on Dispositions and Properties', in *Midwest Studies in Philosophy IX 1984, Causation and Causal Theories*, see French.
Rosenberg, Jay F., and Travis, Charles, *Readings in the Philosophy of Language*, Prentice Hall, Inc., Englewood Cliffs, NJ, 1971.

— *Linguistic Representation*, D. Reidel Publishing Co., Dordrecht, Holland, 1974.

Russell, Bertrand, *Mysticism and Logic and Other Essays*, Longmans, Green and Co., London, 1925.

— *Why I am not a Christian, and Other Essays*, Simon and Schuster, NY, 1957.

'Descriptions', in *Readings in the Philosophy of Language*, see Rosenberg and Travis.

— 'On Denoting', in *Meaning and Truth, the Essential Readings in Modern Semantics*, see Garfield and Kiteley.

— 'Mr. Strawson on Referring', in *Meaning and Truth, the Essential Readings in Modern Semantics*, see Garfield and Kiteley .

— *The Problems of Philosophy*, Oxford University Press, 1959.

— and Whitehead, Alfred North, *Principia Mathematica*, Cambridge University Press, Cambridge, UK, vol. 1, 1912, vol. 2, 1913.

Ryle, Gilbert, *The Concept of Mind*, University of Chicago Press, Chicago, IL, 1949.

Sanford, David, 'The Direction of Causation and the Direction of Time', in *Midwest Studies in Philosophy IX*, see French.

Samuels, Richard, Stich, Stephen, and Bishop, Michael, 'Ending the Rationality Wars: How to make Disputes about Human Rationality Disappear', in *Common Sense, Reason and Rationality*, Vancouver Studies in Cognitive Science, vol. 11, ed., Renee Elio, Oxford University Press, Oxford, UK, 2002.

Searle, John, *Speech Acts*, Cambridge University Press, Cambridge, UK, 1969.

— *Intentionality, An Essay in the Philosophy of Mind*, Cambridge University Press, Cambridge, UK, 1983.

— *Minds, Brains, and Science*, Harvard University Press, Cambridge, MA, 1984.

— 'Is the Brain a Digital Computer?', PresidentialAddress to the Pacific Division of the American Philosophical Association, printed in *TheProceedings and Addresses of The American Philosophical Association*, vol. 64, no. 3, November 1990, University of Delaware, Lancaster Press, Lancaster, PA, 1990.

— *Mind, Language and Society*, Wiedenfeld and Nicolson, The Orion Publishing Group, London, UK, 1999.

Shepard, Roger N. and Cooper, Lynn A. *Mental Images and Their Transformations*, MIT Press, Cambridge, MA, 1982.

Shoemaker, Sydney, *The First-Person Perspective and Other Essays*, Cambridge University Press, Cambridge, UK, 1996.

Shwayder, D.S., 'Hume was Right, Almost; and Where He Wasn't, Kant Was', in *Midwest Studies in Philosophy IX*, see French.

Skinner, B.F., *Science and Human Behavior*, Macmillan Publishing Co., NY 1953.

Soames, Scott, *Understanding Truth*, Oxford University Press, Oxford, UK, 1999.

Spinoza, Baruch, *Works of Spinoza*, trans, R.H.M. Elwes, Bell, London, 1883, Dover Edition, NY, 1955.

Stalnaker, Robert C. *Inquiry*, MIT Press, Cambridge, MA, 1984.

Stevenson, Leslie, *The Study of Human Nature*, Oxford University Press, NY, 1981.

Strawson, P.F., 'On Referring', in *Meaning and Truth, the Essential Readings in Modern Semantics*, see Garfield and Kiteley.

Stich, Steven, *From Folk Psychology to Cognitive Science*, Bradford Books, MIT Press, Cambridge, MA, 1983.

— and Warfield, Ted A., eds. *Mental Representation*, Blackwell Publishers, Oxford, UK, 1994.

— *Deconstructing the Mind*, Oxford University Press, Oxford, UK 1996.

Tarski, Alfred, 'The Semantic Conception of Truth and The Foundations of Semantics', in *Meaning and Truth, the Essential Readings in Modern Semantics*, see Garfield and Kiteley .

Taylor, Charles, *The Explanation of Behaviour*, Routledge and Kegan Paul, Ltd., London, UK 1964.

Taylor, Richard, ed., *The Empiricists*, Anchor Press/Doubleday, Garden City, NY, 1974.

Metaphysics, 4th edn., Prentice Hall, Englewood Cliffs, NJ, 1992.

Thompson, Evan,ed., *Between Ourselves, Second–person Issues in the Study of Consciousness*, Imprint Academic, Exeter, UK, 2001.

Tooley, Michael, 'Laws and Causal Relations', in *Midwest Studies in Philosophy IX*, see French.

Turing, Alan, 'Computing Machinery and Intelligence', in *Mind,* vol. LIX no. 236, October, 1950, Oxford University Press, UK.

Weiskrantz, Lawrence, *Blindsight: a case study and implications*, Oxford University Press, Oxford, UK, 1986.

Wisdom, John, 'Gods', The Aristotelian Society, reprinted in *Journeys Through Philosophy*, eds. Capaldi, Kelly, and Navia, Prometheus Books, Buffalo, NY, 1982.

Wittgenstein, Ludwig, *The Tractatus Logico Philosophicus*, Routledge and Kegan Paul, Ltd., London, UK, 1961.

Philosophical Investigations, Macmillan Co., NY 1958.

Varela, Francisco, 'Present Time Consciousness' in *The View from Within, op. cit.* below.

Varela, Francisco, and Shear, Jonathan, eds., *The View From Within, First Person Approaches to the Study of Consciousness*, Imprint Academic, Exeter, UK, 1999.

Vendler, Zeno, *Res Cogitans*, Cornell University Press, Ithaca, NY, 1972.

Yolton, John W., *Perceptual Acquaintance from Descartes to Reid*, University of Minnesota Press, Minneapolis, MN 1984.

.

Index

A

Affective states 114–115
Agency 115
Algorithm 213–214
Alice in Wonderland 204
Almog 48–49
Analytic 33,45
Analytic a priori 31
Analytic philosophy . . 137,155,167
    linguistic analysis 145
Anscombe 40
Anthropomorphism 87,109
Aristotelian 25
    devil x 215
    hedonistic devil . . 80,86,142,177
Aristotle 6–11,13,17,24,29,89,133–134
    efficient causation . . . 29,82,123
    essence 111
    formal causation 87
    four causes 9
    matter 52,54
    on knowledge 217
    prime matter 85
    relativity in substance . . 110,118
    relativity of matter 53
    scientific revolution 89
    substance 110–111
    the mind is the form of the
        body 89
Artificial Intelligence 169,212
Atkinson 58–59
Ayer, A.J. 137
    linguistic analysis 140

B

Background theory 25

Bayes's Law 172,174
Beethoven 127
Behaviorism 17,81,168,186
    as language analysis 138
    behavioristic reduction of
        language use 138
    denial approach to
        psychological drives . . . 121
    denial of direct experience of
        psychological needs . . . 120
    in Ryle 128
    methodological 21
Being 152
    as limited by logical
        possibility 152
    beliefs 22
Benardete, José 43
Berkeley, George . 29,51,68,116–117
    sense-data 118
    solipsism 70
    to be is to be perceived 68
Binocular disparity 59
Binocular parallax 59
biological naturalism
    naturalistic thinking 168
Biological naturalism 157
    and judgement 159
    hierarchies of needs 93
    pica 93
Biology 38
Bleuler 66
Blindsight 82
Bostock, David . . 205–207,212,214
    alternative logics 205
Bridge concept 142
Brouwer 207

Buddha 132
    on psychological projection . 121

C

Carnap, Rudolph 103
Carroll, Lewis 204
Cartesian dualism 23
Castaneda, Hector-Neri . . . 15-16
Causal laws
    as counterfactual
        conditionals 183
    causal powers in 184
    platonic versions of 105
Causation 8,10,23,29,34,86
    according to Hume 15, 94
    agent 36-37,39,89,107
    billiard balls . . . 34,38,89,98,100
    cause and effect 81
    counter-factual conditional
        accounts of 186
    deductive-nomological
        41,87,102,104-107
    efficient 30,37,81-82,89,91,99,107
    mechanical 82
    motion transfer view 34
    non-linear 81
    platonic account of 185
    projected understanding . . . 94
    projected agency 29-30,41,99-100
    property-oriented accounts . 184
    retroductive 41,102
    singularist 88
    statistical co-relation 30
    time in 10,104
    transuent 29,99
Cause 123
Causity 16, 99
Certainty 47
    in causal laws 98,106
Cheating detection algorithm . 176
Chemistry 67
Chomsky, Noam 173
Churchland, Paul & Patricia 121,141
Clark, Andy 78,80,87
Cognitive penetrability 156
Cognitive science 9,82,85,168
    cognitive scientists 141

linguistic analysis in 145
    on propositions 142
Cognitive states 115
Computational reasoning 212
Computational structure
    in Searle 30
Computational systems 6,22
    logical systems 11
    structure 12
Computational thinking processes
    . . 9,13
Computer
    as symbol cruncher 143
Computers 22,124
    garbage in, garbage out . . . 204
    not candidates for experience 138
    proposition-driven 142
Concatenation rules 13,18
Concepts . . 8,28,47,49,55,83-84,90,
        94,162,218-219
    autonomy of 183
    certainty in 168
    checking for verification . . . 47
    clarity of 151
    conceptual schemas 160
    conceptual systems 152
    contents of 162
    de dicto 185
    describe possibilities 182
    event-structure 83
    explanatoriness of 184
    in causal theories 40,184
    judgements about 162
    logical limits on 151
    modal 185
    of an object 137-138,145
    of being or existence 181
    of self 66
    of truth 206
    platonic universals 24
    set and inference 160
    triangles, recursive sequences,
        etc 150
Conceptual systems
    classical, quantum, and
        intuitionist logics 206
    cosmologies 218-219

elegant fantasies 218
formal structures 190
  incompleteness and
    inconsistency in. . . . 201,212
  linguistic 67
  logical/mathematical. . 185–186
  Quine's. 197
  syntactically structured . . . 199
  systematic considerations . . 198
Consciousness. 68
  isolated ego. 66
  transparency of. 69–70
Consciousness studies 75
Correspondence view of truth. . 83
Cosmic reason 202
Creative mental play 115,127
Cretan Liar, paradox of 190
Cummins, Robert 23
  psychological explanation . . 22

D
Dali Lama. 132
  self-knowledge 132
Darwin, Charles
  evolution 83
  evolutionary theory 213
  natural selection 214
Davidson, Donald. 38
  on propositions. 157
Daydreams 115
De dicto predication . . . 9,147,149,
              160,163,166,185,218
De re predication . 13,19,22,147,149,
              163,166,185,217
Deducibility 149–150,152
Deductive reasoning. 177
Dennett, Daniel 76,213
  on propositions. 141
Denotation 106,137
  denoting in a formal kause . . 91
  in propositions 145
  in symbolic logic 105
  of names. 145
  Russell 18
Descartes, René 63,82,133
  Cartesian isolated ego. 66
  solipsism 70

Determinism. 81–82
Detlefsen, Michael 207,209,
              211–212,214
  mathematical knowledge . . 207
Dewey, John. 81
Dilthey, Wilhelm 62
Direct experience 7,36
Direct realism. 32–33,59,70
  and the pythagorean
    theorem 147
  awareness of psychological
    needs and drives 120
  direct awareness. . . 45,109–110,
      115,118,120,122,134,147,159
  direct experience. 132,217
  direct perception 203
  in Humean induction 95
  in hunger 44
  in identity. 43
  in religious experience. . . . 131
  in retroductive kausation . . 106
  range of sensory awareness . 117
DNA. 213
Donnellan-type reference 22
Dorsal perceptual processes . . . 80
Dreams 115,122
Dretske, Fred
  causal theory of mental
    representation. 34
  on irrelevance of 'genetic' or
    'motile' cause markers . . . 35
  on propositions 141
Ducasse, C.J. 40

E
E= mc² 8
Efficient Causation 9
Einstein, Albert. 133
Ellwood, Robert
  unconditioned reality 129
Embodied metaphors
  Lakoff and Johnson 84
Empiricism 7,26,116,134–135
  and logic. 205
  anti-empirical views of
    knowledge 168
  empirical evidence. 11–12

empiricist accounts of sensory
  data 116
math is an empirical science. 210
of geometry 205
Enc, Berent 50
Essence 111
Evolutionary psychology 175
Existence 23,86
  notion of 25
  of concepts 182
  of forms 182
  of unicorns 182
  platonic account of 185
Existential quantifier 10,25,152-153,
                                    86
  for Quine 186
  of names 142
Experience. . 30-31,35,38,70,85,143,
149,152-153,162-163,168,204,212,215
  articulating experience 78
  as a burst from the blue . . . 134
  as explanatory 184
  collective human 220
  connection to possible worlds 199
  de re 185
  direct, but misunderstood . . 31
  Eureka! 132
  experiential data 158
  first person
    singular . . . 138-139,168,220
  generalized through y-type
    thinking 218
  home of truth 202,215
  how concepts apply 182
  impinging on consciousness
    34,90,99,107
  in dogs 138
  in Humean induction 95
  in kausation 33,95,185
  indexical knowledge of 31,55,219
  indexing names, and labels . 143
  influence on logic 205
  is temporal 89
  logic is a tool for understanding
    of 204
  not in computers 167
  not modal 185

of affective states 115
of creative mental play . 115,127
of dreams and memories 115,122
of intellectual
  synthesis 132,209,217
of kinesthetic sensations 115,117
of mathematics 209-210
of psychological drives and
  needs 115,120,122
of reality 186,188,199,220
platonic dogmas about 88,202,204
points of view in 37,111
priority of 145
psychological, memory, dreams,
  etc. 209
relationship to sense and
  meaning 64,140,142,144
religious or mystical
  115,129,131,132,220
understanding of 132
wide range of 135
Ezekiel 132

F

Falk, Ruma 172-173
Feminism
  on rationality 179
Field, Hartry 157
  possible worlds 150
  propositional mental states . 157
Fodor, Jerry 6,11,13
  cognitive science 121
  compositionality 61
  language of thought 7,127
  mental language 168
  on propositions 141
Formal causation 9
Fra Angelico 133
Free-floating thoughts 203
Freeman, Walter J. 80
  circular causality 81-82
Frege, Gottlob . . . 133,155,163,202,
                              210-211
  'the Thought' 141
  autonomy of logic 202,206
  certainty of math and logic . 209
  compositionality 157

deducibility 149
definitions. 162
disembodied thoughts . 162,202
ideas. 141-142,155,159
learning that p implies p. . . 204
limits on the real 152
metaphysical realism on
  thoughts 150
mind-dependent ideas. . . . 155
on Husserl 62,160-162
on relations 162
on sense 141-142
Peano's axioms 207
platonic entities. 157
propositions 146,148,157
the pythagorean theorem 147,149
the third realm. 141,146,149-151,
  160,162,186,199,202,207-210,
  215
Freud, Sigmund 133

G
Gestalt psychology. 59,61,75
figure/ground 62
gestalten 60-62,70,81
self consciousness 63
Gandhi, Mohandas 119
as a religious leader 132
Gigerenzer, Gerd 176-177
domain specific reasoning. . 176
Gilman, Leonard. 177
Gödel, Kurt 212-213
logical transposition 213
theorem 215
Goodall, Jane
on gorillas 145
Goodman, Nelson. 10
Gricean intentionality. 13

H
Hartmann, George. 62-63,66
Hedonistic devil . . . 3,10,13,16,134
Hempel, Karl 80,103-104,106
bridge principles 103
covering laws and
  observations 103

deductive thinking
  procedures. 104
deductive-nomological
  causation. 102
internal principles 103
theoretical entities 104
Heraclitus
Heraclitean flux 11
Hierarchically invidious monism 179
Hintikka, Jaakko. 75,85-87,210-212,
  214
descriptive games 85
game theory. 210
interrogative games 85
Skolem functions. 87
Hobbes, Thomas 113
Holland, John 169-170
quasi-morphism 171
Holyoak, Keith 169-170
Homonyms 39-40,123
Homunculus 37-38,94
in causation. 99
Hug, Klaus 176-177
domain specific reasoning. . 176
Hughes, Langston 122
Human nature 202
heavy bones 203,205
limits on thinking. 203
Human needs 119
Hume, David 30,173
contentlessness of logic . . . 204
contentlessness of tautologies 204
critique of induction. 30
induction. 36,62,95
knowledge 217
necessity and causes. 98
on causation 14
on sensation 116
statistical co-relation. 94
stream of consciousness . 95,116
using the past to predict the
  future 98,101
Husserl, Edmund. . . . 109,155,159
abstraction 62
experientialized logic 162
in Gestalt Psychology 62
necessity and self-evidence . 162

on arithmetic 161
on logic. 161–163
on objects 154
phenomenology 160–161
presentational view of third
    realm concepts. 160

I

Idealism 31,71,77,87
Identity 137,148,149
Imagining, ... 156
Incompleteness and inconsistency
. . . 212
Independence friendly logic . . 210
Indexicals . . . 9,13,20,37,49,86,143
    in experience. 109,111,218
    in kausation. 185
    in logical systems. 152
    in meaning 139
    in naming 219
    names and labels, denotation 143
Induction. 169,171
    quasi-morphism 171
    inductive reasoning . . . 170,176
Inference 64
    rules of 65
    from sense-data to
        things 56–57,59,61,64
    logical 64–65
Innovation 133
Insurance company statistics
. . . 100–101
Intellectual insight
    and the Pythagorean theorem147
Intellectual synthesis 115
    psychological projection. . . 217
Intentionality . 13,39–40,46,59,69,75,
        77,80–81,84185,199
    conditions of satisfaction . . 139
    eliminated from inference by
        Frege 142
    in creative mental play. . . . 127
    in kausation 38
    in object-positing 138
    in perception 163
    in Stalnaker 155
    intentional states 113–114

of kausation 107,205
of objects. 109
of sensation. 22
Intentions . . . 18,31,54,67,70,87,115
    blinding. 46
    formulated via points of view112
    in creative mental play. . . . 128
    in intellectual insight. 134
    in kausation 37
    in mystical insight 132
    in naming. 32
    in religious experience. . . . 130
    intentional states 111
    role in knowledge 107,219
    role in meaning. 139
    sharing in language 140
Introspection. 84
Intuitionism 210,212
Intuitionist 210
Isomorphism. 77

J

James, William. 76
    on religious experience . 129–130
Jesus. 132
Johnson, Mark 75,82–85
Johnson's rock. 24
Judgement 59–60,87
    human. 89
    in intellectual insight. 134
    in kausation 37–39
    in object-positing 36,95
    in perception 58,97
    in religious experience. . . . 129
    in statistical applications. . . 102
    intentional 39
    mistakes of equivocation . . . 40
    of a kause. 45
    of perspective 60
    practical. 98

K

Kant, Immanuel 32,203
    category of apperception . . . 33
    contentlessness of tautologies204
    ethics. 178
    Kantian causation 30

noumena . . 31–32,43,54,,203,220
phenomena 31–32
schemas 171
transcendental objects . 32,43,46
Kausation 29,75,30,33,36,47,
        72,83–84,87,171,176,199
    agency is projected
        understanding 94
    and experience 39,217
    deductive-nomological
        102,104,107
    efficient 99
    equivocation and mistakes . . 40
    experiential impact, not transfer
        51
    impingement 85,109,111
    intentionality and judgement . 38
    kausal knowledge 219
    kause in intellectual insight . 134
    kause of dreams 123
    mechanics of 33
    not syntactical 185
    recalcitrantly determinate . . 107
    relata of 62
    Retroduction 106
    retroductive 105
    singularist 41
    status as kause 37
    structure of 37
    summary 107
    teleological 94,107
    temporal order in 108
Kause 55,65,70,123
    formal 81,88–90,91–92,
        94,97,99,102,107,114
Keller, Helen
    connecting names to
        experiences 49
Kinesthesis
    is learned 63
Kinesthetic experience 115
Knowledge 6,83,215
    acquisition 6,51
    analytic truths are pristine but
        useless 204
    Aristotle's formula 142
    basis of knowledge claims . . 134
    by acquaintance or
        recognition 26
    by computers 138,168
    collected sum of human
        knowledge 46,219
    de dicto 218
    de re 217
    Dretske and Enc 50
    egotistical knowledge claims 168
    encoded in propositions . . . 218
    eureka type insights 133
    fantastically structural 219
    growth 89
    humility recommended for
        claims to 201
    ignorance of observers 31
    inarticulately experiential . . 219
    Kant's limits on 32
    knower's active participation
        in 107
    limits on 54
    no dichotomies 219
    not had by computers 138
    object-positing 106
    of a theorem 147
    of logic 207
    of mathematics . 207–208,210,214
    of reality 47
    of reality = knowledge of
        logical structure 197
    of things 32
    omniscience . . . 31,33,38,46,168
    prescient intuitive of H2O . . 49
    recalcitrant parameters of . . 203
    respective roles of logic and
        experience 168
    roadblocks in 113
    role of probability in 98
    scientific 83
    self-knowledge 132
    sources of 104,117,131–132
    static vs. dynamic views . . . 26
    summary and overview . . . 217
    things humans know 202
    transcendentally accurate . . . 46
    understanding 205
Kohler, Wolfgang 63

Kosslyn, Stephen, and Pomerantz,
James . . . .
   propositions vs. images . . . 159
Kripke, Saul 185
   as a basis for Mackie's account of
      causation 185
   counter-factual conditionals. 185
   denotation and reference . . . 49
   initial baptisms 49,144
   natural kinds. . . 15,17,19,49,185
   on names 145
   possible worlds 14
   puzzle about beliefs 139
   social meanings of words . . 144

L

Lakoff, George 75,82–85,87
Language
   a dynamic and evolving
      entity 138
   modeled by a computer . . . 138
   no need to standardize into rigor
      mortis. 140
   Peano and the logic of 207
   prerequisite for propositions 158
   private 140
   tied to experience. 140
   vagaries and variabilities of . 146
Language of thought 12
Lao Tzu 132
Lewis, David
   possible worlds 150
Linguistic
   life of names. 142
   notions. 137
   terms. 145
   thinking. 80
Locke, John. 54,116–117
   matter 52
   sense-data 118
   sensory data. 116
   simple ideas. 116
Logic . . 84–85,133,149,152–153,210
   alternative 211–212
   analysis of relationships between
      propositions 146
   basic concepts 137,146,207

deducibility 142,146–147
deductive 108
existence or being in 146
for quantum physics 167
formal systems 214
functions. 211
identity 146
in phenomenology . . . 160–161
independence from
   psychology. 141
independence-friendly 85
independent of experience . 161
inferences and proofs 85
logical constant. 86
logical reductivism 83
material implication . . . 148,151
modal 158
of language 137
of mathematics 13,208
opacity in 184
possible alternatives to . 201,205
relations in 162–163
rigor mortis. 87
role in knowledge . . 54,168,219
sequences. 190,192
sling shot argument 147
substitutional. 87
valid inferences. 141
variables. 146
Logical opacity 77
Logical structures
   classical. 206–207
   contradictions. 212
   entailment. 218
   existential quantifier. . . 166,218
   formal validity 204
   functions 195,197
   Implication 204
   in Lewis Carroll. 204
   law of excluded
      middle 206–207,209
   logical theorem 198
   logical truths. . 192–193,197–198
   metalogic 198
   monolithic logico-
      mathematical 201

preserving truth across
  inferences 204
principle of distribution . . . 206
protosyntax 198
proxy functions . . . 193–194,196
Proxy functions 192
reductio ad absurdum . 195–197
rules and formulas 212
satisfaction relations 193
sequences 192
tautologies 202,204
the Frege-Russell view 207
Logical systems 147
  as purely formal structures . 147
  complete science 201
  existential quantification in . 152
  Frege-Russell view of 208
  Incompleteness and
    inconsistency 198,212
  intuitionist 209
  monolithic 208
  non-classical 206
  paradoxes 212
  regress problems 185
  sameness of structure 148
  structural relationships
    in 148,150
Logical truths 192
Lowenheim-Skolem theorem . . 25

M
Mackie, J.L. . . . 13,104,183–185,188
  counterfactual conditionals . 183
Mad Hatter's Tea Party 204
Magenta thing 144,151
  that-that-color-thing 144
Mangan, Bruce 76–77,87
Maslow, Abraham 118
  hierarchy of needs 93
Mathematical
  ability 213
Mathematical intuitionists . . . 167
Mathematical reasoning 215
Mathematics 207,209
  algebra 208
  Detlefsen-Poincaré view . . . 208
  discoveries 214

Euclidean Geometry 205
Euclidean space 60
geometry 208
incompleteness and
  inconsistency 212
insight 209
Intuitionist interpretations of
  204,206,207–208,210
Lobachevskian geometry . . 205
logic 198,208
Lowenheim-Skolem Theorem
  193,197
mathematical truths 213
non-denumerable sets . 195–197
non-linear 81
not equivalent to logic 201
Peano's axioms 207,210
quadratics 220
Riemannian Geometry 205
Matter 13,55,68
  mind-independent 70
McMullin, Ernan 105
Meaning 137,214
  and names 142
  carried in deductions 150
  carried in unequivocal names 145
  dictionary 139
  identity of 148–149
  in language 40,48,116,137
    Hellen Keller 49
  is not symbol crunching . . 49
  meaninglessness for a person 143
  of propositions 147
  relation to sense 142,152
  social or community 139
Mechanism 89
Memories 115,122
  types of experience 123
Memory 124
  iconic 125,126
  long term 125
  of concepts 151
  reconstructive 125
  sensory 125
  short term 125
Mental processes 22
Merleau Ponty,Maurice 81

metaphors
   primary 83
Metaphysical drift 10–11,25,134,145
   between objectified properties &
    property-reduced objects. 144
   in objectified properties . . . 144
Metaphysics 84
Metatheories 198
Mid-sized objects . . 8,12–21,53,70,
              115,199
   abstract objects 134
   as named 145
   constant and kausative Humean
    impressions 95
   direct experience of. 218
   expanded explanation of . . 135
   identification of 64
   in kausal object-positing . . . 184
   in propositions 147
   ontological commitment to . 166
   Quine's 'ascent' away from . 190
   sources of kausal influence . 118
   stability. 109–110
   Stability 110
   stable objects 12,14,19,20,27,37,97
Milner, D., and Goodale, M . . . 79
Mind games 204
   with systems of structures. . 199
Mind-to-world . 37,40,46–48,80–81,
              90–91
Minnich, Elizabeth 169,179
Modal concepts 201
Modal contexts 22
Mohammed. 132
Montessori 111,133
Monty Hall problem. 172
Moore, G.E. 68–71,116
   refutation of idealism . . . 68,71
   sense-data. 69–70
Moses 132
Mother Theresa of Calcutta
   self-knowledge 132

N

Names 13,90,107,109,152,218
   bridge concepts 144
   denotation of 18,49,145
   for Kripke. 19
   for objectified properties. . . 144
   identity 43,148
   in kausation 39
   in propostions. 147
   in sense and meaning 142
   index experience and
    communicate 142
   indexed to experience . . 31,145
   labels or terms 143
Naming
   activity. . . 67,71,89,91,97,217
   regress of for Tarski 187
Natural kinds. 13,15
Necessary truths 13
Necessity
   in D-N causal laws 104
Newton, Isaac 133
Next-to relation 162
Nisbett, Richard 169–170
Noumena. 68
Numbers
   recursive sequence 150
   zero and the square root of
    two 183

O

Object-positing. . . 7,9,11,24,26–27,
35–36,38–41,46–47,50,56,67,81,89,98,
102,104,107–111,135,144,159,161,
166,186
   according to Quine . . . 186–187
   and Fregian ideas. 142
   and meanings 138,142,145
   as active interaction. . . 33,44,90
   as an act. 55
   by Fido. 158
   in creative mental play . 127–128
   in Humean causation 95
   in intellectual insight . . 133–134
   in kausation 34,45
   in psychological projection . 122
   in religious experience. . . . 132
   in retroductive kausation . . 105
   in science 104,106
   names and labels. 143,145

neither static nor pre-packaged
. . . . 135
not done by computers . . . 138
'objectified' properties 144
observer's role 37
of a song 127
presents actual existence
. . . . 44,153,185
singularist kausation 40
via dreams and memories . . 122
why d-n causation is not. . . 103
world-to-mind side. 217
x-type
thinking . . . 199,209,215,217
Object-positing process 77-78,83-85
Objects 86
Omniscience
not attainable by humans . . 220
Opacity
in causal contexts 39
in object positing. 46
of causal contexts 38
of objects to logical analysis . 138

P

Paradox of rationality 173
Paranoia 66
Parmenides, ... 10
Passing show 12
Peano, Guiseppe 207
Penrose, Roger 212-214
Perception 80
content in. 99,114
perceptual intentions. 114
Perception . 9,14,34,46-47,69-70,163
as projected agency 36
biochemical chain of events in 34
by Fido. 158
cognitive penetrability 46
constancies in. 57
content in 97
direct. 10,59
figure and ground 57
gestalten in 61
in kausation 36,43
in Searle. 91
not propositional. 50

of a chemical 67
of a child 67
perceptual system features . . 59
Perceptual-motor
coordination. 63
psychological research on. . . 57
segregation 57
selectivity in 13
sensory 56
spatial and distance
judgements 60
veridical. 39
Perspective. 83
first-person singular. 78
Physics 38
fluid mechanics 46
mathematical purity of. . . . 184
Newton 99
non-linear. 81
wave/particle location
problem 206
Piatelli-Palmarini, Massimo 172-173
Picasso, Pablo 133
Plato 6,88,151,182,188
derision of lovers of sights and
sounds 89
forms. 5,134,144,181-182
lovers of sights and sounds . 204
on objects. 9,16,155
platonic. 78,179
platonic accounts of existence
and causation 185
platonic causation 15
platonic certainty 82
platonic D-N causal laws . . 104
platonic dogmas about
experience and logic . . . 202
platonic dogmas about
experience and logic . . . 204
platonic entities 10,202
platonic equations 47
platonic forms 85
platonic heaven . 88,108,134,144,
167,177,185-186,197,201-202,
210,212,215
platonic notions of truth . . . 46
platonic property sets 20

platonic purists 159
platonic view of reality 25
properties, i.e. colors 143
regress of explanations . . 14,184
the third man 163,186
theory of predication 181
third man paradox 179
Poincaré, Henri 207–209
Point of view . . . 15,19,32,36–37,39,
54–55,57,62,67,69–70,83–84,109,171,
175–176,178,218
  and objectivity 67
  content of 112
  dynamic 33
  egocentric 111
  first person singular 139
  generated in creative mental
    play 128
  human 89
  in agency 107
  in intellectual insight 134
  in kausation 30,91
  in object-positing 115,138
  in x=r 43
  of a parent 67
  of language users 138
  point-of-viewless world 89
  related to education and
    experience 112
  relationship to ofness 35
  religious 132
  time and space limits 38
  variety possible 38
Possible worlds 20,150,151,
157–158,185,199,218
  do not contain real causation 185
  for Stalnaker 156-157
  in conceptual systems 186
  in D-N causal laws 104
  semantics 13
  transition 104
Pragmatism 87
Predication
  of properties 146
Price, H.H. 116
Primary metaphors
  Lakoff and Johnson 83

Prisoner's dilemma 178
Probability 31,41,97,107,172,177,178
  costs vs. benefits 177
  formal kause basis 97
  object-positing account of . . . 98
  role in understanding 100
  systematic statistical studies . 97
Properties,
  causal powers 184
Property-attributing . 3,5,7,22,46,85,
102,104,107,144,160,166
  concatenation rules 134
  identity in 148
  in retroductive causation . . 105
  inferences 46
  mathematics in 209
  names and labels in 145
  objectivity in 87,88
  'propertizing' objects 144
  propositions as vehicles in . 146
  relationships 147,150
  role of definitions 162
  singularist kausation 40
  statistical co-relation in . . 98,101
  structures in thought . . 103,201
  y-domain is not unitary . . . 210
  y-type reasoning processes . 148
  Y-type thinking . . . 103,199,203,
    215,218–219
Propositions 5,45,64–65,86,147–149,
152,155–157,201,218
  and names 142,144–145
  as logical concepts . 146,150,157
  content of . . 2,22,114,141,143,146
  deducibility 9,147
  eternal
    sentences . . 10,22,131,141,202
  identity of 148
  in Frege 141
  in property-attributing 46
  in cognitive science 142
  in Stalnaker 155,157
  logical isomorphism 47
  propositional structure 50
  reduction of thought to . . . 121
  relationships 147
  role in memory 124

role of objects in 147
sense in 142
subject to dynamic revision . 219
truth-functional. . . . 46,103,157
understanding of 218
unite x and y-type thinking
   processes 219
variables as space markers . 146
Psychological
   limits on knowledge. 54
Psychological explanation. 7
Psychological projection 33
   in art 128
   in bigotry and fear 121
   in creative mental play. . . . 128
   in Eastern Philosophy 121
Putnam, Hilary
   Dopplegangers 139
   on propositions. 157
Putnam's sociological view of
      reference 13,20
   quantum logic 205–206
Pylyshyn, Zenon. 166
   cognitive penetrability . . 46,156
Pythagorean theorem
   141,147,151,153,157,208
Pythagoreanism 193,195–197
   ontological reduction to . . . 186

Q

quantifiers. 210–211
Quine, W.V.O. . 6–7,9–10,16–18,22,
   75–77,103,163,167,186–188,190,
      198–199
   background
      theories. 186–188,192–198,212
   behaviorism 18,121
   critique of 201
   desire for relief from
      slooplessness 92
   empirical influences on logic 206
   existential quantifier 166
   incompleteness and
      inconsistency in math. . . 212
   incompleteness of mathematical
      logic. 198
   indefinability of truth 212

indeterminacy of translation . 21
knowledge claims 168
logical structures 152
logical truths 192
modeling 187

objects are posits of theories . 17
on existence 21,152
on symbolic logic 147
ontological commitment. . . 196
ontological reduction
   194,193–197
ontological relativity
   21,152,171,188,192–193
proxy functions . 21,188,187–188,
   192,196–197
reality anchors . 192,194,197–198
reduction of an
   economic theory . . . 194–197
regress in metatheories . . . 186
satisfaction relations 189
self-rebuilding ship metaphor 20
semantic ascent
   . 21,188–190,192–193,197,201
sense-data. 23
the third man 185–186,198
truth predicates 190–192
unitary view of science and
   language 166

R

Rationality 169,173
Realism 211
   embodied 83
Reality 71,85,104,215
   anchors in Quine
      . . . 187–188,192,194,197–198
   and objectivity 67

   complexity of 169
   de re 147
   denial approach in behaviorism
      121
   direct realism. . . 70,134,199,217
   distinction between direct
      perception and
      dreams, etc. 123

impingement on
  consciousness 107
in retroductive scientific
  entities 105
limned by symbolic logic 147,186
limning the true and ultimate
  structure of 197
looking in the wrong place
  for. 188
lost in sling shot argument . 149
marked by intentional
  states. 114,183
mind-independent. 53
not in a y-type system 199
not in formal structures . . . 147
not in Frege's third realm . . 199
not in platonic heaven 108
not in possible worlds. . 182,186
not modal 185
of cars, tables and trees . . . 151
of concepts 182
of fear, hunger, mice, and
  chairs 122
of forms 181
of sky-hooks. 199
of time 130
of triangles, recursive
  sequences, etc. 151
psychological 146
recalcitrance of reality 85
structural properties of . 160,185
summary and overview . . . 217
unconditioned 130
used to check validity in
  logic. 205
Reasoning
  non-computational 214
Recognition 44,89,91
  in Dretske and Enc. 50
  of a mouse 45
  of hunger 45
Reduction
  of properties to objects and
    vice versa. 144
Reductivism. 84,215
Reference. 187,192–193,197
  in Quine. 187,192

indeterminacy of 188–189
preservation in translation . 193
Regress
  in a counter-factual conditionals
    account of causation . . . 184
  in logical/mathematical
    systems. 186
  in metatheories 186
  in ontology 187
  in the semantics of truth . . . 187
Relations. 8
Relations and properties 146
Relativism 83,87
Relativity 8
Religious experience. 115
Representation 77,85
  mental representation 86
Robotic scanners 58
Robots. 214
Rosenberg, Alexander . . . 183–185
  regress in a counter-factual
    conditionals account of
    causation. 184
Rosenberg, Jay 173
Rules of transition. 16
Russell, Bertrand 6,13,22,103,173,210
  and Whitehead 133
  compositionality 61,157
  deducibility 149
  dream tables 55
  Euclidean space 60
  matter 53
  on objects 20
  on religious experience . 130–131
  Peano's axioms 207
  propertizing objects 144
  propositions 148,157
  reduction of objects to property
    sets. 17,144
  sense-data . . . 51,55–56,63,66,68
  symbolic logic. 146
  the autonomy of logic 202
  the pacifist. 131
  unity of math and logic . . . 210
Ryle, Gilbert 26
  a clown's pratfalls 128
  category mistakes 89

S

Salmon, Weseley 105
Sanford, David 11–12,104
Scholastics 29,133
Schulte 66
Science 199
  complete and logical
    structure 201
Searle, John 22,109
  agent causation 91
  causally self referential 35
  chinese room 49
  conditions of satisfaction . 90,114
  content of a belief 114
  efficient causation 100
  Fido's thoughts 157
  intentional states 111,114
  intentionality 35
  on imagination 156
  on intentional identification of
    objects 33
  on Kripke on beliefs 139
  on perceptual judgements . . 159
  on propositions 141
  privacy of the mental 23
  psychological modes 114
  simulation 210
  teleological causation . . . 89–90
Seaweed
  knowledge of 33
Self-organizing systems 81
Semantic
  nature of x and r 35
Semantics . . . 13,35,85–87,161,210
  according to Tarski 187
  as kausal manipulation 90
  denotation 47
  identity 43
  in kausation 34
  in Kausation 37
  in perception 163
  in the mind-to-world
    relationship 40
  meaning in language 49
  'ofness' 35
  possible world 14
  role in knowledge 219

semantic
  ascent . . 188,190,197–198,201
semantic identification
  of objects 33
semantic judgements 40
Sensation . . . 13,18,26,56,68–70,122
  attuned to
    object-positing 57,61,63
  content 122
  imagistic 217
  in animals 158
  kinesthetic 217
  of Kantian phenomena 32
  role in memory 125
  sensory experience . . . 15,22,24
  sensory knowledge 54,217
Sense 148
  'making sense' 143
  a bridge concept 142,144
  in a proposition 147,152
  irrelevant in deducibility . . 150
  of a statement 142
  of 'pineapple flavoring' . . . 142
Sense-data 22,61–62,67,134
  as intermediaries 71,135
  dogmas about 43,56,68
  in Price and Moore 116
  in Quine 22
Set theory 18
Shoemaker, Sydney . . 183,185,188
  counterfactual conditionals . 183
Schwayder, D.S. 38
Skinner, B.F. 133
Skinnerian behaviorism 26
Sky-hooks 199
Sling shot argument 6,21,149
Social policy 178
Sorting-box view of thought . . . 33
Spinoza's one substance world . 39
Stability of objects 15
Stalnaker, Robert . . 109,121,155,159
  a dog's thoughts 157
  mental entities 157
  on objects 154
  on propositions 141,157
  propositionalized
    ideas 14,142,156

Statistics 174,178
  legitimate conclusions from . 101
  on macho bravado 101
  social. 169
Stimulus-response 81
Stich, Stephen
  on propositions 141
  rationality wars. 169
Subconscious drives 115
Subject matters 178,205
  in mathematics 207–208
  relatively existent. 144
Substance 11–12,53
  a composite, stable, mid-sized
    object. 11
  a product of object-positing . 13
  in a felt position of rotational
    balance 118
  in Aristotle 110
  in cartesian dualism 23
  of particulars in experience . . 11
  relatively existent. 8,144
  the four causes. 9
Substitutional quantification
 10,12,25,103
Symbolic logic . 25,134,166,173,176
  as a system 147
  as an empirical tool . . . 201-205
  canonical notation 187
  causation as entailment . 103,184
  counter-factual conditionals. 183
  formal structures . . 105,148–149
  in language analysis 138
  independent of, not opposed to
    mystical experience 131
  necessary incompleteness of 198
  open sentences . . . 189–190,192
  platonic dogmas about. . . . 202
  protosyntax 198
  pure abstract structures . . . 150
  Quine's system 186
  role of propositions. 146
  rules in. 152
  satisfaction
    relations 186–189,192
  substitutivity property . 194-195
  timelessness of. 130–131

truth-functional relations in . 104
universal generalization . . . 64
variables and
  constants. 137,150,152,166,187
y-type notion of identity 148,194
Syntax 22,46,86–87131,161
  and reference 49,198
  as symbol crunching. 49
  in Aristotle's definitions of
    essences 111
  in causal laws 40
  in cognitive science. 168
  in computers. 22,138
  in deductive nomological
    causation. 108
  in property-attributing 26,163,199
  in Searle. 30
  protosyntax for mathematical
    logic. 198
  role in knowledge 219
  syntactical definability. . . . 198
  syntactical relations in
    deductions 108,218
  syntactical structures. . . . 173
Synthetic a priori 31

T

Tarski, Alfred. 77,86
  metalanguage 86
  truth definition. 86
  truth predicates 190–193
Thagard, Paul 169–170
Thau, Stewart 43
Theoretical entities
  in science 41
Thinking 87,121,149153,155
  about linguistic concepts . . 145
  about relations and
    properties 147
  autonomy of the x and y . . . 166
  by dogs 157
  creative 130
  data . . 12-14,20,22,50,93,95,106,
    110,115,128,158,206,217
  deductive thinking
    procedures. 104
  disembodied thoughts 202

differences between x and y type
   processes 165
first person singular 140
Fregian senses 142
how experience makes a
   difference 12,15,113
how the x and y are
   tied together. 9,143,153
human. 26,167,215,220
imagination in 128
in property attributing. . . . 162
intellectual insight 45
intellectual synthesis 132
intellectual tools . . 102,106,108,
   205,215
manipulating and manipulated
   by experience 33,37
mental activity 88
methods and
   procedures. 10,201,205
mistakes of equivocation . 40,123
organizational capacity . . . 107
perceptual data 108
philosophical theory of . . . 137
points of view. 107
processes 7,12–13,21,215
psychological projections . . 122
recalcitrant parameters of 203,205
relevance in data. 98
rigor mortis in 135
role of judgement in. 39
role of mystical intuition in . 130
role of psychological needs
   in 120
sensory data. 127
statistical judgements in . . . 98
syntactical structure in . 160,199
'understanding crisis' 113
y-type, not about reality . . . 199
Third man . 6,14,16,22,149,163,185,
   99,212
in a logical system 186
in background
   theories. 194,196–197
in counterfactual conditional
   causal accounts. . 105,183,185
in Plato. 181

in Quine. 187,198
in Quine's semantic ascent . 193
regress of explanations. . . . 184
Thisness . . . 4,19,37,45,109,111,143
'this' 13
'What is that?'. 134
indexical pointing 142
'magenta-thing'. 144
'that' 143
that thing 149
that-that-color-thing. 144
this something 26
Thought
   non-computational. 212
Three prisoners' paradox 172
Tooley, Michael 40
Transforming Knowledge . . . 169
Transition
   action at a distance 44–45
   adjectival and transitory
     Humean impressions . . . 95
   motion is not a part of
     any object 99
   physical transfer relationships 50
   retroductive scientific account
     of motion 99
Transition. 34,38
   in properties. 104
   understanding of 100
Transitory properties 144
Truth 204,215
   about experience 202
   concept of 206
   formal definition of in
     classical logic 206
   game-theoretical conception
     of 87
   ideal conception of 219
   indefinability of. 215
   indefinability of 212
   pragmatic understanding of. 219
Truth conditions. 13
Truths
   mathematical and logical . . . 85
   scientific. 84
Turing, Alan 133, 212–213
   Turing machines 214

U

Understanding 83–84
Unitary structure of science
    blind faith in 215,219
Utilitarian ethics 177

V

Varela, Francisco 75–78,81,87
Ventral skills. 80
Visuomotor skills 80
Vos Savant, Marilyn 177

W

Whitehead, Alfred North. 17
Wisdom 129
Wittgenstein, Ludwig 86, 146
    language games 86
    private language 23
World-to-mind 37,46,48,80,90

X

X=r 40,148
    identity 45,47107
    the redundancy of the
        relationship 33
X-type experience 212
X-type reasoning process. . . 77,80,
            84–85,171,176,178,210

Y

Yin and Yang 177
Y-type reasoning process . 78,80,84,
            85,176,178,210,212–213
Y-type thinking processes . . . 215

Z

Zen Masters 132
Zermelo-Fraenkel
    logic system 213

WITHDRAWN